Download Forms on Nolo.com

You can download the forms in this book at:

 www.nolo.com/back-of-book/PNUP.html

We'll also post updates whenever there's an important change to the law affecting this book—as well as articles and other related materials.

More Resources from Nolo.com

 ### Legal Forms, Books, & Software
Hundreds of do-it-yourself products—all written in plain English, approved, and updated by our in-house legal editors.

 ### Legal Articles
Get informed with thousands of free articles on everyday legal topics. Our articles are accurate, up to date, and reader friendly.

 ### Find a Lawyer
Want to talk to a lawyer? Use Nolo to find a lawyer who can help you with your case.

NOLO
LAW for ALL

7th Edition

Prenuptial Agreements

How to Write a Fair and Lasting Contract

Katherine E. Stoner, J.D.

SEVENTH EDITION   JANUARY 2023

Cover Design   SUSAN PUTNEY

Book Design   SUSAN PUTNEY

Proofreading   CATHLEEN SMALL

Index   ACCESS POINTS INDEXING

Printing   SHERIDAN

ISSN: 2472-596X (print)

ISSN: 2472-5978 (online)

ISBN: 978-1-4133-3003-8 (pbk)

ISBN: 978-1-4133-3004-5 (ebook)

This book covers only United States law, unless it specifically states otherwise.

Please note

Accurate, plain-English legal information can help you solve many of your own legal problems. But this text is not a substitute for personalized advice from a knowledgeable lawyer. If you want the help of a trained professional—and we'll always point out situations in which we think that's a good idea—consult an attorney licensed to practice in your state.

Acknowledgments

This book would never have been written without the foresight, enthusiasm, and patient support of the folks at Nolo, especially Janet Portman and Jake Warner. Nor could I have done justice to the sheer breadth of the legal landscape without the diligent efforts of the Nolo research team.

No amount of thanks could ever be enough for the contributions of my original co-author, Shae Irving. Rarely does a collaboration proceed with as much grace and good humor as this one did.

I am indebted to all the Nolo editors I have had the pleasure of working with over the many editions of this book and, most recently, to Ann O'Connell for her skillful and incisive assistance on this edition.

A special note of thanks to Mickey for hanging in there, as always.

About the Author

Katherine E. Stoner is a superior court commissioner in Monterey County, California. Prior to that, she was a certified family law specialist with a practice focused primarily on family law and mediation. She is an adjunct faculty member at Monterey College of Law, where she has taught community property, family law, and mediation since 1980. She is the author of *Divorce Without Court, A Guide to Mediation and Collaborative Divorce* (Nolo).

Table of Contents

Appendixes

Your Prenup Companion

If you're planning to be married and considering a prenuptial agreement—a "prenup" for short—this book is for you. It will help you and your fiancé sort through the questions that most couples have about making this type of contract.

This book explains what prenups are, what you can do with one, and how to figure out if a prenup is right for you and your spouse-to-be. If you decide you want a prenup, we show you what terms to include and how to put those terms into an agreement that's legally sound and fair to both of you. We also explain the benefits of using a prenup to make your own rules about the financial aspects of marriage, rather than leaving everything up to the laws of your state.

Although a prenuptial agreement might not seem romantic, working together to consider and choose the terms of a prenup can actually strengthen your relationship. After all, marriage is a partnership in every sense of the word. Learning to deal respectfully and constructively with each other about finances is a benefit in itself. So even if you conclude that you don't need a prenup, using this book can help you converse with each other about the important financial matters that are sure to arise in the course of your years together.

Turn the page to start learning the basics of prenups. And please accept our congratulations on your upcoming marriage—may it be long, joyful, and prosperous.

Get Updates, Forms, and More at This Book's Companion Page on Nolo.com

You can download the worksheets, forms, and state law summaries that are discussed in this book at:

www.nolo.com/back-of-book/PNUP.html

See Appendix A for a list of what's available on this companion page, along with instructions for how to use and edit the customizable documents. Also, when there are important changes to the information in this book, we'll post updates on this same website.

A Prenup Primer

The pages that follow take you step by step through the process of making a prenuptial agreement, from deciding whether to have one to preparing a final written agreement. This book has worksheets to help you assess your finances and goals, plus sample agreements and clauses that you can tailor to meet your needs.

To help you see how the prenup process works, we follow three couples through the entire process: Ted and Grace, Karen and Russ, and Steven and Freda. You'll have a chance to see how they deal with each stage as they come to it, and you'll be able to read selected parts of the agreement each couple signs. You'll also see examples using other fictional couples that illustrate particular issues that might arise as you negotiate and draft your agreement.

This chapter covers how prenups work and what you can accomplish by preparing one. Before you get started, though, consider a few points that are essential to making a responsible, legally valid agreement.

Other Names for Prenups

In some states, a prenuptial agreement is known as an "antenuptial agreement" or in more modern terms as a "premarital agreement." Sometimes the word "contract" is substituted for "agreement," as in "prenuptial contract." For the sake of brevity, we'll stick with "prenup" in this book, but occasionally you'll find us using one of the other terms if it's appropriate.

Our Assumptions

A prenuptial agreement is more than just a legally binding contract. It is the material and financial counterpart to wedding vows.

When you marry, you make what you expect and hope will be a lifetime commitment to be there for each other in every way.

Unfortunately, prenups aren't always negotiated in this spirit—but they should be. Your prenup should support and reflect the spirit of partnership with which you make your wedding vows.

This book makes certain assumptions about how you will approach your prenup. They are:

1. You want to be fair.
2. You are prepared to make full disclosure about your property and finances.
3. You are willing to communicate about finances.
4. You'll each work with a lawyer.

Let's look at each of these assumptions more closely.

Assumption 1: You Want to Be Fair

Almost every person who's about to get married would claim that they want to be fair to their future spouse. But there's often more to "fairness" than meets the eye.

A prenuptial agreement is fair when:

- its terms benefit both of you (it's not one-sided), and
- it was negotiated in a balanced manner (neither party was subject to undue pressure or coercion).

As for the first of these criteria, you might discover that each of you has a different view of your respective situation. It might take some talking and a little compromising to come up with an agreement that seems fair to both of you.

Negotiating fairly means taking the time to make sure that both of you participate in making the agreement and that neither of you feels pressured into signing an agreement you're not comfortable with.

A prenup that meets both criteria of the fairness test—its terms are equitable and you've mutually negotiated it—is most likely to stand the test of time in your marriage. An agreement that fails the fairness test will be at best a reminder of an unpleasant experience that you put away and hope to forget about. At worst, it can erode the trust between you and your betrothed, and it could even be the source of bitter and expensive court battles in a later divorce.

On the legal front, courts in most states will not enforce prenups that don't meet both of these criteria. So paying attention to fairness also makes it more likely that a court will enforce your premarital agreement, if it comes to that.

CAUTION

A premarital agreement is a binding legal document. If you have reservations about a proposed agreement, don't sign it with the hope that you can get out of it later. Although it's true that courts sometimes disregard prenups on various grounds, don't take any risks—you never know exactly what a particular court or judge might do.

Assumption 2: You're Prepared to Make Full Disclosure

This assumption is closely related to the first. A premarital agreement is most likely to be viewed as fair—by you and by the courts—if it is based upon complete and accurate financial information. This means that you should both disclose everything you own (including approximate values) and all of your debts (including any obligations from a prior marriage, such as child support or alimony). Virtually every state requires that any premarital agreement be accompanied by complete written disclosure of both parties' financial circumstances.

This book will help you figure out exactly what you own and what you owe. You can use the worksheets provided to prepare the written financial disclosures that will accompany your prenup.

Assumption 3: You're Willing to Communicate About Finances

Although most people marry for love rather than money, marriage is a financial partnership as well as a spiritual, emotional, and physical union. Sooner or later, the two of you will need an understanding about how to handle your finances, even if it's just day-to-day stuff like whether to have a joint bank account or who will pay the bills. This means that you'll need to communicate well about money and finances.

If you intend to sign a premarital agreement, you must have complete and clear communications about finances before you sign. If your communications aren't clear, it will be next to impossible to come up with a written document that truly represents a mutually negotiated agreement.

Bringing up the topic of money can be hard. Having a sustained conversation about it is even more difficult. At a time when romance is on your minds, talking about money can feel out of place. And just the thought of disagreeing can be enough to make you avoid the subject. Maybe it feels awkward to discuss old debts when you're in the process of clearing them up and you're confident that they'll soon be ancient history. Or maybe it's your partner who has the outstanding debts and you hesitate to bring up an embarrassing subject.

Whatever the reasons, money and finances can be a difficult topic for many of us to broach. If this is true for you, don't be alarmed, but don't let it be an excuse to delay the inevitable, either.

Read on for lots of tips on how to have good conversations about money, plus guidance on working with financial counselors, mediators, or other advisers.

Assumption 4: You'll Each Work With a Lawyer

If you want to end up with a clear and binding premarital agreement, you should get help from two good lawyers—one for each of you. This advice might sound surprising in a self-help legal book, but it's essential. Here's why.

Our legal system views marriage as a matter of contract between two consenting adults. The terms of the "marriage contract" are dictated by the laws of the state where the married people live, unless they have a premarital agreement containing different terms.

The laws governing marriage contracts vary tremendously from state to state. This book provides some general information on each state's laws relating to marriage and prenups, and gives you some tips on doing your own legal research. (See Chapter 4.) If you don't want to take the time to learn the ins and outs of your state's matrimonial laws, a lawyer who knows the law will be an important resource. The lawyer can help you put together an agreement that meets state requirements and says what you want it to say.

This explains the desirability of having one lawyer, but why two? If your prenuptial agreement ever ends up in court, expect the judge to scrutinize its terms. If you want your agreement to pass muster, having an independent lawyer advise each of you can be critical. While most states don't mandate that each party to a prenup have a lawyer, the absence of separate independent advice for each party is always a red flag to a judge. Some states even require additional paperwork for couples choosing not to be represented. If the technical requirements aren't satisfied, the prenup won't be valid.

All of this assumes that you select and use lawyers who are not only competent and experienced in matrimonial law but who are also capable of supporting the two of you in negotiating and writing up a loving, clear, and fair agreement. You also don't want to spend a fortune on lawyers doing background work you could handle yourselves. Finding the right lawyers can take some time, but it's worth the effort. This book gives you some suggestions on how to find and work with good lawyers in a way that both cuts your costs and supports your relationship. (See Chapter 10.)

How Prenups Work

People have been making prenuptial agreements for thousands of years. Scholars tell us that the practice dates back to the ancient Egyptians and that prenups have existed for many centuries in Anglo-American tradition. In previous times, the parents of the bride and groom negotiated the agreement on the new couple's behalf. These days, engaged couples do their own negotiating, although it's not uncommon for family members to exert influence behind the scenes (especially when family money is involved).

Prenups are not just for the rich. While prenups are often used to protect the assets of the wealthy, couples of more modest means are increasingly using prenups. For example, a couple with children from prior marriages might use a prenup to spell out what will happen to their property when they die, so that they can pass on separate property to their children and still provide for each other, if necessary. Without a prenup, a surviving spouse might have the right to claim a large chunk of the other spouse's property, leaving much less for the kids.

Couples with or without children, wealthy or not, might simply want to clarify their financial rights and responsibilities during their marriage. Or they might want to avoid potential arguments if they ever divorce by specifying in advance how their property will be divided. Prenups can also be used to protect spouses from each other's premarital debts and can address a multitude of other issues as well.

Exactly what you decide to do with your prenuptial agreement depends on your particular circumstances and wishes. But before getting into the specifics of what you want to accomplish with a prenup, it's wise to have a basic understanding of what you're doing when you make this type of contract. To put it briefly, you're deciding how you each want your property to be treated—during your marriage, when you divorce, or when one of you dies—rather than letting your state's law make these decisions for you.

A Note for Same-Sex Couples

Now that same-sex couples can marry in every state, all of the laws that apply to prenups for heterosexual couples also apply to same-sex couples—even if the state's law doesn't make this explicitly clear. Some states' laws are still behind the times and might refer to "him" and "her," or "husband" and "wife." But no matter the terminology, the laws apply the same to all married couples.

Making Your Own Rules

If you don't make a prenuptial agreement, your state's laws will determine who owns your marital property and what happens to it at divorce or death. State law might even have a say in what happens to some of the property you owned before you were married.

> TIP
>
> **Good to know.** Property that is acquired by either spouse during marriage is known as either marital or community property, depending on the state. See Chapter 4 for an in-depth discussion of marital property and the laws that might apply in your state.

Under the law, marriage is considered a contract between spouses, and with the contract of marriage comes certain automatic property rights for each spouse. For example, in the absence of a prenup stating otherwise, a spouse usually has the right to:

- share ownership of property acquired during marriage, with the expectation that the property will be divided between the spouses in the event of a divorce and will transfer to a surviving spouse at death
- incur debts during marriage that the other spouse might have to pay for, and
- share in the management and control of any marital or community property, including the right to sell it or give it away.

So what do you do if some of these laws—called marital property, divorce, and probate laws—aren't to your liking? Enter the prenup, which (in most cases) lets you decide for yourselves how your property should be handled.

As part of making your prenup, you'll review your state's laws. You'll compare your own preferences about property ownership, division, and distribution with the state's rules. If state law already provides for what you want, there might be no need to make a prenup. But if you find that the law won't meet your needs, you'll probably want to go ahead and craft your own agreement. (In Chapter 4 and on the book's companion page, we discuss state laws in more detail and tell you how to find the laws for your state.)

TIP

Head off disputes by making a prenup if your state's law is unclear.
When you familiarize yourself with the laws of your state, you might feel that they'll work just fine for you. But the law isn't always clear or predictable. Going without a prenup can increase the likelihood that there will be contentious and expensive court battles at the time of a divorce or even after death. Often, the law says something that seems straightforward at first glance, but it turns out that there's room for argument on the finer points. If you agree in advance on a fair approach to things like separate versus shared ownership of property and inheritance rights of the surviving spouse, you can save yourselves and your inheritors the risk of legal expense, uncertainty, and acrimony by making a prenup.

Making Sure Your Prenup Is Valid

Traditionally, courts scrutinized prenups with a suspicious eye, because they almost always involved a waiver of legal and financial benefits by a less wealthy spouse. In the days when married women had far fewer legal rights than today, many courts believed that a woman was at too great a disadvantage when negotiating with her prospective husband. Even more unacceptable legally was a prenup that spelled out the couple's rights in the event of a divorce. Prior to 1970, such an agreement was considered unenforceable in all states because it was seen as a way to encourage divorce.

As divorce and remarriage have become more prevalent, and with growing equality between the sexes, courts and legislatures are increasingly willing to uphold premarital agreements. Today, every state permits them, although a prenup that is judged unfair or otherwise fails to meet state requirements will still be set aside—and some state laws are stringent about prenup procedures such as waiting periods. Because courts still look carefully at prenups, it is important that you negotiate and write up your agreement in a way that is clear, understandable, and legally sound. As you progress through the steps in this book, we'll show you how to avoid the pitfalls that could invalidate your agreement.

What a Typical Prenup Covers

Most prenups begin with a brief description of each party's circumstances —such as age, occupation, and any children. And prenups almost always include disclosures of both parties' finances—that is, assets, liabilities, and incomes. (These disclosures are usually attached to the end of the prenup as separate lists.)

Beyond that, the contents of the prenup vary, depending on the needs of the couple. Many prenups include:

- A declaration that each spouse's separately owned property will remain their sole and separate property during the marriage. (Sometimes this refers only to assets owned before the marriage, but it can also include property acquired during the marriage, especially gifts and inheritances.)
- A confirmation that each person is responsible for their own premarital debts.
- A waiver of the surviving spouse's legal right to claim a share of the other spouse's separate property at death.

Here are some other typical but less common inclusions:

- A provision that all property acquired by a spouse during marriage will be their separate property, and that there will be no marital property to be divided in a divorce or upon death.
- A waiver of property rights, sometimes in exchange for one or more of the following:
  - a sum of money (either right away or according to a specified timetable)
  - life insurance coverage, or
  - establishment of a trust for the spouse who is giving up rights.
- A plan for dividing property in the event of a divorce.
- A requirement that each spouse sign documents after the marriage reaffirming any waivers contained in the prenup. (This usually applies to waivers of rights to retirement benefits or an interest in real estate.)

- A description of how household expenses will be paid.
- An automatic termination clause specifying that the prenup will terminate on a certain date in the future—often called a "sunset clause." Alternatively, a schedule for adjusting the terms of the prenup as time passes.

Some prenups also include provisions that are enforceable in some states but not in others. The most notable examples are waivers of alimony if there is a divorce or legal separation, and the so-called "bad-boy" (or "bad-girl") clause requiring financial compensation if one party is caught cheating on the other. (These aren't very common, but a few states still allow them.)

In addition to the typical provisions, many prenups contain terms that are tailor-made to the couple's circumstances. For example, there might be an agreement that the couple will own a home in certain percentages or a promise to take turns supporting each other while obtaining an education.

Finally, every prenup contains standard clauses that go into almost all legal agreements. Lawyers often call these clauses "boilerplate" (a newspaper term referring to preset or syndicated features). The boilerplate in a prenup would most likely include clauses naming the lawyers who represented each party, a statement about who prepared the agreement, the agreement's binding effect on the couple and their inheritors, which state's law will apply in any legal dispute over the agreement, and other terms relating to the legal interpretation or enforcement of the agreement.

All of the above discussion is just to get you started thinking about the issues that might be involved when you set out to make a prenup. In Chapter 2, we dive into much more detail about what a prenup can —and can't—do. And in Chapters 5 through 9, we provide plenty of sample clauses that you can include in your contract.

How to Make a Prenup

From getting started to getting married, there are eight basic steps to making a prenup. Here's an introduction to the steps you'll learn about in this book.

Step 1: Start Early

Begin planning for your prenup as soon as possible—at least three months before the wedding. If you wait until the last minute, you might not have time to decide what you want and get everything in writing before the wedding. (An agreement signed after the wedding is a postnuptial—or postmarital—agreement and is covered by more stringent legal rules. See Chapter 12.)

Plan to sign your prenup about a month before the wedding. The closer you get to that all-important day, the greater the risk that your agreement won't stand up in court later—you might miss a legal waiting period, or the court might find that there was undue pressure on one of the spouses to get it signed before the marriage.

Before signing, you should allow a couple of months—or longer, if you can—for piecing together the details of your agreement, getting it reviewed, and putting it into final form for signing. Although it's possible to plan and finalize a prenup in less than three months, moving too fast will add unneeded stress and could doom your efforts to create a clear and fair agreement.

> CAUTION
>
> **Timing is everything.** While it is important to get an early start on your prenup, it is possible to be too early. You want all of your information, including your financial disclosures, to be current when you sign your contract. As a rule, you should start working on your prenup no less than three or four months before your wedding and no more than eight or nine months before. If you end up postponing your wedding date after signing a prenup, take the time to update the prenup in writing before you marry.

Step 2: Decide Whether You Need a Prenup

If you're reading this book, you might have already decided that a prenup is what you want. Even so, it doesn't hurt to take a little time to examine your situation (together, if possible) to figure out whether a prenup is what you need. Chapter 2 is devoted to this step.

Step 3: Agree on the Specifics

Once you've decided to go forward, the next step is to figure out exactly what your agreement should say. This involves doing some list making and some soul searching, both separately and together. Clear communication is essential to success in this endeavor, and it doesn't hurt to know a little about constructive negotiating, too. Chapter 3 explains how to decide on the specifics of your agreement, and Chapter 11 offers tips on communicating and negotiating.

Step 4: Create a Draft Agreement

As Chapter 3 explains in detail, you'll almost certainly be better off if you have your final prenuptial agreement written up by a lawyer. A good lawyer can ensure that you put together a contract that meets the requirements of your state and says exactly what you want it to say. In fact, as we explain later, you will greatly improve the odds that your prenup will stand up in court if each of you has a separate lawyer review and sign off on the agreement.

Taking the time to write up a draft of what you've agreed on before you meet with your lawyers can have significant cost savings. By working out the details early on, you and your partner will be in sync on the fine points before you ask a lawyer to prepare the final agreement. You'll also minimize the risk of having a lawyer put together a one-sided agreement that doesn't reflect what either of you wants, wasting time and legal fees. You can use your draft to check the lawyer's work, making sure nothing's been missed or misunderstood. Of course, if you elect not to use a lawyer to write up the formal agreement, then your draft will eventually become the document you sign.

Chapters 5 through 9 provide a format for your draft prenup, with sample clauses covering the most common situations and suggestions for customizing your agreement.

Step 5: Write Up the Formal Agreement

After you've made a draft agreement, each of you should read it carefully to see whether you need to make changes to it. Once that's done, you'll either prepare the formal document yourselves or hire a lawyer to help you; the best way to proceed is to hire separate lawyers for each of you. Chapter 10 takes you through the process of finalizing your prenup, including suggestions for finding good lawyers and tips on how to work with them.

Step 6: Ask Your Lawyers to Review the Agreement

After the formal agreement is prepared, the next step is to have your separate lawyers review the agreement to confirm that it's legally sound.

Step 7: Sign the Agreement

Signing the agreement should be something you remember without regret. Plan to sign at a time when you can pay attention to the moment. If the agreement will be notarized, you'll need to arrange to sign when a notary is available. You might also have to contend with your lawyers' schedules, so it's important to plan ahead. You might even want to make a ceremony out of the event or plan a little celebration afterward—just the two of you. After the hard work you've done getting to this point, do what you can to make signing the agreement a relaxed and positive experience for both of you. (Chapter 10 provides more details about signing your prenup.)

Step 8: Enjoy Your Wedding

Your wedding day promises to be one of the happiest moments of your life. When you get there, put away this book, file away your prenup, and enjoy the day. Our best wishes will be with you.

Is a Prenup Right for You?

T his chapter can help you decide whether you want a prenup. We explain what you can and can't accomplish with a prenup. We also outline a step-by-step approach to assessing whether a prenup is right for your particular situation.

The two of you can read and use this chapter together or separately, depending on what is more comfortable for you.

SKIP AHEAD

If you know you want a prenup, skip ahead. To get right to the specifics of what your agreement will say, turn to Chapter 3.

What You Can Do With a Prenup

When deciding whether you want a prenup, it helps to consider the kinds of things that you can—and can't—do with this type of contract. Prenups are most often used to:

- keep finances separate
- protect each of you from the other person's debts
- provide for children from prior marriages
- pass on family property
- define who gets what in the event of separation or divorce, and
- clarify each person's responsibilities after getting married.

CAUTION

Each state has its own laws about what can be addressed in a prenup. This chapter gives you general rules about what you can and can't do, but you'll need to check the laws of your state to be sure that what we say here applies to you. For an overview of state laws, see Chapter 4. You can find a summary of some applicable laws for your state on the book's online companion page (see Appendix A).

Keep Your Finances Separate

Every state has laws designating certain assets and income accumulated during marriage as marital or community property, even if these assets are held in the name of just one spouse. (For a detailed explanation of marital versus community property, see Chapter 4.)

If you want to avoid having your individual accumulations during marriage divided up as dictated by state law, you can do so with a premarital agreement. The prenup can be customized to fit your situation. For example, if you want to keep absolutely everything separate, you can specify that no assets accumulated during your marriage will be considered marital property. Or you can specify that certain types of property or items that you plan to acquire will be separate property and the rest will be marital property, or vice versa.

Steven and Freda

Steven, a sales manager, and Freda, a schoolteacher, are considering a prenup. They are in their mid-30s and this is a first marriage for both of them. Steven watched his brother Tom go through a bitter divorce two years ago. Tom has suggested that Steven use a prenup to protect the property he owns before the marriage. When Steven mentioned the idea to Freda, it occurred to her that she might also want a prenup to keep her own premarital investments separate.

CAUTION

Rules for retirement plans. Most retirement plans require a separate written waiver of spousal death benefits—that is, the survivor's right to receive money from the plan if the other spouse dies. The waiver can't be signed before you marry and must be on a form provided by the retirement plan. Your prenup can spell out your intentions to waive spousal death benefits, but both of you must also sign the necessary forms after you are married.

Protect One or Both of You From the Other Person's Debts

Some of us bring debts, as well as assets, to a marriage. If there's no prenup, creditors can sometimes turn to marital or community property to satisfy the debts of just one spouse. But if you want to make sure that saying "I do" does not mean saying "I owe," you might be able to use a prenup to limit your liability for each other's debts in two ways. First, your prenup can state that each of you is solely responsible for your own debts. Second, you might be able to place certain assets out of the reach of bill collectors by designating those assets as separate property rather than marital or community property.

Karen and Russ

Karen and Russ are both in their late 40s and about to get married, each for the second time. They live in California, a community property state. Karen is a veterinarian who has two teenage children. Russ is a bookkeeper who has a six-year-old daughter. Each of them owns a home. After they marry, they plan to rent out Russ's house and live at Karen's place.

Both Karen and Russ want to protect their property from the other person's debts. Although Karen's veterinary practice is quite successful, Karen and Russ want to be sure that there will not be any liens placed against Russ's home if a disgruntled pet owner sues Karen or if her business runs into financial troubles.

They are equally concerned about protecting Karen's assets and income from Russ's business debts and any child support obligations to his ex-wife.

Karen and Russ might be able prevent these problems by using a prenup to designate their assets and earnings as their separate property, and to spell out their intention to be responsible for their own debts.

> CAUTION
> **You can't hide property.** Every state has laws making it illegal to give away your own property to protect it from debt collectors. These laws are known as "fraudulent transfer" laws. While you can use a prenup to protect your fiancé's separate property from your debts, you probably cannot save your own assets from your creditors by transferring ownership to your fiancé. It might be more problematic to declare property acquired after you marry off-limits from creditors. If you want to protect each other's property (or your marital property) from your separate debts, it will be important to get legal advice from a competent lawyer.

Provide for Children From Prior Marriages

A prenup is helpful (perhaps essential) if either of you has children from another relationship and you want to make sure that your children inherit their share of your property. Consider the following examples.

Ted and Grace

Ted, age 70, is a retired real estate developer. He owns several parcels of commercial real estate as well as his own home, which is furnished with valuable antiques and artwork. Ted has three grown children. Grace is 48 and has worked for the past 15 years as a county social worker. She owns her own home and has a modest retirement plan from the county. She has no children of her own. Ted wants to make sure that Grace will be comfortably provided for if he dies first, but he also wants to make sure that his property will revert to his children after Grace dies.

Without a prenup, Ted can do some estate planning and make a will or trust that lets Grace use (but not actually own) Ted's property during her lifetime, with the assets going outright to Ted's children when Grace dies. But even with a good estate plan in place, Grace could still be entitled to a share of Ted's estate, as Ted's surviving spouse. If Ted and Grace agree, Grace can waive her rights, in a binding premarital agreement, to take the share of a surviving spouse. This guarantees that Ted's estate plan will work the way that Ted intends.

Karen and Russ

Karen's divorce settlement with her first husband states that each of her two children is to receive at least $50,000 from her estate if she dies before the youngest child turns 25.

Even if Karen makes sure that her will sets aside $50,000 in a custodianship for each child, Russ's rights as a surviving spouse could affect Karen's estate plan unless they sign a prenup in which Russ agrees to waive those rights.

Pass on Family Property

In a prenup, you list all of the property each of you owns at the time of your marriage. If your property includes something you want to keep in your birth family, such as an heirloom or a share in a family business, you can specify in your prenup that it will remain in your family.

Ted and Grace

Many of the antiques in Ted's house are family heirlooms. Ted wants to leave some items to his children and let Grace enjoy the use of all the other items until she dies, at which time they will also go to his children. Ted can designate the items going to Grace and to his children in a will or trust. Then Ted and Grace can use a prenup to list Ted's family heirlooms so that there will be no question about which items in the house were Ted's and which ones belong to Grace.

On her side, Grace owns a 10% share of a family farm, together with her mother and sister. Her mother is planning to give Grace and her sister a larger share of the farm over the next few years. Grace and Ted can include in their prenup a statement that Ted waives any spousal claim to Grace's current and future share in the family farm so that Grace's will or trust can leave her share to her sister.

> CAUTION
> **Follow through by making your estate plan.** In addition to using your prenup to waive inheritance rights and state your intentions for passing on your property at death, it's vital that you prepare the estate planning documents—your wills, living trusts, and so on—that actually transfer your property as you intend. See Chapter 12 for more information about estate planning.

Reassuring Family Members

Sometimes the main impetus for a prenup comes from your grown children or other family members. Your children might worry that they will be left out when you die. Other family members might fret over possible dilution of the family wealth. Still others might be concerned about messy disagreements after you are gone. Even if you know that there is no reason for alarm, you could reassure nervous family members by spelling things out in a prenup.

On the other hand, it's important that you not let others dictate what is best for the two of you. A prenup reflects your commitments to each other. Balancing your concerns for family members with your best interests as a couple will take some careful thinking, discussion, and planning. For help, see Chapter 11.

Define Who Gets What If You Divorce

Without a prenup, state laws will specify how your property will be divided if you ever divorce. These laws might dictate a result that neither of you wants. (Chapter 4 provides an overview of how state divorce laws work.) You can use a prenup to establish your own rules for property division and avoid potential disagreements in the event of a divorce.

Even if you're uncomfortable talking about the possibility of a future divorce, spelling out your rights in advance can be a wise thing to do. You might be surprised to find that talking about these things brings the two of you closer together. In fact, communicating honestly about important issues such as money, property, and how to avoid future disputes might even *prevent* divorce in the long run. And if you ever do part ways, having clear terms in your prenup will almost certainly make the passage easier.

> **EXAMPLE:** Daniel and Chanee plan to buy a house together. Chanee's parents have agreed to give them the money for the down payment. In the state where Chanee and Daniel live, the law is not clear whether the gift from Chanee's parents is considered joint property or Chanee's separate property. Furthermore, state law says that in the event of a divorce, even if the down payment were found to be Chanee's separate property, she would be entitled to reimbursement for only the amount of the down payment, without appreciation, unless she and Daniel have a written agreement stating otherwise.
>
> In talking about this, Daniel and Chanee agree that if they ever split up, Chanee would get back the money from her parents, plus appreciation if the value of the house goes up after they buy it. Chanee and Daniel ensure that their agreement about the down payment will be carried out in a divorce by including it in their prenup.

Some people use a prenup to simplify potentially complicated property issues. This can save money and time if there is a divorce. It can also streamline the settlement of your estate by clearly stating what will belong to the estate and what will belong to the surviving spouse.

Karen and Russ

Naturally, Karen and Russ hope to stay together. They expect Karen's veterinary practice to provide both of them with a comfortable lifestyle and retirement savings as they grow older, supplemented by Russ's more modest earnings as a bookkeeper.

Karen and Russ are aware that under state law, a portion of any increase in the value of Karen's veterinary practice will be considered community property. This seems fair to them, especially since Russ contributes his time to the veterinary practice by doing the books on the weekends.

Karen's lawyer has advised her to put into the prenup a formula for calculating the community property share in Karen's practice. According to the lawyer, there are numerous methods for computing community property rights in a business at the time of divorce. Settling on the most appropriate method in advance will eliminate the possibility of a long and expensive duel between experts in a contested divorce case. This can also cut down on expenses of probate, since the community property share of Karen's practice might need to be determined then, too.

Clarify Each Person's Responsibilities After Getting Married

A prenup can specify how to handle issues that might arise after marriage, such as:

- deciding whether to file joint or separate income tax returns (and allocating income and deductions if you choose to file separate returns)
- paying the household bills and deciding whose funds will be used for payments
- opening and contributing to joint and separate bank accounts
- making decisions about specific purchases or projects, such as buying a house together or starting up a business
- using (and paying for) credit cards
- setting aside money for savings
- assisting each other financially while one of you completes college or other education
- providing for the surviving spouse, and
- settling any future disagreements.

Most topics covered in prenups are financial. Some people are tempted to include nonmonetary matters in their premarital agreements as well—

from critical issues such as having children to more mundane matters such as who's responsible for household chores. Nonmonetary issues are best left out of a prenup, for reasons discussed in the next section.

What You Can't Do With a Prenup

There are some things you can't legally accomplish with a prenup. State laws differ as to what matters are considered off-limits. However, as a general rule, any agreement to do something that is illegal or against state-defined public policy will be considered unenforceable—and might even jeopardize other valid aspects of the premarital agreement.

Agreements That Violate Public Policy

State law might block you from including a number of issues in your prenup. For example, no state will honor agreements limiting or waiving future child support. The same holds true of agreements limiting future custody and visitation rights. This is because state lawmakers consider the welfare of children to be a matter of public policy. Private agreements that would impair a child's right to be supported or to have a relationship with a parent in the future are void.

In some states, a similar public policy limitation applies to agreements waiving alimony—also called "spousal support" or "separate maintenance"—if there is a divorce. Other states permit such waivers, so you will need to know what your state laws say if you are considering this kind of agreement.

A third example of a public policy limitation is any agreement that would "promote" divorce. At one time, it wasn't unusual for a court to hold a prenup unenforceable on the grounds that it somehow encouraged divorce. Although courts no longer take this approach, judges in some states still scrutinize prenups with a suspicious eye. If the agreement appears to offer a financial incentive for divorce to one party, the judge might set it aside.

The Case of the Dubious Dowry

In a famous California case called *Marriage of Noghrey,* the court threw out a premarital agreement specifying that the wife would receive a house and half of her husband's premarital separate property if they divorced. The prenup was arranged by the families of the bride and groom, who were members of a traditional culture where a husband could divorce his wife at will and the wife could not. In that culture, a prenup guaranteeing a wife a substantial divorce settlement was designed to discourage a husband from divorcing his wife. But in California, Mrs. Noghrey was able to sue for a no-fault divorce a few months after the wedding. She then tried to claim the property specified in the prenup. The court invalidated the premarital agreement because it violated public policy by giving Mrs. Noghrey an incentive to file for divorce. (See *Marriage of Noghrey,* 215 Cal.Rptr. 153 (1985).)

The Practical Limits of a Prenup

Even if your prenup doesn't contain anything that's illegal or against public policy, there are practical limitations to what you can do with a prenup. While you can take care of the most obvious and most important aspects of your finances, there's no way you can—or should try to—anticipate every possible contingency that might arise during your marriage. A better approach is to periodically review your prenup to see if it still makes sense or if changes are needed to bring it in line with your new circumstances. For more on this, see Chapter 12.

You also shouldn't try to dictate every aspect of your personal life in a prenup. While communicating about what's important to each of you is a vital part of preparing for marriage, a prenup isn't the best place to address lifestyle agreements—such as who's responsible for taking out the garbage and what kind of schedule you will keep around the house, or whether you will have kids.

Nonmonetary agreements aren't binding in court, and including them could cause a judge to take your entire prenup less seriously. Your views on these issues could also change over time. Rather than include such matters in your prenup, write them down in an informal memo so you have a record of your most important concerns that you can discuss and update from time to time.

Here is a partial list of nonfinancial matters you might be tempted to include, but that are better dealt with outside of a prenup. Of course, the possible issues are endless and you may well think of many that aren't mentioned here:

- responsibility for household chores
- use of last names after you marry
- agreements about having and raising children, such as birth control, having children, children's names, child care responsibilities, and education, and
- how you will relate to in-laws or stepchildren.

Will a Prenup Work for You?

Whether to have a premarital agreement is as personal and unique a decision as whether to marry in the first place. Here, we'll take you through several steps to help you figure out whether a prenup is what you need.

Step 1: Consider the Pros and Cons

No matter your personal situation, a good first step is to review the general pros and cons of making a prenup. We'll start with the advantages, then we'll take up a couple of the downsides.

Benefits of a Prenup

Some of the pros we've already discussed are that a prenup can:

- protect your separate property
- support your estate plan
- define what is considered marital or community property
- reduce conflicts and save money if you divorce
- clarify special agreements between you, and
- establish procedures and ground rules for deciding future matters.

In addition, remember that creating a prenup may strengthen your relationship. While people often focus on the fact that negotiating a prenup can be potentially divisive, it is easy to lose sight of the fact that communicating about money matters can actually improve the quality of your marriage. Even if you don't end up signing a written agreement, just sitting down and hashing out the basics about money and property can eliminate misunderstandings that might otherwise derail your marriage.

How can you tell whether negotiating a prenup would help or do damage to your relationship? Obviously, there's no way to know for sure. But you probably have a pretty good sense of how well the two of you can talk now about money matters. You probably also know your own temperament. Are you the type to plan in advance and confront things directly, or are you more inclined to let things take their course and deal with problems if and when they arise? How about your partner—do they like to plan or take things as they come?

Balancing such intangibles against your legal and financial objectives will help you decide the right course for you. Remember, sooner or later you and your intended will be talking about money. If you think you can handle it, most psychologists and legal experts would tell you there's no time like the present.

Everybody's Got an Opinion

Many experts who work with couples in conflict—and those familiar with statistics on divorce rates—believe that having a prenup strengthens a relationship. Some even believe prenups should be mandatory. Why? Because making a prenup forces a couple to grapple with the difficult but necessary questions of money and property. By working through money issues in advance, couples start out their economic partnership on a firm foundation.

Other experts say prenups are not all that useful: They cite examples of couples who put away the prenup once it is signed and never look at it or think of it again.

Interestingly, very few scholars believe prenups are harmful. Nevertheless, the idea meets with resistance among many couples. Not only does having a prenup run counter to our romantic ideas about love and marriage, but there is also the potential for dissension and divisiveness. A couple negotiating a prenup might even discover that they have such fundamental differences that they decide to call off the wedding. While some would say that it's better to find out about such differences sooner rather than later, others disagree and argue for a wait-and-see approach. You and your partner must consider this question and be the final judges of whether negotiating up front is likely to help or hurt.

Disadvantages of a Prenup

While there's a lot to be said for a carefully considered, clearly written prenup, there are some downsides to consider before proceeding.

It's not romantic. Let's face it, a prenup is not romantic. Although marriage is a financial partnership as well as romantic one, if you feel that discussing anything as mundane as property and finances will mar an otherwise beautiful time of your lives, you might not be candidates for a prenup.

The time might not be right. The need for a prenup is partly a question of timing. The issues covered in a prenup will probably arise sooner or later in your marriage: money management, property rights, responsibility for debts, estate planning. And if your marriage doesn't work out, you will certainly need to deal with divorce decisions. If you decide to create a prenup, you will confront many of these issues now, at a time when your relationship is still new and perhaps untested. The process of discussing what goes into a prenup could be unpleasant and stressful, leaving one or both of you with bad feelings about the relationship. (If now isn't the time to make a written agreement, you might be able to make a contract after you marry—called a "postnup." But postnups have their own disadvantages. See Chapter 12 for more information.)

State law might protect you without a prenup. It could be that the laws of your state do a fine job of accomplishing what you want. For example, you might live in a community property state where assets owned before marriage are separate property and all assets accumulated during the marriage are community property that is owned 50/50. If this is essentially what you would want in your prenup, or maybe even better than what you expected, why go through the hassle, expense, and possible unpleasantness of negotiating a prenup? Still, you will want to be certain that you're not facing any special circumstances in which your state law is unclear. Proceed to the next step to take a careful look at your situation.

Step 2: Examine Your Situation

Now that you have an overview of the basic uses for and pros and cons of a prenup, it's time to focus on the specifics of your situation and figure out if a prenup is what you need.

Take a Prenup Quiz

If you're not sure whether you would benefit from a prenup, ask yourself the questions in the chart below. If you're using this book together, each of you should answer the questions that apply to you. If you're doing this on your own, answer as many questions as you can for both of you.

If either of you answers "yes" to any question, there is a good chance a prenup would be helpful. If you answer "no" to all the questions, a prenup might not be necessary, but you might still benefit from having one.

Prenup Quiz		
	Partner 1	**Partner 2**
1. Do you own any real estate?		
2. Do you own more than $100,000 in assets other than real estate?		
3. Do you own a business (with or without other partners)?		
4. Do you owe more than $10,000?		
5. Are you currently earning a salary of more than $100,000 per year?		
6. Have you contributed to a retirement plan for more than a year, or do you have other valuable employment benefits, such as profit sharing or stock options?		
7. Does one of you plan to pursue an advanced degree or other education while the other works?		
8. Will all or part of your estate go to someone other than your spouse?		

Identify Important Issues

Make a list of the things you might want to include in a prenup, such as separate property identification, decisions about how you will handle money and property while you are married, retirement benefit agreements, and agreements about how you want to leave property at your death.

Common Prenup Topics

Here's a quick reminder of some of the issues that can be included in a prenup:

- separate versus joint property
- estate planning issues, such as providing for children from prior marriages or leaving family property
- how to handle a separate business
- retirement benefits
- debt allocation and responsibility
- who gets what if you separate or divorce
- procedures for filing tax returns, including allocating income and deductions
- who pays household bills—and how
- whether to have joint bank accounts and, if so, how to manage them
- agreements about specific purchases or projects, such as buying a house together or starting up a business
- how you will handle credit card charges
- agreements to set aside money for savings
- agreements for putting each other through college or professional school
- provisions for a surviving spouse in your estate plans or through life insurance coverage, and
- how to settle any future disagreements, such as with the help of a mediator or by a private arbitrator acting as judge.

Assess Your Comfort Level

Next, ask yourself this question: On a scale of one to five, how comfortable am I with the idea of having a prenup? A one is not comfortable at all and a five is very comfortable. Make note of the number that best describes your comfort level.

If you gave yourself a one or a two, try to identify the reasons for your discomfort. If the source is uncertainty about how your negotiated rights under the terms of a prenup might differ from your legal rights without one, you might want to investigate the laws of your state before making your decision. (See Chapter 4 and the book's online companion page.) If you're pretty sure you want a prenup and your discomfort comes from fear of starting an argument or offending your partner, then you might take this as an opportunity to practice talking about difficult matters in a loving way, using some of the techniques we discuss in Chapter 11. You might even find it helpful to work on your communication and negotiation skills with a counselor who specializes in premarital counseling. (This is also discussed in Chapter 11.)

If you scored a three, four, or five on the comfort scale, you're ready to start discussing specifics. Even so, bear in mind that every good conversation involves some give and take. Don't assume that you and your future spouse will see eye to eye on everything, especially when you first start talking. Allow plenty of time to talk—and be willing to get help if you need it.

Step 3: Share Your Thoughts

If you think you want a prenup and you've been using this book by yourself up until now, then it's probably time to broach the subject with your fiancé. If the two of you have been using this book together, it will be a natural progression to share with each other what you've learned about your attitude toward a prenup.

It might be that you've both concluded that a prenup isn't right for you. In that case, you can close this book and go back to planning your wedding and honeymoon.

If one or both of you has some interest in a prenup, you're ready to work on the specifics and you can move on to Chapter 3. But before you do, you might want to read through Chapter 11 for some suggestions and advice on how to successfully communicate and negotiate when drafting a prenup.

If you've been working alone so far and you're ready to raise the topic with your future spouse, how to proceed is a matter of individual style and preference. You probably know better than anyone what is best. Some people prefer a direct and forthright approach. Others will want to introduce the idea more slowly and indirectly.

Ted and Grace

Remember Ted? He is the direct type. When he approached Grace about a prenup, he said, "I've been thinking about our financial future and how best to provide for you and protect you from hassles with my kids when I die. I've heard that having a premarital agreement is a good way to do this. What do you think? Can we talk about it? I've got a good book about prenups, and a few suggestions and ideas. Let's arrange a time to take a look at this together."

Karen and Russ

Karen's approach was similarly direct. She said to Russ: "I went to see my lawyer about the contract with the new vet we're hiring. We talked a little about coverage for the office when you and I are gone for the honeymoon, and she told me that we really should have a prenup to spell out what happens to the practice if I die or if we get divorced. I know it's not a very pleasant subject to have to deal with, but we probably should talk about it soon."

Steven and Freda

Steven favored a more indirect approach when talking to Freda. Here's how he got the ball rolling: "You know, I'm starting to realize that there's a lot more to getting married than just planning the wedding. The human resources manager at my office said there are a lot of forms that I'm going to have to sign after we're married, including beneficiary designations for my retirement benefits and insurance forms. You've probably got similar paperwork to deal with at school. Maybe we should sit down sometime soon and go over all this stuff together." Freda and Steven then arranged a time to talk. When they met, Steven brought up his brother's remark about protecting the property he already owns. This led to a conversation about using a written premarital agreement to specify that all the property owned by Steven and Freda before their marriage would remain their separate property.

These are just a few examples of how you might approach the subject of a prenup. You will know best what will work for you. The most important thing is to clearly and kindly express what you want—and to be open to your partner's point of view.

Deciding on the Specifics

O nce you've decided you want a prenup, it's time to work out the details of your agreement. But where to start? Here's a step-by-step approach to figuring out what to include in your prenup.

Evaluate Your Situation

Before you even begin discussing details with your partner, it's a good idea to make some notes about your individual financial position and goals for the prenup. Having a written summary of your situation will help you stay on target when you're face to face with your partner. It will also be useful when you compile the written financial disclosures for the prenup and prepare an outline of terms to include in the prenup itself.

Step 1: Inventory Your Finances

A good way to start determining guidelines for your financial future as a married couple is to get a clear picture of your current financial circumstances.

To develop a snapshot of your finances, we suggest that you and your fiancé each prepare a financial inventory. When you've finished, you'll share your inventories as you decide what your prenup should say about property ownership and other financial issues. Your financial inventory will also be the basis of the written financial disclosures attached to your prenup, so be sure to make the inventory as complete and accurate as possible.

> RESOURCE
>
> **Having trouble getting started?** Thinking about money isn't everyone's cup of tea. Some of us are comfortable working with financial information, while others find the very idea overwhelming. If you fall into the latter category, talking with a good financial adviser might help ease your fears. You might also find the following books helpful:
>
> - *The Energy of Money: A Spiritual Guide to Financial and Personal Fulfillment,* by Maria Nemeth, PhD (Wellspring/Ballantine)

- *Money Harmony: A Roadmap for Individuals and Couples*, by Olivia Mellan and Sherry Christie (Money Harmony Books), and
- *Emotional Currency: A Woman's Guide to Building a Healthy Relationship With Money*, by Kate Levinson, PhD (Celestial Arts).

To prepare your inventory, you can use Worksheet 1: Financial Inventory (available in Appendix B and on the book's online companion page) or you can choose some other format. (See "Don't Reinvent the Wheel," below.)

Don't Reinvent the Wheel

If the inventory we're describing sounds familiar, that's probably because you've already made one. Many of us have prepared a personal financial statement (or net worth statement) for some other purpose, like applying for a mortgage or other loan. If you still have a copy of that financial statement or loan application, you can use it as a starting point and update it if needed.

Even if you haven't previously prepared a financial inventory, you might have access to one without realizing it. For example, many personal finance programs and apps—such as Quicken or Mint.com—have the capacity to generate net worth reports and income/expense (cash flow) statements. If you already keep track of your finances in this way, you might be able to generate a complete report at the push of a button. (You could also take this opportunity to start keeping track of your finances through a software or online program. Then you can update the information and print out a report whenever you need it.)

Choose whatever method works best for you. Just be sure to include the basics that we discuss below: what you own, what you owe, how much you make, and how much you spend.

SKIP AHEAD

Have you already done an inventory? If you've already prepared a thorough inventory, you can skip the rest of this section and go on to the next step, "Step 2: Examine Your Credit History and Spending Habits."

Even if you and your fiancé are working through this book together, we recommend that you complete separate financial inventories. Each of your inventories should include a thorough breakdown of your individual:

- assets
- debts
- income, and
- expenses.

Here's how to get started with your inventory of each of these categories.

Listing Your Assets

An asset is any property you own that has value, such as cash, real estate, investment accounts, retirement plans, personal property, and money that others owe you.

When describing and valuing your assets, you should be as thorough, specific, and accurate as possible. Obviously, we don't expect you to list everything you own down to your paper clips and the leftovers in your fridge, but you'll want to make sure to include everything that's important to you—financially or sentimentally. Use Worksheet 1 on the book's companion page and in Appendix B to jog your thinking about what you might include in your inventory.

Categorize assets to save time. You don't need to list every item of property separately—you can use categories for similar types of property. For example, you might list all of your household furnishings, linens, kitchenware, appliances, and the like as "household goods." You can then estimate the total value of all of the items in that category. When you prepare the written disclosure that will be attached to your prenup, you might decide to be more detailed with some assets, but that's not necessary at this stage.

Specify your ownership percentage. If you own less than 100% of an asset because you share ownership with another person, indicate your percentage and the value of your share.

Use market values. Include your best estimate of the current market value of each asset or category of assets. If you have a recent appraisal, that can be a good point of reference. Here are some tips on how to determine the value of particular items of property:

- **Real estate.** Use online property listing estimates—such as those on Zillow.com or Redfin.com—as a starting point in determining the value of real estate. In addition, you can ask a local real estate agent for a list of "comps" (records of recent sales of comparable properties): Many agents are happy to promote their services by providing a complimentary "property profile" that estimates your property's value.

- **Vehicles.** You can get values for vehicles from one of the "blue book" type services available online (try kbb.com or Edmunds.com), or check your local library for the most current volume of one of the popular vehicle value reports. It's best to use a "private party sale" value rather than wholesale (which tends to be low) or retail (which is often high).

- **Household goods.** Classified ads or websites like craigslist.org or eBay.com are good sources for valuing large household items. For more valuable items, such as antiques, collectibles, jewelry, and art, consider checking its worth on a site such as ValueMyStuff.com or WorthPoint.com.

- **Stocks, bonds, and mutual funds.** If you own investments like these through a broker, your monthly or quarterly statement will show their values as of the statement date. You can obtain current values from your broker, from any daily newspaper, or from one of the many stock trading websites on the Internet.

- **Small businesses.** If you own all or part of a small business—that is, one that is not publicly traded on the stock market—determining the market value of the business might be tricky, unless you just purchased the business or recently had it appraised for some other reason, such as applying for a loan or buying out a partner.

Appraisers use many different methods for valuing businesses. Some methods are as simple as multiplying the yearly gross receipts of the business by a certain number (typically a number between one and four, depending on the type of business).

Other methods are much more complicated. Which method to use depends on the circumstances and the type of business. If you don't have recent data on the value of your business, ask your accountant to help. The accountant might have an easy way to estimate the market value of your particular business. If not, the accountant can give you a balance sheet showing the "book value" of the business.

Book value first considers the original cost of the assets owned by the business, then adjusts that amount for depreciation and outstanding liabilities. Book value might not accurately reflect the market value of the business assets, nor will it take into account the intangible "goodwill" value of the business. Nevertheless, it is a good starting point for your discussions about a prenup, and it can be replaced by a more accurate market value later, if you decide that is necessary. If you do use book value, make a note of this on your inventory.

Listing Your Debts

A debt is a legal obligation to pay money now or in the future. Common debts include:

- mortgages
- car payments
- amounts owed on lines of credit
- unpaid taxes (along with penalties and interest)
- judgments
- student loans, and
- personal loans.

Bills that get paid in full when due, such as utilities and insurance premiums, are in a sense debts too, until they're paid. But you don't need to include those recurring monthly bills in the "debts" section of your financial inventory unless they are overdue. The same is true of revolving credit arrangements or credit card charges; don't list them unless the balance due is more than what you will pay off in the current month.

A special category of debt is any obligation owed to a former spouse—or to the other parent of your child. Include child support and alimony (spousal support) obligations on your list of debts, even if you are current in your payments. If you owe a property settlement or reimbursement payment under a divorce decree (judgment), include that in your list. Sometimes a divorce decree requires you to do something other than pay money. For example, you might be required to maintain dependent medical insurance coverage for your children. Or you might have to keep a life insurance policy for your children or your former spouse. If so, list those obligations. Even though they are not technically debts, these obligations should be considered when you decide what goes in your prenup.

Listing Your Income

The financial inventory you are preparing should include a reasonably accurate picture of your current income from all sources. If you filed a federal income tax return for last year (Form 1040), and if your income hasn't changed significantly since then, you can put down the same amounts that appear in the income section of your return. The income section of our financial inventory worksheet includes the most common income categories, with a space to insert others.

If your income in any category has changed significantly since the time covered by your last income tax return—or if you haven't filed an income tax return recently—then you'll need to insert the current amounts using whatever records you have, such as pay stubs or monthly investment statements. This might involve converting monthly or quarterly figures to yearly amounts.

Sometimes income varies substantially from year to year. This is particularly true of business or investment income. If this is your situation, take a look at your annual income for the last three to five years and come up with a reasonable average. Indicate that average on your worksheet.

Listing Your Expenses

Unless you and your future spouse are already living together, you might not know what the other spends on housing, food, clothing, and other personal items. Sharing with each other a summary of your current expenditures will help you assess differences and similarities in spending patterns, so that you can decide whether to include an agreement about budgeting in your prenup.

Because your monthly expenses will probably change after you marry, you don't have to go into great detail when listing your expenses. Just summarize your expenses in major categories. Our financial inventory worksheet breaks expenses down in four categories:

- housing
- transportation and auto
- necessities (such as food, clothing, and medical expenses), and
- other (such as entertainment, travel, gifts, and charitable giving).

Feel free to be flexible in your approach; you might come up with different categories that work better for your lifestyle. You can insert a total amount for each category or break down a category into smaller ones, as we do on the financial inventory sheet.

Not every expense comes due on the same schedule, so you might decide that an annual, a monthly, a quarterly, or another period of accounting will provide the most accurate numbers. Any approach will work, as long as you indicate which one you're using and are consistent.

Step 2: Examine Your Credit History and Spending Habits

In addition to sharing information about your assets, debts, incomes, and expenses, the two of you should have an honest discussion about your credit ratings and your philosophies on spending and saving. And if you have had credit problems in the past, the sooner you bring this up the better. Putting off this discussion is not a good way to start your financial partnership, even without a prenup.

To prepare for your conversation about spending and credit, continue your separate inventory process by taking a look at your individual credit history and your own approach to spending and saving.

Credit History

The best way to start investigating your credit history is to order a copy of your current credit report. Under a federal law, you are entitled to receive one free credit report from each of the major credit reporting agencies every 12 months. To request your free annual reports, you must use the central source established for this purpose. For more information, visit AnnualCreditReport.com or call 877-322-8228.

In addition to the free service, you can order your credit report directly from any of the three major credit bureaus listed below:

- Equifax: 888-378-4329, Equifax.com
- Experian: 888-397-3742, Experian.com, and
- TransUnion: 833-395-6938, TransUnion.com.

TIP

Cleaning up your credit. Nearly 70% of credit reports contain at least minor errors—and many contain mistakes that can seriously damage your creditworthiness. If you haven't checked your credit report recently, this is a good time to review it for errors and make any necessary corrections. For detailed information on checking your credit report and cleaning it up, see *Credit Repair*, by Amy Loftsgordon and Cara O'Neill (Nolo).

In addition to getting a copy of your credit report, we recommend that you jot down the answers to the following questions about your credit history. (We've included a worksheet for you to use to note your answers; see Worksheet 2: Credit History and Spending Habits on the book's companion page or in Appendix B.)

1. Do you currently owe any debt that is more than 60 days overdue? If so, specify the debt and the amount you owe.
2. Have you been turned down for a loan or credit card in the last two years? If so, give details (when, by whom, and the reason given for the denial of credit).
3. Have you ever been sued for failing to pay a debt? If so, give details (when, by whom, what court, amount of the claim, and the outcome).

Spending and Saving Habits

After you've taken a look at your credit history, spend some time thinking about your financial philosophy. Are you a saver or do you spend money as fast as you earn it? Do you believe in borrowing to take advantage of financial opportunities or are you more comfortable keeping spending within the limits of your income? The answers to these and similar questions reveal a lot about how you will approach spending decisions in your marriage.

To get started, answer the following questions. This will give you a snapshot of your own financial philosophy, both in theory and in practice. You can record your answers on Worksheet 2, if you like.

1. On a scale of one to five (one being least important and five being most important), how important is it to you to set aside savings on a regular basis?
2. On a scale of one to five (one being least comfortable and five being most comfortable), how comfortable are you with going into debt to take advantage of an investment opportunity?
3. Do you usually pay bills early, on time, a little late, or very late?
4. Of the following methods, which ones do you use to pay bills and everyday expenses (list all that apply):
   - cash
   - check
   - automatic transfer from a checking or other bank account
   - online bill pay
   - credit card, or
   - other (specify).
5. How many credit card accounts do you currently have?
6. Do you pay credit card bills in full each month? (Always, Never, Frequently, Occasionally)
7. How often do you balance your checkbook? (Always, Never, Frequently, Occasionally)
8. Do you participate in a voluntary savings program?
9. Have you set aside money in a savings account or other investment (including retirement accounts) in the past 12 months?

10. How many secured loans have you obtained in the past 12 months? How much money did you borrow?

11. How many unsecured loans have you obtained in the past 12 months? How much money did you borrow?

12. Is there any other information you consider significant in analyzing your spending and saving habits?

Step 3: Scan the Financial Horizon

The next step in your financial self-assessment is to look at the road ahead. Are you planning a major investment sometime soon—such as buying a house or starting a business? Will you be changing jobs or going back to school in the foreseeable future? Has a parent or another relative informed you that you will be the recipient of a substantial inheritance?

If possibilities such as these are on your financial horizon, it's important to think about how they might affect what you say in your prenup. For example, you might not own any separate property now, but if your parents have informed you that you are the beneficiary of a trust, you might want your prenup to identify any property or funds that you receive from the trust as your separate property.

Here are the questions that will help you focus on upcoming financial developments. If you like, you can jot down your answers on Worksheet 3: Financial Outlook (which is in Appendix B or on the book's companion page).

1. Do you plan to make a major purchase or an investment of more than $10,000 in the next two years?

2. Are you planning a career change in the next two years?

3. Are you planning to retire from your current occupation in the next five years?

4. Are you planning to enter a college, vocational, or professional school in the next few years?

5. Do you expect to receive a significant inheritance or gift in the next few years?

6. Do you know of any other approaching events that are likely to affect your financial status?

Step 4: Identify Your Goals

After you complete your financial inventory, focus on what you hope to accomplish in the prenup. Your goals will likely fall into one or more of these categories:

- identifying which assets you will keep separate and which you will share
- protecting yourself from your future spouse's debts
- clarifying each spouse's financial responsibilities
- supporting your estate plan, with an emphasis on providing for children from prior marriages or passing on family property
- providing for each other after one of you dies, or
- defining who gets what if you divorce.

Within these general categories, your goals will be unique to your situation. You might also find that your goals change or that you add new goals after the two of you explore things further. At this point, your list of goals is merely a starting point for your discussion.

As you list your goals, note which ones are most important to you. By prioritizing your goals, you can distill what you'll consider essential to include in your prenup.

You can each use a copy of Worksheet 4: Prenup Goals, found in Appendix B and on the book's companion page, to record your goals and note which ones are most important to you.

 Ted and Grace

Ted wants his prenup with Grace to accomplish two main goals:

- to affirm and preserve his plan to leave the bulk of his estate to his children and grandchildren, and
- to anticipate and prevent any potential disagreements that might arise between Grace and his children over his estate after he dies.

Karen and Russ

When Karen considers a prenup, she comes up with these main goals:

- to protect her separate assets, including the veterinary practice, from Russ's child support obligations
- to agree on an equitable way of settling Russ's potential community property claims on the practice and other assets if she and Russ divorce, and
- to ensure her ability to fulfill the obligation in the divorce agreement from her previous marriage to provide an inheritance for her children if she dies before the children reach age 25.

Talk It Through

After completing the steps outlined above, make copies of all four worksheets so that you have a set and your fiancé has a set. Now you're ready to sit down together and exchange the information you've compiled. Follow the approach outlined in the remaining sections of this chapter. For more detailed help on talking together and negotiating the terms of your prenup, see Chapter 11.

Share Your Results

You might be a little apprehensive about the conversation you are about to have. Here are several simple things you can do to help your conversation go smoothly.

Choose the Time and Place With Care

Optimize your chances of having a productive and relaxed discussion by setting aside enough time to go over all four worksheets without feeling pressured. A couple of hours should do it. And be sure to select a time when you're not too tired or stressed from other demands.

Pick a place that's comfortable and free of distractions. Choose whatever location will be conducive to a relaxed and distraction-free discussion.

Pace Yourselves

Some people can easily review their worksheets in a single conversation. Others prefer to conduct the conversation in segments. Choose whatever approach seems right for the two of you and be prepared to adapt if you need to go slower or faster. There is no "right" way to go about it. Just be sure you allow enough time to cover everything thoroughly and thoughtfully.

Take Turns

It's possible that you and your future spouse are coming into the marriage with very different financial backgrounds. It's important to discuss these differences (and similarities) without feeling embarrassed or uncomfortable. To stay on the right track, consider taking turns when sharing the contents of your worksheets.

For example, Ted might start by showing Grace his financial inventory (Worksheet 1: Financial Inventory). He would answer any questions Grace has about the financial information on the inventory. Grace would then show Ted a copy of her Worksheet 1, and they would discuss his questions about it. Then Grace would start first with Worksheet 2, and they would continue to alternate in this way through all four worksheets.

Stick to the Facts

At this point in your conversation, your goal is to understand each other's financial circumstances and perspectives as clearly as possible.

Your discussion might reveal some key differences between you and your future spouse—not just in the financial specifics but also in how you approach decisions about property and finances. If so, resist the temptation to short-circuit the information exchange by minimizing or quickly negotiating away these differences. First, get a firm grasp on the reality of your separate finances and how you approach them.

Stay honest, even when your approaches appear to differ. Then, when you really understand each other, you'll be ready to look for mutually acceptable arrangements. It's worth hanging in there even if things get a little bit uncomfortable: The result will be a prenup that works for both of you.

> **TIP**
>
> **Ask for what you want.** As you talk together about your goals and how to achieve them, don't be afraid to be specific about what you want, no matter how wild and crazy—or mundane—your hopes and preferences might seem to you. In all likelihood, your fiancé will want to make you happy by saying yes to your request, if it's within reason and doesn't interfere with something else that's important. If you don't say what you want, there's much less chance you'll get it.

Agree on the Basics

After you've analyzed all four worksheets, you'll be poised for the next step in making a prenup. This step, like the preceding one, will take an hour or two. As you did when exchanging information, pick a time and place that will be conducive to a relaxed but focused discussion. Pace yourselves by breaking the discussion into two or three different sessions if necessary, and take turns expressing your views.

Each of you should have your list of prenup goals (Worksheet 4: Prenup Goals) in front of you. Go over each person's goals. Highlight or mark each goal that you both want your prenup to meet. If you disagree about a goal, make a note of that and set it aside to return to later.

Think about what you might include in your prenup to meet each of the goals you both want to address. Then write down what you want to put in your agreement. For example, Ted and Grace want to ensure that the bulk of Ted's estate will pass to Ted's children when he dies. So they agree that their prenup should include waivers of surviving spouse rights that could interfere with that goal. (Chapters 5 through 9 will supply the clauses you need to cover each goal in the prenup itself.)

Use Worksheet 5: The Basics of Our Prenup to record your results. (You can find it on the book's online companion page—see Appendix B for details.) Below is a sample worksheet showing how Ted and Grace listed the essential points for their agreement.

Once you've gone through all the goals once, ask yourselves whether there is anything else you'd like to include in the prenup. Add any additional items to your list in Worksheet 5.

Next, go back to the goals you disagreed about. Do you still disagree? (Sometimes what initially looked like a conflict can be easily resolved after you've talked about other matters and taken a second look.) If you still differ on a particular goal, decide how you will resolve those differences. (See Chapter 11.)

After you've completed these steps, the contents of Worksheet 5 will serve as a list of the basic elements of your prenup. Congratulate yourselves on a job well done and take a break before you continue.

Will Your Prenup Pass the Fairness Test?

Now that you've outlined what you want in your prenup, you're almost ready to start preparing a draft. But before you proceed, you should ask yourself:

- Are you on your way to making an agreement that's fair?
- If you didn't make a prenup, would the laws of your state (or federal law, if it applies) accomplish your goals?

This section explains in detail what you must do to make an agreement that's fair. Chapter 4 will help you understand the laws that affect prenups.

You'll recall from the introduction that a prenup will likely pass the fairness test when:

- its terms reflect a balanced arrangement that benefits both parties, and
- you've negotiated the agreement without subjecting each other to undue pressure or coercion.

10/14/20xx
Date Prepared

Ted Bedford and Grace Nelson
Your Names

Worksheet 5: The Basics of Our Prenup

1. Premarital assets will be:
   - ☑ Separate property
   - ☐ Marital property
   - ☐ Community property
   - ☐ Exceptions or special provisions (specify): _____

2. Any of the following assets we acquire during our marriage will be:

	Separate	Marital Property	Community Property
a. Real estate purchased	☑	☐	☐
b. Each person's salary earned during marriage	☑	☐	☐
c. Retirement benefits earned during our marriage	☑	☐	☐
d. Stock options and other employment benefits earned during our marriage	☑	☐	☐
e. Any increase in the value of a premarital business	☑	☐	☐
f. Other investments	☑	☐	☐
g. Joint bank accounts (see below #3)	☑	☐	☐
h. Other: _____	☐	☐	☐

3. Special provisions concerning assets acquired during marriage. Details:
   Joint bank accounts: Funds will be shared in proportion to contributions. Reconcile each January. Gifts to each other will be separate property of the person receiving the gift.

4. Our prenup will provide the following regarding each person's premarital debts. Details:
   Each person's debts are his or her sole responsibility.

5. Our prenup will provide the following regarding business debts or other debts incurred during marriage. Details:
   Ted's business debts incurred during marriage are his sole responsibility.

6. Our prenup will spell out a process for deciding whether to file joint tax returns and how to allocate income, deductions, taxes, and refunds. Details:

   Consult with accountant each year: Compare filing jointly and separately then pick the most advantageous. If separate returns allocate all past income and deductions to each, each pays own taxes. Ted pays all accountants' fees and all taxes on joint returns. Any refund to person who paid tax.

7. Our prenup will define each person's responsibility for household expenses. Details:

   Ted will pay all. Deposit necessary amount in joint checking account.

8. This is how our prenup will support our intended estate plans (this might require waivers of surviving spouse rights). Details:

   Both waive surviving spouse rights.

9. Our prenup will provide for our estate plans to include the following terms. Details:

   Ted's trust will leave $500,000 to Grace, plus the right to stay in the house and $5,000 per month for one year.

10. Our prenup will provide for support of the surviving spouse. Details:

    See #8 and #9 above.

11. Our prenup will specify what should happen to our property if we separate and divorce. Details:

    N/A

12. Our prenup will limit, avoid, or provide for alimony if we separate and divorce. Details:

    Ted waives alimony. Grace gets $5,000 per month to age 62,
    unless she remarries.

13. Our prenup will include other agreements that apply if we divorce. Details:

    N/A

14. Other provisions of our prenup. Details:

    N/A

Fair Terms

Take some time to make sure that the plan you've outlined for your prenup is well balanced so that you won't make an agreement that obviously disfavors one of you. And commit to reevaluating the terms of your agreement periodically, even after you've signed it. If your circumstances change significantly, what's fair now could seem otherwise later on. (See Chapter 12 for more information on giving your prenup occasional checkups.)

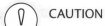

CAUTION

Making an agreement that appears imbalanced. We don't recommend it, but you might find yourself wanting to make an agreement that seems to disproportionately benefit one of you. Be aware that some courts will assume that such a prenup is fraudulent, putting the pressure on you to prove otherwise. For example, a court might be inclined to overturn a prenup in which a much less wealthy person gives up rights to spousal support in the event of a divorce or waives all inheritance rights. You'd have to show that such an arrangement was actually fair. If you even suspect that there's something in your document that might look suspicious to a court, you should follow each of the tips in "What's Fair?" below, being especially sure to seek advice from separate lawyers.

Fair Process

Ultimately, *how* you negotiate your prenup could be even more important than what it actually says. Not only is an equitable process critical to making a prenup that's enforceable in court, but—probably much more important—negotiating fairly is what will leave the two of you with good feelings about each other and your agreement. We suggest that you stick to the following guidelines:

What's Fair?

Courts take different approaches when deciding whether or not a prenup is fair. Some look only at how the agreement was negotiated, but most give at least some consideration to the terms of the agreement itself. Courts commonly consider the following factors when analyzing the fairness of a prenup:

- your goals in entering the agreement
- the amount of income and property that each of you owns
- your family relationships and obligations
- your education, occupation, and earning capacity
- the expected contribution one of you will make to the education, training, or increased earning power of the other
- your future needs
- your age and health (physically and emotionally)
- your expected contribution to the marriage (pay careful attention to the value of contributions such as caring for the house or children), and
- your ability to support yourself after divorce or the death of your spouse.

The last of these factors is particularly important. Consider your plan in light of what might happen if the two of you divorce or if one of you dies. If your prenup would leave one of you struggling to make ends meet while the other—or the other's heirs—are well off, you've clearly got some balancing to do.

- Understand the property rights you would have in the event of a divorce or at death, without a premarital agreement (we'll discuss this in the next chapter).
- Understand every provision of the agreement before you sign it.

- Be impeccably honest in your negotiations, especially when it comes to disclosing information about your financial situation.
- Allow sufficient time for negotiating the terms of the agreement (as mentioned earlier, we think it's wise to allow at least two months for this part of the process).
- Have your document reviewed by separate lawyers before you sign it (see Chapter 10).
- Don't sign the agreement under any kind of pressure, whether it be mental or emotional stress or a simple lack of time to consider and reflect upon what you're signing (remember, we suggest signing the agreement at least one month before your wedding).

Understanding Your State's Law

There's one more step to take before you start drafting your prenup: You'll want to cross-reference your prenup goals with the laws of your state (and federal law, if necessary). This will help you make a final decision about whether you need a prenup.

To see how your prenup plans compare to existing law, you will need to do some legal research or consult a lawyer versed in these matters—or both. This chapter will:

- help you determine which laws will govern your prenup
- provide an overview of the law itself, and
- give you guidance on how to look up more details.

Which Laws Apply to Your Prenup?

If you consult a lawyer at this stage, the lawyer can tell you which state or federal law applies to each provision of your prenup. If you'll be doing your own legal research, you'll need to make sure you are looking at state law when appropriate and at federal law when it applies. And because laws vary from state to state, you'll also want to decide which state's laws are going to govern your prenup.

State or Federal Law?

The law that applies to your prenup will usually be state law, which covers most aspects of family and estate planning law. Federal law comes up only when a federal benefit or federal program is involved. For example, federal laws typically regulate:

- pension and retirement benefits for federal government workers and members of the military
- private sector retirement plans that are approved for favorable federal tax treatment
- Social Security benefits
- Medicare benefits, and
- matters related to bankruptcy.

If you are thinking of making agreements about such matters in your prenup, you will need to consult both federal and state law.

Which State's Law Applies to Your Prenup?

As for which state's laws to consider, start with the laws of the state where you maintain your permanent residence (your "domicile"). Your domicile is typically the state where you live and work most of the time, own or rent your home, and vote.

If you plan to move to a different state after you marry, or even if you think a future move is a possibility, you might want to compare the states' laws to see which one provides you with the best options. Then you can include in your agreement a "choice of law" clause designating the state whose laws will govern your prenup regardless of what state is your current domicile. (We provide an example of such a clause in Chapter 9.) For example, if you live in New York but plan to move to California, you would compare the laws of the two states and then designate the one that best supports your prenup in a "choice of law" clause.

Preparing to Review the Law

To prepare for a meeting with your lawyer or for doing your own research, refer to the prenup topics listed on Worksheet 5, "The Basics of Our Prenup." For each item on Worksheet 5, you'll ask the following questions:

- What does the law say about this item?
- Will the law allow us to create a different result in our premarital agreement?
- Is there any special legal restriction, procedure, or consideration that applies to this item?

You can use Worksheet 6 in Appendix B and on the book's companion page to record your answers to these questions.

Russ and Karen

Russ and Karen want Karen's veterinary veterinary practice to be considered her separate property. If the practice grows in value during their marriage, however, they want to come up with an equitable formula for sharing the increase. When Russ volunteers to do some research on the subject, he discovers these answers to his three questions about the veterinary practice:

How does the law cover this item? California (a community property state) provides that a business owned before marriage is the separate property of the spouse who started it. If the value of the business increases during the marriage, then a portion of the increase in value may be considered community (jointly owned) property.

Will the law allow us to come up with a different result in our prenuptial agreement? Yes. State law will honor a written prenuptial agreement providing that some, all, or none of the value of the veterinary practice is to be considered community property. If there is to be partially shared ownership, the prenup may specify a formula to be used in determining the shared portion.

Is there any special legal restriction, procedure, or consideration that applies to this item? Yes. If Karen and Russ divorce, or when one of them dies, there is the possibility of an expensive and complicated court procedure (with dueling experts) to determine the community share of Karen's veterinary practice—unless Karen and Russ have already specified their own approach in a written prenuptial agreement.

An Overview of State Law

When learning about the law, one of your tasks is to gain some understanding of how your state regulates the property of married people who don't make written agreements. It might turn out that in your circumstances, state law takes care of some or all matters just as well as a prenup would.

Short of compiling a 50-volume treatise, it would be impossible for us to cover every complexity and nuance of marital property law for every state. This section provides some fundamentals to get you started. (You can find additional information for your state on the book's online companion page.) If you have a question about state law that isn't answered in this book, you'll need to ask your lawyer or do some more research on your own. (See "Researching State Law," near the end of this chapter, to learn about doing your own legal research.)

SKIP AHEAD

When to skim or skip this material. If you're already working with a lawyer, you might prefer to have the lawyer tell you how your prenup plan compares to state law. In that case, you can quickly review this section for general information—or skip it altogether and turn to Chapter 5 to begin drafting your agreement.

There are a number of important issues to consider when learning how your state governs marital property. This chapter covers:
- who owns property that either of you acquires before or during your marriage
- who is permitted to manage or control any property you own together
- who is responsible for debts incurred before or during your marriage
- what property each of you will be entitled to claim from the other's estate at death, and
- what will happen if you divorce, including how property and debts will be divided and whether either of you must pay alimony.

Keep in mind that you can use a prenup to choose among most of the rules discussed in this chapter and, in most cases, craft your own guidelines if you don't care for the laws of your state. The main goal of this chapter is to introduce you to some options and help you understand what rules apply to your property if you don't make a prenup.

Ownership of Property During Marriage

Without a prenup, state law determines what property you own before and during your marriage. If you decide to make a premarital agreement, you can use it to either confirm or override state law by designating certain assets as nonmarital (or separate) property and other property as marital (or community) property. In Chapter 8, you'll get lots of guidance about how to do this. Before you begin, however, you'll need to know whether you live in a "community property" or "equitable distribution" state (also called a "common law" state) and how your state treats the property of married couples.

A handful of states follow community property laws, while most states use an equitable distribution system.

Community Property and Equitable Distribution States	
Community Property	**Equitable Distribution**
Arizona	All other states and the District of Columbia, except as follows:
California	Alaska: spouses may create community property by written agreement or community property trust; Kentucky, South Dakota, and Tennessee: spouses may create a community property trust
Idaho	
Louisiana	
Nevada	
New Mexico	
Texas	
Washington	
Wisconsin	

Community Property States

A number of states, mostly in the West, use what's known as a "community property" system to govern marital property. (These laws originated with ancient Europeans and came to the western United States through Spanish and French explorers and settlers.) The community property states are Arizona, California, Idaho, Louisiana, Nevada, New Mexico, Texas, and Washington. Wisconsin follows a system so similar that it is usually considered a community property state, though its laws use the term "marital property" instead. And in Alaska, South Dakota, and Tennessee, a couple can elect to have their property treated as community property if they make a written agreement or trust to that effect.

The basic rule of community property law is simple: During a marriage, all property earned or acquired by either spouse is owned 50/50 by each spouse, except for property received by only one of them through gift or inheritance.

More specifically, community property usually includes:

- All income received during marriage by either spouse from employment or any other source (except gifts to or inheritance by just one spouse)—for example, wages, stock options, pensions and other employment compensation, and business profits. This rule generally applies only to the period when the couple lives together as spouses. Most community property states consider income and property acquired after the spouses permanently separate to be the separate property of the spouse who receives it.
- All property acquired with community property income during the marriage.
- All separate property that is transformed into community property under state law. This transformation can occur in several ways, including when one spouse makes a gift of separate property to both of them or when property is so mixed together that it's no longer possible to tell what property is separate (lawyers call this "commingling").

- In a few community property states, income derived during marriage from separate property—for example, rent, interest, or dividends—is community property. Most community property states consider such income to be separate property, however.

EXAMPLE: Beth and Daniel live in Idaho, one of the few community property states where income derived from separate property belongs to the community. Beth inherits 22 head of Angus cattle from her father. Those cattle go on to breed a herd of more than 100 cattle. All the descendants of the original 22 animals are considered income from Beth's separate property and are included in the couple's community property estate; the original 22 head of cattle remain Beth's separate property.

Since a title document doesn't necessarily indicate whether an asset is community property or separate property, making a prenup can help avoid confusion about your intentions by specifying what's community property and what's separate, even if you want state law to apply to what you own. And of course, if you live in a community property state but don't want community property laws to apply, a prenup is essential. In your agreement, you can write down your own rules for what is separate property and what is community property, regardless of how you hold title or what your state's law says. Chapters 5 through 9 will help you craft the rules that you want.

Equitable Distribution States

States that have not adopted a community property system are typically called "equitable distribution states." In these states, the spouse who earns money or acquires property during the marriage owns it separately, unless it is transferred into a form of joint ownership such as joint tenancy, tenancy by the entirety, or tenancy in common. (See "Ways to Own Property Together," below.)

What Is Separate Property?

In all states, spouses are permitted to treat certain types of earnings and assets as separate property. This means that the spouse can do pretty much anything with the property—for example, borrow against it, sell it, give it away, or leave it in a will—without the consent of the other spouse. What qualifies as separate property depends on state law.

Community property states. The following property qualifies as separate property in virtually all community property states:

- property that a spouse owns before marriage
- property that a spouse receives after marriage by gift or inheritance
- property that a spouse purchases using only separate property, and
- property that a spouse earns or accumulates after permanent separation.

In some states, additional types of property—such as one spouse's personal injury award received during marriage—may also be separate property.

States differ in how they treat income earned from separate property. In most community property states, such income is separate. But some take the opposite approach, treating income from separate property as community property.

Normally, separate property stays separate as long as it is not:

- mixed with marital property so that it is impossible to tell what is separate and what is not, or
- transferred in writing into a form of shared ownership.

Just as separate property can be transformed into shared property, community property can become separate property by a gift from one spouse to the other. The rules differ from state to state, but in general, gifts that transform one type of property into another must be made with a signed document. Chapter 7 explains how you can use your prenup to specify whether your property will be considered community or separate.

Equitable distribution states. In equitable distribution states, all property that a spouse owns before marriage is that spouse's separate property. Although property earned or acquired by one spouse during marriage is that spouse's separate property, it might be subject to division if the couple divorces. If you make a prenup, you can keep separate property separate by specifying that it will not be considered marital property if you later divorce. Chapter 8 explains how.

The twist here is that even though equitable distribution states technically allow spouses to own and accumulate more separate property than spouses are allowed to in community property states, they don't get to keep all of that property in the event of a divorce—or leave it without restrictions at death. Most property acquired during marriage is considered marital property, which means that the property is subject to division in the event of a divorce even if just one spouse owns the property on paper. (We discuss this in "Property Rights If You Divorce," below.) In this limited way, marital property functions very much like community property. And for inheritance purposes, even though a spouse is permitted to leave property held in their name to anyone at all, there are rules that guarantee that a surviving spouse will receive a portion of a deceased spouse's property, no matter what that spouse's will or other estate plan says. (See "Property Rights at Death," below.)

Managing and Controlling Property During Marriage

If you live in an equitable distribution state, you will need a prenup if you want to opt out of the equitable distribution rules. For example, you can provide that certain property held in one person's name is still to be considered jointly owned (marital) property during your marriage. Or you can state the reverse: that certain property held in your joint names is actually the solely owned (separate) property of one of you. When a marriage is going well, the issue of who owns a particular asset or item of property rarely arises. It usually comes up only if there's a question or disagreement about who gets to control the property—for example, if one spouse wants to sell or give away property and the other spouse objects, or if one person wants to manage money or other property in a way the other doesn't agree with. This section will give you an idea of who is legally entitled to control property when there is no written agreement covering the matter.

Ways to Own Property Together

When two or more people are the legal owners of a piece of property, they are generally called "joint owners." There are several different ways that spouses can own property together. Here are the most common:

Joint tenancy. This type of property is held with a written ownership document identifying the owners either as "joint tenants" or "joint tenants with right of survivorship" (some states require minor variations to this language to make a joint tenancy legal). Each joint tenant owns an equal share of the property. The share of the first tenant to die must go to the survivors—that's what's meant by "right of survivorship."

Tenancy by the entirety. This form of ownership, limited to married couples, is recognized in about half the states. It is almost identical to joint tenancy and creates a right of survivorship between the spouses. Like a joint tenancy, it must be created in writing.

Community property. In the community property states (listed in "Ownership of Property During Marriage," above), any property spouses earn or acquire during marriage is shared community property. This is true even if only one spouse's name is on the title document.

Community property with right of survivorship. This form of community property functions just like joint tenancy—the surviving spouse automatically inherits the property when the other spouse dies. It is available only in Alaska, Arizona, California, Nevada, and Wisconsin.

Tenancy in common. Any jointly owned property that doesn't fall into one of the categories listed above is held as tenants in common. This usually includes much of the property spouses own together in common law states. Unlike joint tenancy, owners' shares don't have to be equal. You can own any percentage of tenancy in common property—for example, 5% or 95%. And also unlike joint tenancy, at your death you can leave your portion of property held as tenants in common to anyone you choose, unless you are either restricted by an agreement or your spouse defeats the gift by exercising inheritance rights. (See "Property Rights at Death," below.)

Community Property States

In almost all community property states, either spouse has the right to manage, control, or dispose of community property. But most states have created exceptions to this general rule. For example, in California (the most populous community property state), spouses must act together to sell, convey, or mortgage community property real estate or to lease it for more than one year. (Cal. Fam. Code § 1102.) And one spouse is not permitted to give away community property without the written consent of the other. (Cal. Fam. Code § 1100(b).) Other states have similar laws restricting one spouse's ability to dispose of certain types of community property without the consent of the other spouse.

In addition, while spouses can usually share in the management and control of community property, many states impose restrictions on the management of certain assets. For instance, in many states, if just one spouse operates a business that consists mostly of community property, that spouse has primary management rights over the business property. (Cal. Fam. Code § 1100(d); Nev. Rev. Stat. § 123.230(6); Wash. Rev. Code Ann. § 26.16.030(6).)

> **EXAMPLE:** Alicia and Sam live in California. When they got married in 1999, they each put all the money they brought to the marriage (which wasn't all that much) into joint bank accounts. Since then, they have continued to mix all of their property together—including $250,000 that Alicia inherited from a wealthy aunt—so that everything they own now is considered community property. In 2013, Sam decides to open a small retail business specializing in fine local wines, something he knows a great deal about. With Alicia's blessing, he funds the new venture by withdrawing money from a brokerage account that contains a mix of Alicia's inheritance and his own savings. Even though the business is funded with community property—much of which was formerly Alicia's separate inheritance—Sam is entitled to run the business on his own; he doesn't have to consult Alicia about day-to-day business matters. However, if Sam takes a significant action, such as selling the business or pledging its assets as security for a loan, he must get Alicia's written consent.

Texas has taken a somewhat unique approach to community property management, calling certain assets "sole management community property." This is defined as all property that a spouse would have owned if single, including job earnings, income from separate property, and personal injury awards. (Tex. Fam. Code § 3.102(a).) Each spouse has the exclusive right to manage, control, and dispose of that spouse's sole management community property. All other community property in Texas is known as "joint community property," meaning that both spouses are entitled to participate in its management, control, and disposition. (Tex. Fam. Code § 3.102(c).)

> **EXAMPLE:** Elena and Paul live in Texas. Elena deposits part of her monthly pay into a money market savings account in her name only. The money in this account is part of her sole management community property. When her sister needs help, Elena decides to lend her most of the money she's saved. She can do so even if Paul objects.

Wisconsin, too, takes a different approach. Even though it is considered a community property state, the management and control of marital property (Wisconsin's term for community property) usually depends on whose name is on the title document. (Wis. Stat. Ann. § 766.51.) For example, let's say that one spouse acquires a boat with money earned during marriage (so the boat is considered marital property) and takes title to it in his own name. The boat-owning spouse is permitted to manage and control the boat; the other spouse has a say over that property only in very limited circumstances.

Wisconsin law imposes restrictions on gifts of marital property by just one spouse, but otherwise allows one spouse to sell or encumber marital property if that spouse is permitted to manage the property alone.

The one thing that all community property states absolutely agree about is that spouses are required to act ethically with regard to community property. In other words, one spouse is never permitted to defraud the other of an interest in their shared assets.

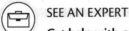 SEE AN EXPERT

Get help with questions about management or control of community property. Clearly, this is a complicated issue in every state. If you're unsure about your rights to buy, sell, give away, or invest community property, talk with your lawyer.

Equitable Distribution States

Each spouse usually has complete control of that spouse's separately titled property, even though some of that property might be deemed marital property and divided between the spouses in the event of a divorce. A handful of states have created an exception to this rule for the family home, which can't be sold or used as collateral for a loan without the consent of both spouses, no matter whose name is on the deed.

The Duty to Treat Each Other Fairly

As we discussed in Chapter 3, if you make a prenup, you must approach your negotiations with the utmost good faith and honesty. But once married, whether or not you've made a written agreement, you've entered into what's called a "confidential relationship" with your spouse. People in confidential relationships have a duty to act fairly toward each other—sometimes termed a "fiduciary duty." This means that you may not conceal or misappropriate property from one another, or incur debts holding the other liable without authorization—and it means that you must be open and honest with each other even during divorce. If a spouse breaches any of these duties, that spouse may be awarded a smaller share of marital property in the event of a divorce.

Most equitable distribution states give both spouses the right to manage and control their own shares of jointly owned property. This means that either spouse can sell, borrow against, give away, or invest the portion that they own. But there are exceptions to this rule in most states. One common exception is for property held in tenancy by the entirety (defined above in "Ways to Own Property Together"): Neither spouse is permitted to sell or encumber their own half of the property without the written consent of the other.

Debts: Who Is Responsible?

This section sets out the general rules about how spouses must pay debts during marriage in either community property or equitable distribution states. How debts are divided at divorce is covered in "Dividing Property and Debts," below. And of course you can use a prenup to specify your own rules about who is responsible for debts; that's discussed in detail in Chapter 7.

Under the laws of any state, which spouse is responsible for paying a debt may depend on several things:

- whether the debt was incurred before or during the marriage
- who agreed to the debt, and
- what the money was used for.

How these factors are applied depends on whether the state follows a community property or an equitable distribution system.

Community Property States

To understand which spouse is responsible for a debt in a community property state, you should first look to when the debt was incurred—that is, whether the spouse agreed to the debt before or during the marriage.

Debts incurred before marriage. Debts incurred by a spouse before marriage are primarily the responsibility of that spouse. In no case is the separate property of one spouse liable for debts incurred by the other spouse before marriage. However, creditors may turn to the couple's community property to collect one spouse's premarital debt. The spouse who did not incur the debt would then have to ask the other spouse for reimbursement.

All states place some restrictions on the amount and type of community property that can be taken to satisfy one spouse's premarital debts—or provide spouses with a method to protect a share of the community property. For instance, in California, the community property earnings of a nondebtor spouse may be shielded from the other spouse's premarital debts if the earnings are kept in a separate bank account and not mixed with other community property. (Cal. Fam. Code § 911.)

> **EXAMPLE:** When Marie and Pierre marry in California, Marie has a student loan debt of $45,000. She defaults on four payments of $250 each, and then continues not to pay. During the marriage, Pierre deposits his paycheck into a separate bank account in his own name. When the bank that lent Marie the money sues her for repayment, it can go after Marie's separate property and most of Marie and Pierre's community property—but Pierre's separate savings account can't be touched.

Debts incurred during marriage. In community property states, debts incurred during marriage by either spouse are considered "community debts." Usually, both community property and the separate property of the spouse who incurs the debts are liable for community property debts. In other words, if just one spouse binds the community to a debt, the separate property of the other spouse is normally protected. (There is usually an exception if the debt is for "necessaries of life" of either spouse—for example, food, housing, clothing, or medical care.) But if both spouses enter into a community debt, the separate property of each spouse is liable for that debt.

Equitable Distribution States

As in community property states, who is responsible for paying a debt depends on a number of factors. Again, one of the most important is when the debt was incurred.

Debts incurred before marriage. A spouse is generally not responsible for paying the debts the other spouse incurred before marriage. These debts are considered separate debts, and creditors will look first to the debtor-spouse's separate property for payment. In no case can the separately owned property of one spouse be taken by a creditor to pay the premarital debts of the other spouse.

> EXAMPLE: Martin is having financial troubles at the time of his marriage to Ellen. Just before they married, he closed his small construction business after failing to pay several subcontractors who are now threatening to sue him. If Ellen keeps her property clearly separate from Martin's, it will be safe from any court judgments these subcontractors obtain against him. If Ellen and Martin buy property together, however, or mix their money together in joint accounts, Ellen's interest in that shared property will be at risk for Martin's debts if Martin's separate property is not sufficient to cover what he owes.

Debts incurred during marriage. In most states, a spouse is individually liable for only those debts that they incur during marriage. In other words, a spouse can't be forced to pay bills that the other spouse runs up. However, both spouses are usually responsible for paying the following debts:
- debts incurred with joint accounts
- debts where the creditor considered both spouses' credit information (many debts incurred during marriage are likely to be this type)
- debts incurred for the necessities of either spouse or their children, such as food, clothing, housing, or medical care, and
- debts incurred for the care or education of the spouses' children.

Creditors will first look to jointly owned property to satisfy joint debts. But if there is not enough jointly owned property to cover what's due, the separate property of one spouse can be taken to pay debts that the spouses incur together. And of course, the separate property of one spouse is always liable for that spouse's separate debts.

> **EXAMPLE:** Clare and Saul purchase an expensive Lexus sedan and register it in both of their names. When they fail to make the payments, the car is repossessed. To cover the balance remaining on the car loan after it is sold at auction—as well as collection costs—the bank that holds the loan first looks to see whether it can reach any of the couple's joint assets for payment. When the bank discovers that nothing is available, it obtains an order to garnish Clare's wages for the amount due.

Property Rights at Death

As we discussed in Chapter 2, many couples make a prenup to specify how they will leave property at death. Usually, this amounts to making sure that children from a prior marriage receive their intended inheritance and that valuable property remains in the family. Without a prenup and some basic estate planning documents such as a will or trust, it's possible that state law could defeat these wishes.

In all states, spouses are guaranteed an inheritance when the other spouse dies. These laws are often called "election" laws because the surviving spouse "elects" to take property other than what was left under the deceased spouse's will or other property transfer documents. Below, we explain in general terms what election laws are and how they work. We also discuss the rules that you must follow if you want to waive any or all election rights in your prenup. State lawmakers justly consider inheritance rights to be important protections for surviving spouses, so many states are quite particular about the requirements you must meet to waive them.

If You Die Without a Will

Every state has laws setting out what a surviving spouse and other family members will inherit if someone dies without a will or another valid estate plan. These are called "intestate succession" laws. This book doesn't discuss intestate succession laws for one important reason: We assume that in addition to preparing a prenup, you'll each make a will and any other documents necessary to plan for what happens at death. As we've discussed, prenups go hand in hand with estate planning. It wouldn't make sense to make a prenup and overlook your wills.

Spouses' Election Rights

For couples without prenups, how much property one spouse is entitled to when the other spouse dies depends in part on whether the state follows a community property or an equitable distribution system. (See "Ownership of Property During Marriage," above, for a list of community property and equitable distribution states.)

Community Property States

When one spouse dies, what happens to assets in a community property state is fairly straightforward: One-half of all community property belongs to the surviving spouse. Each spouse is free to leave their half of the community property—and all of their separate property—to whomever that spouse chooses.

In a few community property states—and under limited circumstances—a surviving spouse may elect to take a portion of the deceased spouse's community or separate property. These election rights are designed to prevent spouses from being either accidentally overlooked—for example, if one spouse makes a will before marriage and forgets to change it to include the new spouse—or deliberately deprived of their fair share of property. These spousal protections are detailed in the "Summary of State Prenup Laws" on the book's companion page (see Appendix A).

Allowances

In all states—community property and equitable distribution alike—surviving spouses are entitled to ask a court for certain benefits, known as allowances, after the death of a mate. Allowances typically fall into three categories: homestead, personal property, and family allowances (individual states may use different names). As with other spousal inheritance rights, the right to allowances can be waived in a prenup.

Homestead allowance. In most states, the surviving spouse has a homestead right of some sort. Often, the spouse is permitted to remain in the family home during the probate proceedings—and sometimes longer—even if the deceased spouse left the home to somebody else. In many states, the spouse can take a sum of money from the estate instead of the homestead right.

Personal property allowance. In the majority of states, a surviving spouse is entitled to claim a certain amount of the deceased spouse's personal property, such as household furniture, appliances, and other items.

Family allowance. Most states allow a surviving spouse to ask a court for money to support the spouse and any children while the deceased spouse's affairs are being settled. The majority of states say simply that this amount must be "reasonable," leaving it up to a judge to decide how large the allowance will be.

A Bit of History: Dower and Curtesy

The methods that equitable distribution states use to protect surviving spouses were developed hundreds of years ago by English courts. These courts crafted legal concepts called "dower" and "curtesy." Dower refers to the property rights of a surviving wife; curtesy is the share received by a surviving husband. Most of the states in this country originally adopted these concepts, and you might find dower and curtesy mentioned in your state's laws. However, most states have dropped the old terminology and now provide for "spousal election rights," "spousal inheritance rights," or something similar.

Equitable Distribution States

Equitable distribution states give a surviving spouse legal rights to claim a certain portion—usually one-third to one-half—of the other's estate, no matter what the will or other estate planning documents say. As mentioned, these rights are usually known as a spouse's "election" rights, because the spouse can elect to take property other than what's offered by the will or other estate plan.

When determining the total value of the deceased spouse's estate—that is, the amount from which the surviving spouse's share will be calculated—some states provide that all of the deceased spouse's property, including any that was transferred by means other than a will, is subject to the surviving spouse's claim. Other states take a different approach: They include not only all of the deceased spouse's property, but some or all of the separate property owned by the surviving spouse as well. (The total amount of property used to calculate the surviving spouse's share is called the "augmented estate.")

A surviving spouse does not automatically inherit the share that's guaranteed by law; they must go to court and ask for it. So if a person leaves nothing to a spouse or leaves less than the spouse is entitled to under state law, the surviving spouse has a choice of either taking what the will or other transfer documents provide or rejecting the gift and instead claiming the minimum share allowed by state law. Taking the share permitted by state law is often called "taking against the will."

For details about your state's spousal election law, see the state summaries on the book's companion page. (See Appendix A.)

Waiving Election Rights

When a surviving spouse uses a spousal protection law to take more property than the deceased spouse left in a will or other estate planning document, the property comes out of what was left to others. In other words, other beneficiaries will get less. As we've discussed, preserving the deceased spouse's estate for beneficiaries other than the surviving spouse—usually children from an earlier marriage—is a primary goal of many couples who make prenups. To accomplish this, one or both spouses may explicitly waive (forgo) any or all rights to inherit the other's property. But because inheritance rights are so important, a number of states have explicit rules for waiving them.

Some states simply require that any waiver of inheritance rights be written down and signed by the person who is giving up the rights. Other states have more complex rules. Florida, for example, requires that a waiver of inheritance rights be signed in front of two witnesses. (Fla. Stat. Ann. § 732.702.) And California has a rather elaborate law governing waivers of inheritance rights. In California, even if a waiver is written and signed (as it must be), it is not valid if the surviving spouse can prove either of the following:

- The surviving spouse did not receive fair disclosure of the deceased spouse's finances (unless the surviving spouse waived disclosure after receiving advice from his or her own lawyer).
- The surviving spouse was not represented by a lawyer when the waiver was signed. (Cal. Prob. Code § 143.)

But the law does not end there. Even if the surviving spouse can prove that the waiver isn't valid for one of the reasons listed above, a court may enforce the waiver if it determines either of the following:

- At the time it was signed, the waiver was fair to the surviving spouse.
- The surviving spouse had, or reasonably should have had, adequate knowledge of the deceased spouse's finances—and the deceased spouse did not mislead the surviving spouse in any way. (Cal. Prob. Code § 144.)

You can see that if one or both of you will waive inheritance rights in your prenup, it is important to familiarize yourself with your state's requirements. Otherwise, your waiver might be invalid and a court could refuse to enforce it. The state summaries on the book's companion page list all waiver rules that were in effect at the time this edition of this book was published, and the book's companion page will have updates.

Property Rights If You Divorce

Even if you don't want your prenup to cover what will happen to your property in the event of a divorce, it's helpful to know some basics about how states handle the property of divorcing couples who haven't made written agreements. Here, we discuss:

- how property and debts are divided at divorce, and
- how states handle alimony payments.

SKIP AHEAD

When to skip this section. Some couples are quite sure that they don't want to spend time before their marriage contemplating the details of divorce. While we understand that it's not a very appealing conversation, it can save you a lot of time, money, and heartache later, so we really encourage you to consider including these provisions in your prenup. But if you really want to leave that subject alone, go ahead and skip this section. You can jump to the end of this chapter to learn more about researching your state's law, or turn to Chapter 5 to begin drafting your prenup.

Dividing Property and Debts

In any state, when a couple divorces, they are free to decide together how to divide their property, rather than leaving it up to a judge. But if a couple hasn't already set out their intentions in a prenup and can't work things out during the breakup, they can submit their dispute to a court, which will divide the property according to state law.

While there are many similarities in divorce procedures among the 50 states, a number of rules for dividing property and debts depend on whether the state follows community or common law principles. (See "Ownership of Property During Marriage," above.) Here are the basics for spouses in each type of state.

Community Property States

First we'll look at how judges tend to divide community property when a couple divorces. Then we'll briefly discuss how a judge may allocate debts in a community property state.

Dividing property at divorce. Courts attempt to divide community property equally. To keep things even, a spouse who contributed separate property to a community asset might be entitled to reimbursement for that contribution. On the other hand, the community estate might be reimbursed for community property contributions to a spouse's separate property. For example, the community might be entitled to compensation if the spouses used community money to fix up a house that one spouse owns separately. Or, the community might be reimbursed for something less tangible—such as using community property to fund an education that greatly increases the earning capacity of one spouse.

> **EXAMPLE:** Meg and Gordon married in Wisconsin in 2005. Gordon started medical school while Meg got a job as an elementary school teacher. Though they never wrote anything down, they agreed that Meg would work so that Gordon could go to school. After Gordon finished school, Meg would stop working for a while so they could start a family. For the first four years of their marriage, Meg entirely supported the couple except for student loans that Gordon obtained to cover his education expenses. She also took care of all the household chores. Shortly after Gordon completed his residency and began practicing medicine, the couple separated and filed for divorce. When dividing the couple's community property, the court found that it would be unfair to deny Meg a share of the education's benefits while Gordon prospered from all the advantages of the degree. Meg was therefore awarded 80% of the couple's community assets and Gordon was required to make support payments to her for several years.

In most community property states, if the court thinks that dividing community property equally would result in unfairness to one party, the court may distribute property in whatever proportion it thinks is right.

> **EXAMPLE:** After a brief courtship, Than and Li get married in Washington state. Than doesn't have much property when they marry, but Li is financially comfortable because of a large inheritance from her grandfather. Certain that their marriage will succeed, they mix whatever property they have in joint accounts, but the marriage lasts only five years. When the court divides the couple's property, Li receives a much larger share to compensate her for contributing all of her inheritance money to the community.

That said, one thing courts generally are not permitted to do is award all or part of one spouse's separate property to the other spouse.

Several community property states—including California, Louisiana, and New Mexico—require courts to adhere to the standard of equal division of community property, with very limited exceptions. Even in these states where property division appears to be straightforward, however, thorny questions may arise when attempting to determine what is and what is not community property or how much certain property is worth. Life insurance, retirement benefits, and business interests are examples of property that can be particularly difficult to divide.

> **EXAMPLE:** Greta owns and runs a successful art dealership in Santa Fe. After she marries Jim, her business continues to thrive and she opens a number of galleries throughout New Mexico. The assets of Greta's business are separate property because she began the business before she married Jim and he has never been involved with it. But what about all the work that Greta puts into the business during the marriage? Without a written agreement specifying otherwise, the benefits of Greta's labor belong to the community. Valuing and allocating such intangibles can be extremely complicated in the event of a divorce.

Quasi-Community Property

Quasi means "like." In some community property states, including California, Idaho, and Washington, the term "quasi-community property" refers to property accumulated by a married couple while living in a non–community property state. If a couple moves to a community property state that recognizes quasi-community property, the property acquired in the non–community property state is treated exactly like community property in the event of death or divorce.

Wisconsin recognizes a similar type of property, but calls it "deferred marital property."

Allocating debts. How courts divide debts in community property states depends on whether the debts are community or separate debts at the time of the divorce. For help understanding the difference between community and separate debts, see "Debts: Who Is Responsible?" earlier in this chapter.

Debts Incurred Between Separation and Divorce

Community property states take different approaches when assigning liability for debts incurred after a couple separates but before a divorce is final. Often, a court's determination of whether this debt is community or separate depends on whether the debt was incurred for a purpose that is related to the community, which is not formally dissolved until a divorce is finalized. For example, the community may be held responsible when debts are incurred for necessaries of life for one of the spouses—or, especially, for their children. The community is unlikely to be held responsible for debts that are more clearly separate, such as a debt related to one spouse's gambling losses or the purchase of nonessential property.

When a couple divorces, community property debts (like other community property) are usually divided equally. However, the court may divide debts according to who is better able to pay them. For example, if a couple has many debts but also has a lot of property, a common result is for the spouse who is better able to pay the debts to assume their payment and also to receive a larger share of the property to even things up.

EXAMPLE: Scott and Lyn divorce after almost 30 years together. Scott is a partner in a large law firm and Lyn is a successful freelance graphic designer. Their only child has recently graduated from college and is embarking on a career of her own. At the time of their separation, Scott and Lyn are quite wealthy. They own three homes—their primary residence in California and vacation homes in Hawaii and Colorado. They also have many secure investments. While Scott intends to continue with his law practice, Lyn wants to scale back a bit. Taking all these factors into consideration, the court orders that Lyn take ownership of the house in Colorado, which is paid for. Scott is ordered to take the more valuable homes in California and Hawaii and assume responsibility for the mortgages. The rest of their investments are divided pretty much equally between them.

Equitable Distribution States

If a court in an equitable distribution (common law) state divides your property and debts, the judge will look to state law to determine what property should be considered marital property and split between you. (Remember from our earlier discussion that marital property has legal significance only if a couple in an equitable distribution state decides to divorce. Otherwise, all property is simply owned separately or jointly, depending on whose name is on the title document.)

What constitutes marital property differs from state to state. Some states include all property and earnings obtained during marriage, though most exclude certain types of property, such as gifts and inheritances. For the most part, when it comes to dividing property and debts at divorce, marital and community property are very much alike. The rest of this section sets out the general rules.

SEE AN EXPERT

Finding specific information for your state. If you have questions about whether a particular asset would be considered marital or separate property in the case of a divorce, ask your lawyer. The lawyer might not be able to tell you for certain how an asset will be classified (not even a crystal ball can predict what a judge will do in all cases), but you should be able to get a good idea of how the property will be treated. If you want to do your own research to learn more about what constitutes marital property in your state, be forewarned—it's a complicated subject. "Researching State Law," below, provides some tips to get you started.

Dividing property at divorce. In equitable distribution (common law) states, courts divide assets and earnings accumulated during marriage fairly—that is, "equitably." What a court considers to be an equitable division of property depends on the circumstances in each case. For example, a court may award two-thirds of the marital property to the lower wage earner and one-third to the higher wage earner, or any other proportion that the court believes to be fair.

> EXAMPLE: Maureen and Frank, who live in New York, are divorcing after ten years of marriage. During their marriage, they bought a house, some furniture, and a car with their earnings, and they made investments. Maureen earns substantially more than Frank; they shared the work around the house. Upon divorce, a court is likely to divide the property in a way that takes into account the money and work put into the marriage and property as well as the economic realities of the parties. Maureen, because of her higher earnings, will probably keep the house (and its mortgage), the furniture will be divided, the party who needs the car more will get it, and Maureen will pay Frank a sum of money equal to his portion of the house—probably near half.

Here are some of the factors most courts consider when deciding what's fair in the absence of an agreement between the spouses:

- **Separate property.** If one spouse owns a great deal of separate, nonmarital property while the other spouse has little, the court may give more marital property to the less wealthy spouse.
- **Earning capacity.** Similarly, if one spouse has an obvious capacity to earn more money than the other spouse, the court may award more marital property to the spouse that has less earning power.
- **Effort.** The court may consider whether one spouse worked harder or invested more than the other to acquire or maintain property. In the case of a business, it is common for a court to award all or most of the business ownership to the spouse who operates it. (The other spouse may, of course, be compensated with an award of other marital property.)

- **Nonmonetary contributions.** Most states now recognize that a spouse's nonmonetary contributions to a marriage should be valued in the event of a divorce. Nonmonetary contributions include work such as homemaking, childcare, or assisting without a salary in a spouse's business. The spouse who contributed these services is likely to be compensated from the couple's property for their value. (If a stay-at-home spouse's earning capacity has been impaired because of a lengthy absence from the income-earning world, that spouse may also be compensated by a large alimony award.)

- **Fault.** Most states no longer consider fault—such as infidelity—when dividing property at divorce. But in some states, whether or not a spouse obtains a divorce based on fault, a "guilty" spouse may receive less than what would otherwise be considered an equitable share of the marital property.

- **Duration of marriage.** Though times have changed, if a marriage has been a long and traditional one, it is not unusual for a woman or a spouse who was the stay-at-home parent to have diminished earning power and less wealth at the time of divorce. A judge is likely to take this into account, awarding more property to the spouse who will find it more difficult to earn enough to enjoy a standard of living comparable to the one established during the marriage.

- **Spouses' needs.** If one spouse is significantly older than the other or has health problems, a court may grant that spouse more marital property.

- **Tax consequences.** Dividing property at divorce can affect the taxes of both spouses—for better or for worse. A court may look at the various tax consequences when attempting to craft a fair property settlement. For example, if selling a house would result in large capital gains taxes, the court may avoid ordering the sale of the house and find another way to balance property between the spouses. A judge will likely consider only those tax consequences that are immediate and specific, rather than speculating about what might happen years down the road.

Allocating debts. When a couple divorces, responsibility for joint debts is allocated in accordance with the property division laws of the state. This usually means that the debts are divided equally or equitably, especially if they were incurred for necessities (food, clothing, housing, or medical care). The court also considers who is better able to pay the debts—usually the spouse with the higher income and/or lower living expenses. If a couple has a lot of debt and also a lot of property, the spouse who is better able to pay the debts often assumes the debt payments in exchange for a larger share of the marital property.

Regardless of the court's assignment of responsibility for a joint debt, a creditor collecting on an unpaid debt may sue either or both spouses and will do so on the basis of who is more likely to pay. Although spouses may make an agreement between themselves about which of them will pay these debts, the agreement is not binding on creditors; it does, however, entitle a spouse to reimbursement if the other spouse does not honor the agreement.

> EXAMPLE: During their marriage, Alan and Don purchased a valuable painting for cash, bought a car on credit, and charged a cruise to Europe on their credit card. When they divorce, Alan agrees to pay off the car in exchange for keeping the painting, and Don agrees to pay off the credit card. If Alan doesn't make the car payments or if Don fails to pay for the vacation, the creditor can seek payment from the other; the two of them will then have to work out who must pay and who is entitled to reimbursement.

Debts Incurred Between Separation and Divorce

Usually, debts incurred after spouses separate but before the divorce is final must be paid by the spouse that incurred them. There is an exception, however: Both spouses are almost always responsible for paying debts for either spouse's necessities and the children's education, regardless of who incurred them.

Alimony

Alimony (also called maintenance or spousal support) is money paid by one ex-spouse to the other during or after divorce for ongoing support. Without a prenup stating whether a spouse is entitled to alimony (and how much), alimony provisions are typically spelled out in a court order or property settlement agreement following a divorce. In all states—community property and equitable distribution—courts can order either spouse to pay alimony to the other after considering a long list of factors. (See "Factors Used to Determine Alimony Payments," below.)

Traditionally, alimony was granted in most divorce cases: Ex-husbands were usually expected to provide their ex-wives with some form of permanent support. But those days are gone in many states—and quickly disappearing in others. Now, in some states, alimony is awarded in a minority of divorces. And in all states, either spouse can be ordered to pay alimony.

Since the 1980s, the trend in state divorce laws has been to favor short-term support awards over traditional permanent alimony. The idea behind this is that alimony should continue only until the recipient spouse can become self-supporting. Some courts also use property allocation to offset the need for alimony, giving more property to the spouse who would otherwise be entitled to short- or long-term support payments.

Factors Used to Determine Alimony Payments

When determining whether to award alimony and, if so, how much and for how long, courts evaluate a great number of factors. The exact rules vary from state to state, but in most states the court considers the:

- earnings and earning capacities of both spouses
- ages and the physical, mental, and emotional health of both spouses
- sources of income of both spouses, which might include retirement, insurance, or other benefits
- property that either spouse expects to receive by gift or inheritance
- length of the marriage
- contributions by one spouse to the education, training, or increased earning power of the other
- extent to which the earning power, expenses, or financial obligations of one spouse will be affected by the need to care for children
- standard of living that the spouses established while married
- relative education of the parties and the time necessary to acquire sufficient education or training to enable the spouse seeking alimony to find appropriate employment
- relative assets and liabilities of the spouses
- property brought to the marriage by either spouse
- contribution of a spouse as homemaker
- relative needs of the spouses
- marital misconduct of either of the spouses during the marriage (about half of the states no longer consider this factor when determining alimony)
- tax consequences of the alimony award, and
- any other factors the court considers appropriate.

When determining the amount and duration of permanent alimony, courts are not supposed to be governed by the amount of temporary alimony payments. In practice, however—and despite the long list of factors judges are supposed to consider—a permanent alimony award often looks much like the temporary award that preceded it.

EXAMPLE: Barbara and Cindy have a volatile marriage that lasts just two years. At the time of their divorce, Barbara is earning about twice as much as Cindy. Rather than order Barbara to make short-term, monthly support payments to Cindy to help her make the transition to self-sufficiency, the court gives Cindy the family car and the moderate amount of money in their shared savings account, dividing the rest of their property equally between them.

Of course, courts are also free to order long-term alimony payments, and sometimes they do—particularly when there has been a lasting traditional marriage or when a recipient spouse has little hope of supporting themselves due to health concerns, childcare obligations, a very low earning capacity, or other factors.

There are two basic types of alimony payments—temporary and permanent.

Temporary alimony. When a couple separates or files for divorce, the spouses often need the immediate intervention of a court to establish support obligations, especially to help determine who pays the bills and lives in the family home while the divorce proceedings are underway. One spouse might also need temporary support to cover the costs of the divorce proceedings. Either spouse can request a hearing before the judge to have these issues temporarily resolved.

In some states or counties, courts calculate temporary alimony payments using a narrow formula based primarily on each spouse's income. If the parties cannot agree on an amount for temporary payments, a judge will most likely impose this formula-driven amount at a preliminary hearing. The payment amount can be changed later, when the court has a better understanding of what will be best in the long run. As a practical matter, however, courts can be strongly influenced by the amount of the temporary alimony award when setting the amount of permanent alimony.

Permanent alimony. Permanent alimony is usually established in the court order that finalizes the divorce. It is intended to continue at the same payment rate until a time specified in the order—or until the ex-spouses' circumstances change significantly. Most states have laws that clearly establish when permanent alimony payments may be changed or terminated—for example, if the recipient spouse remarries (or moves in with someone, in a handful of states), or if the paying spouse loses a job or has a new child. Of course, permanent alimony may also be modified when both parties agree to the change.

The only time alimony cannot be modified is when the divorce decree or an agreement between the spouses specifically states that it may not be modified, or when it is part of a property settlement where alimony is paid as a part of the property division.

If a spouse fails to pay alimony, the recipient spouse has many options for collecting, including asking a court to garnish the spouse's wages. Federal and state laws make it very difficult to shirk alimony payments, and alimony debts will stick with the spouse who owes them; you can't get rid of alimony you owe by filing for bankruptcy.

Researching State Law

If you want to learn more about the laws that affect prenups, marital property, or inheritance in your state, the easiest way is to ask your lawyer. (See Chapter 10 for more information about working with lawyers.) But learning how to do some of your own research can provide real benefits if you have the energy and the patience. Not only are you likely to save money on professional fees, but you'll also gain a feeling of mastery over an area of law that concerns you.

Once you understand some basic research techniques, it isn't too difficult to look up certain types of law. For example, to confirm that the statutes listed in your state's summary on the book's companion page are up to date or to browse other parts of your state's code, all you'll need to do is look up the statutes on the Internet or in a local library. Below, we provide some simple instructions to help you do this.

On the other hand, if you want to delve into more complex issues—say, looking up court decisions governing prenups or marital property—you will have a more complex task ahead of you. We can't guide you through all the nuances of legal research in this book, but we do give you some information that will help you get started.

Looking Up State Statutes

If you're drafting your own prenup, you should review the summary for your state on the book's online companion page (see Appendix A) that lists some of the basic rules governing your agreement. But it's wise to take your research a step further and check the laws yourself. Fortunately, it's fairly simple to look up state statutes.

Using Citations

It's easiest to look up a state statute when you already know its citation—that is, the number that indicates where the statute is located in the state laws. For example, the state summaries on the book's online companion page list the citations to each statute related to making your prenup.

Citations to state statutes usually refer to a title (or volume) of the state code and the section numbers where the statute can be found. See below for some examples.

Sample State Statute Citations

Mich. Comp. Laws   § 552.13   (1)

Michigan   section   subsection
Compiled Laws   number   number

N.J. Stat. Ann.   § 3B: 8-10

New Jersey Statutes volume   section
Annotated   number   number

Vt. Stat. Ann.   tit. 14,   § 402

Vermont Statutes   title   section
Annotated   number

Some states' laws, such as those in California and New York, are divided up into sections by topic. In these states, citations look like those shown below.

Sample California and New York Citations

Cal. Fam. Code.   § 760

California   section
Family Code   number

N.Y. Dom. Rel. Law.   § 236   (B)(3)

New York Domestic   section   subsection
Relations Law   number   number

When you know a statute's citation, you can find it online or in a local law library.

Finding Statutes Online

All states have made their statutes available on the internet. You can find them by visiting the Cornell University Law School's Legal Information Institute at www.law.cornell.edu/statutes.html or FindLaw at https://caselaw.findlaw.com. Choose your state to search or browse the statutes. You can also find information about any state's legislature through the National Conference of State Legislatures at www.ncsl.org.

Finding Statutes in a Law Library

You can always find state statutes at a law library or, usually, at the main branch of a public library. Depending on the state, statutes are compiled in books called statutes, revised statutes, annotated statutes, codes, or compiled laws. (The term "annotated" means that the statutes are accompanied by information about their history and court decisions that have interpreted them.) The citations in your state summary will indicate what the books are called in your state.

Once you've located the books you need, search for the specific statute by the citation provided in the state summary or, if you wish to research another topic, by looking up keywords in the index.

After you find a law in the statute books, it's important to look at the update pamphlet in the back of the book (called the "pocket part") to make sure your statute hasn't changed or been repealed. Pocket parts are published only once per year, so brand-new laws often have not yet made it to the pocket part. Law libraries subscribe to services and periodicals that update the statute books on a more frequent basis than the pocket parts. You can ask a law librarian to help you find the materials you need.

Looking Up Court Cases

Statutes alone won't tell you the whole story of your state's prenup laws. It's a good idea to also look at court cases, which explain how courts have interpreted the statutes. The state summaries on the book's online companion page list some of the most important prenup cases for each state, including their citations—that is, the location of each case as specified by book title, volume number, and page number. If you want to read one of these cases, you can follow the instructions below to look it up. If you want information about other cases affecting prenups in your state, you should consult your lawyer or use a more detailed legal research manual (see below) to learn how to find cases on the topic that interests you.

Finding Cases Online

If a case is fairly recent it's likely you will be able to find it for free on the internet. Some good places to start are Justia (www.justia.com), Google Scholar (https://scholar.google.com), and FindLaw (https://caselaw.findlaw.com).

If the case is older, you can still find it on the internet, but you might have to pay a private company for access to its database. Fastcase, at www.fastcase.com, maintains an excellent library of older state court cases. You can do unlimited case law research on Fastcase for about $65 per month. You can also get state cases online through the Lexis and Westlaw databases, though these options are much pricier. (A lucky few might live near a law library that offers Westlaw access for free. It's an option worth investigating.) To find out more about these services, visit Westlaw at www.westlaw.com or Lexis at www.lexis.com.

Finding Cases in a Law Library

In the library, state cases are found in a series of books called reporters. For example, California cases are contained in the *California Reporter*. You can also find state cases in books known as "regional reporters." These volumes contain cases from several states in a geographical region. For example, the *Atlantic Reporter* contains cases from several eastern states, including Delaware and Maryland.

If you have a case citation (for example, 21 Cal.App.3d 446), locating the case should be easy. Follow these three steps:

1. Find the correct series of books (in the above example, it would be the *California Appellate Reports, 3rd Series*).
2. Select the appropriate volume (here it's Volume 21).
3. Open the book to the appropriate page (in the example, page 446).

If you don't have a citation but you know the name of one or both of the parties in a case—for instance, in the case named *Jones v. Smith*, Jones and Smith are the names of the parties—you can use a "case digest." Look for the parties' names in the digest's table of cases. If you don't know the name of the case or the citation, then it will be very difficult to find the case in the law library.

Finding Other Information About Prenups

In addition to looking up a particular state statute or case, you can do some background reading about certain aspects of premarital agreements. Such reading can give you an overview of the law applicable to your concerns, possibly provide some initial answers, and refer you to more specific sources.

There are many types of background books; we'll suggest just a couple of them here. Keep in mind that these resources are written by lawyers, for lawyers, and you might have to struggle through loads of legalese to get to the information you want.

Practice Guides

Some states have books for lawyers that discuss a broad range of family law topics, including prenups. For example, in California, the Rutter Group publishes the *California Practice Guide: Family Law*, which contains information about pre- and postmarital agreements, marital property law, and a wide variety of other family law topics. The best way to search for this type of book for your state is to ask a law librarian or look in a library catalog under "family law," "marital property," "premarital agreements," or similar headings.

Journals and Law Reviews

Many legal organizations publish journals (magazines) that contain articles covering current legal issues, including premarital agreements. Law schools also produce journals, called "law reviews," which consist of scholarly articles written by law students, law professors, and practicing attorneys. While law reviews are notorious for their complex and confusing language, they often cover timely topics and can provide leads to relevant statutes and cases.

To locate articles on prenups, you can use the *Index to Legal Periodicals*, the *Current Law Index*, or a computerized index called LegalTrac, found in many law libraries.

More Legal Research Help From Nolo

Nolo offers many tools designed to help you with basic legal research. Start by visiting Nolo's website at www.nolo.com, where you'll find an entire area of the website devoted to helping you look up the law. (You can find the legal research center at www.nolo.com/legal-research.)

If you want to pursue more detailed legal research, Nolo offers a book that will show you the way. *Legal Research: How to Find & Understand the Law*, by the editors of Nolo, is a hands-on guide to research on the internet and in the law library. It addresses research methods in detail and should answer most questions that arise. In particular, it contains a good discussion of how to read and analyze statutes and instructions for looking up court cases.

Do You Still Want a Prenup?

Once you've come this far, it's a good idea to stop and think about whether signing a premarital agreement makes sense for you. For any number of reasons, you might conclude that it doesn't. Perhaps the benefits of a prenup are minor compared with the hassles and expense of completing the written agreement. Maybe you'll discover that you're better protected legally without a prenup. Whatever the reasons, stopping short of preparing and signing a written premarital agreement might be the right course of action for you. If that's the case, you can close this book with a clear sense that, together, you considered the options carefully and made the best decision for the two of you—not a bad foundation for making decisions in the future.

On the other hand, your work thus far might have reinforced your initial interest in making a prenup. If so, it's time to take the concepts outlined on Worksheets 5 and 6 and put them into a draft of a written agreement. So take a moment to congratulate yourselves on your progress; when you're ready, turn to Chapter 5.

Assembling Your Draft Agreement: The Basics

I f you completed Worksheet 5 using the suggestions found in Chapter 3, you've already worked out the main terms of your prenup. Now it's time to put those terms into clear language that you can include in the written document you'll take to your lawyers.

An Outline of Your Prenup

Your prenup will consist of a title such as "Premarital Agreement" or "Prenuptial Contract" and ten basic sections (we call them "paragraphs"), plus any optional paragraphs that you want to add. Each paragraph will consist of one or more clauses. Some paragraphs are pretty much the same for all prenups, except for your personal information, like names and addresses. For other paragraphs, you will choose from several clauses that we provide or craft your own. Here's a summary of what you'll tackle in each paragraph. Chapters 6, 7, and 9 walk you through drafting these paragraphs in detail.

Paragraph 1: Introductory Facts

This paragraph includes information such as your names and addresses, when you plan to marry, whether you have children, and the general purpose of your agreement, plus other optional information about yourselves you might choose to mention. For more details, see Chapter 6.

Paragraph 2: Effective Date and Term

Here, you state that the agreement takes effect when you marry and continues indefinitely or until some specified date in the future. For more details, see Chapter 6.

Paragraph 3: Legal Representation

In this paragraph, you either identify the lawyers who are helping you with the agreement or state that you are opting not to use lawyers. For more details, see Chapter 6.

Paragraph 4: Disclosures

In this paragraph, you confirm that you are making written disclosures of financial or other personal information. Typically, the actual disclosure statements are attached to the end of the agreement; this paragraph simply refers to them. For more details, see Chapter 6.

Paragraph 5: Definitions

As its name implies, this paragraph explains some commonly used terms contained in the agreement, such as "separate property" or "marital property." For more details, see Chapter 6.

Paragraph 6: Ownership of Premarital Assets

You will use this paragraph to specify whether your premarital assets will be considered separate property or shared between you once you are married. For more details, see Chapter 7.

Paragraph 7: Ownership of Assets Acquired During Marriage

In this paragraph, you can lay out whether you'll keep separate any new acquisitions after you marry. For more details, see Chapter 7.

Paragraph 8: Responsibility for Debts and Expenses

This is where you'll clarify who is responsible for premarital debts as well as any new debts incurred during your marriage. For more details, see Chapter 7.

> **TIP**
>
> **Optional paragraphs.** You can choose to include optional paragraphs in your prenup after Paragraph 8. Optional paragraphs are discussed in detail in Chapter 8. If you insert any optional paragraphs, you should renumber Paragraphs 9 and 10, below.

Paragraph 9: Provisions Regarding Interpretation, Modification, and Enforcement of Agreement

This paragraph is the last one before the paragraph containing your signatures. In this paragraph, we've included all the standard provisions that make for a clear and binding agreement (sometimes called "boilerplate"), plus some optional clauses on topics such as how to review the agreement over time and how to resolve any future disagreements about the prenup. For more details, see Chapter 9.

Paragraph 10: Signatures, Acknowledgments, and Attorneys' Certificates

This one's obvious: It's where you and your lawyers sign. For more details, see Chapter 9.

Working on Your Prenup

The following suggestions will help you with the practical part of assembling your prenup. We assume that most of you will use the downloadable form that's available on the book's online companion page (see Appendix A) to prepare your draft agreement, but this section contains tips for working by hand as well.

Using a Computer

The prenup clauses discussed in this book are available for download on the book's online companion page. You can use these clauses to draft your prenup. You'll need to read through the following chapters to learn about each clause and decide which ones you need.

Finding the Clauses You Want

When you go to the online companion page, you'll be able to download each of the clauses, as well as an outline and full sample agreement. You can use these files to assemble a draft that accomplishes your goals.

Drafting Your Prenup

When you're ready to begin assembling your draft prenup, open the file "Outline" (Outline.rtf), which contains the title and paragraph headings for every prenup. After filling in the preliminary information, you can start opening, copying, and pasting from the other clause files into the "Outline" file. When you open a clause file, you'll see that it contains blank lines, which show you where you need to add your own information. In most cases, the blanks contain bracketed instructions telling you what information is required. After pasting a clause into your prenup, fill in the appropriate information, following the instructions and examples in this book. *Delete any blank underlines and the bracketed instructions from your finished document.*

Alternatives. For prenup clauses with two or more alternative versions, all alternatives are included in the same file. Alternative clauses are indicated by instructional text and are always preceded by a checkbox. (The information we provide will help you choose the alternative that's right for you.) *Delete from your prenup file any alternatives you don't want to include as well as the checkbox for the alternative you choose and the italicized instructional text.*

Optional clauses and text. As you choose the clauses for your prenup, you'll find that a number of provisions are optional (indicated by instructional text). Optional clauses are always preceded by a checkbox. *Delete any optional language that you don't want to include in your agreement as well as the checkboxes for any options you include and the italicized instructional text.*

Because the formatting of the files has been simplified, the clauses might look slightly different from the samples in the book. If you want your final agreement to look just like the samples, you'll need to format it with your word processing program.

The optional clauses are not numbered. Blanks are provided for numbering the optional paragraphs and clauses in your final document.

To save your draft prenup, use your word processing program's "Save As" command to rename and save the file.

If you don't know how to use your word processing program to save or edit a document, consult the program's help file. Nolo's technical support department cannot provide help with the use of your word processing program.

Working by Hand

If you're using Appendix C to draft your agreement, rather than the downloadable clauses, you'll want to work through it as you read the next few chapters. It's a good idea to make a photocopy of the appendix so that you can keep the appendix and book side by side as you work.

Starting with Paragraph 1, go through the clauses and explanations for each successive paragraph. Select the clauses that apply to you. Replace the bracketed instructions in each clause with your own information and check off the clause when you're done. Paragraphs and clauses that are mandatory for all agreements are already marked with a ☑. When you've finished, you'll type up your agreement using the clauses you've completed.

TIP

Creating custom clauses. If you don't find a clause that's exactly right for your situation, try using one that's close to what you want as a springboard for writing your own. If you're working on paper, be sure to check off that clause so you don't overlook it when you assemble your draft agreement.

Choosing the Clauses for Your Prenup

Choosing and completing the paragraphs and clauses for your prenup is a task you'll want to complete with your partner. It will probably take you a few hours.

Start by completing the ten basic paragraphs. Then, if you've covered everything you want to, you can go on to the next step—finalizing your agreement—which is discussed in Chapter 10. Or, if you want to include other matters in your agreement, you can expand your prenup by selecting optional paragraphs from Chapter 8.

If you completed Worksheet 5, have that in hand when you begin. You'll also need the complete text of the clauses themselves, which you can find in Appendix C and on the book's online companion page.

Giving Your Prenup a Title

Decide what you want to call your agreement and put the title at the top of the page. The most common titles are:

- Premarital Agreement
- Prenuptial Agreement, or
- Antenuptial Agreement.

Choosing the title is mostly a matter of custom and personal style, even among lawyers. If you want to know how the laws of your state refer to prenups, check your state's summary on the book's online companion page, but don't feel bound by what you find there. Pick a title you're comfortable with. You can even customize your title by including your names, as in "Premarital Agreement of Ted Beckford and Grace Nelsen."

Next: Drafting the Introduction of Your Prenup

Now that we've covered the basics, you're ready to start drafting the first five paragraphs of your prenup. Chapter 6 will walk you through these paragraphs step by step.

Paragraphs 1–5: The Introduction

The tips in this chapter will help you draft the first five paragraphs of your agreement. Most paragraphs contain multiple parts or clauses. To show you how each clause might be used, we provide examples of how fictional couples (some of whom we introduced earlier) facing real-life situations and dilemmas complete each paragraph.

SKIP AHEAD

Using the default clauses to create a simple agreement. If you intend to use a premarital agreement only to identify and keep separate your premarital assets and debts, while leaving everything else to state law, you can create a very simple prenup. If you're working on paper, using Appendix C, select only the paragraphs and clauses that are already marked with a ☑. Then add the clauses that are marked * ; these indicate default selections when you need to choose between clauses. You can also find a simple prenup on the book's companion page. Look for the link called "Simple Prenuptial Agreement." All you need to do is fill in the requested information and your draft is complete. This is what Steven and Freda used to prepare their prenup. You can find their completed basic agreement at the end of Chapter 9.

TIP

Decide whose name comes first—and watch your pronouns. To avoid confusion, we suggest you decide whose name will come first throughout the agreement. When you complete the clauses in Appendix C, put that person's name in all the blanks labeled "Spouse 1." The other spouse's name goes in the blanks for "Spouse 2." As you put together your document, you must also choose the appropriate pronouns as you go along. We've indicated each spot where you must make a choice.

Paragraph 1: Introductory Facts

The clauses in the first paragraph of your prenup are pretty self-explanatory.

A. Parties

Use this clause to identify yourselves as the "parties" to this agreement by inserting your first and last names in the appropriate spaces. You can also include middle initials or names as Karen and Russ do.

> This Agreement is between Karen A. Schonberg and Russell J. Kroger. We refer to ourselves by our first names in This Agreement.

B. Purpose of Agreement

This is where you indicate the date you plan to marry and your general purposes in making a prenup. If you haven't set a date yet, provide a general time frame. (It's a good idea to complete the prenup at least one month and no more than three or four months before your planned wedding date—doing it too close to your wedding could make the prenup unenforceable; signing it too far in advance means the disclosures won't be timely.)

> We plan to marry later this year.

After you indicate the date or time frame of your planned marriage, you should specify the general purposes of your prenup—that is, the topics you will cover. We give you the following options to choose from (you should select all that apply):

- to identify your premarital assets and debts
- to define your mutual rights and obligations regarding property and finances after you marry
- to support your estate plans through waiver of certain spousal rights, and
- to set forth your rights and obligations if you separate or divorce.

Here is what Ted and Grace include in their agreement:

> We plan to marry on June 1, 20xx. The purpose of This Agreement is to identify our premarital assets and debts, to define our mutual rights and obligations regarding property and finances after we marry, and to support our estate plans through waiver of certain spousal rights.

You can also add your own topics. For example, you might want to describe how you will handle joint bank accounts or how you will establish and manage your monthly budget. You can include any agreement you make about your finances or property so you have documentation of your understanding for future reference.

> This Agreement also establishes our plan for setting up and maintaining a monthly budget.

C. Current Circumstances

Use this clause to include some basic information about each of you, such as where you live, your occupations, and the names and ages of any children. Making note of this kind of information is part of the disclosure process required by most state laws. You can also include special facts about yourselves, such as your ages and general state of health, your countries of citizenship, or any other information you consider important enough to include. For example, Karen and Russ both have children from previous marriages, so they make a note of this in their prenup.

> Karen currently resides at 56 Bell Street, Sacramento, California. Her occupation is veterinarian. She has two children: Shawn, age 16, and Kyle, age 13.
>
> Russ currently resides at 247 Stone Creek Drive, Sacramento, California. His occupation is bookkeeper. He has one child: Tiffany, age 6.

D. Future Plans [OPTIONAL]

You have the option here of inserting any specific plans to relocate, change jobs, attend college, or make similar major moves that might affect the agreements contained in your prenup.

For example, Grace plans to quit her job as a county social worker after she and Ted marry so that the two of them can travel. They mention this plan here and refer to the later provisions in the prenup that are intended to compensate Grace for the future earnings and job security she's giving up.

> After we marry, Grace plans to resign from her current employment so that we can travel together. As a consequence, Grace will be giving up future job security and potential earnings. This has been taken into consideration in the provisions regarding estate planning matters and property transfers set forth in Paragraphs 9 and 10 of This Agreement.

Paragraph 2: Effective Date and Term

This paragraph covers two more essential aspects of your prenup: when your agreement takes effect and when it ends.

A. Effective Date of Agreement

The first clause of Paragraph 2 states what should be obvious: The agreement takes effect only if and when you marry. This means that any obligations to take certain actions—such as transferring property, setting up bank accounts, or changing insurance beneficiaries—won't be binding until after your marriage. There are no choices to make or blanks to fill in for this clause. It is the same in every prenup.

> This Agreement will be effective on the day we marry. If we do not marry, This Agreement will be null and void.

B. Term of Agreement

You also need to specify how long your prenup will stay in effect. Ordinarily, a premarital agreement lasts as long as your marriage does. Under some circumstances, however, you might want your prenup to last for a specified period of time, possibly because the main purpose of the prenup is to protect property from debts that will be paid off at some point, or perhaps because you feel that if you stay married for a given length of time, certain waivers of marital property or alimony claims will no longer be appropriate. If so, you can choose a clause that terminates the agreement on a certain date or after a specified number of years. Lawyers call this a "sunset clause." We give you the following alternatives for Clause B.

Alternative 1: Prenup Continues Indefinitely

If you want your prenup to stay in effect for as long as you are married, you will choose this clause. It states that the agreement will remain in effect indefinitely, unless you later decide to modify or revoke it. This is what Karen and Russ elect to do.

> After we marry, This Agreement will remain in full force and effect indefinitely, unless and until we sign a new written agreement revoking or modifying This Agreement.

Alternative 2: Prenup Ends on a Specified Date (Retroactive)

In this sunset clause, you specify that your agreement will end on a certain date and that termination of the agreement is retroactive—meaning that once the agreement ends, your rights will be the same as if you had never signed a prenup.

EXAMPLE: Harry is remarrying after a costly divorce. He wants a prenup that protects his assets from any claims if he and Marta get divorced within five years of marrying. However, he and Marta agree that if they stay together longer, the prenup shouldn't apply at all, even to assets bought during the first five years. So they use Alternative 2, specifying that the agreement will terminate after five years of marriage, and their rights from then on will be the same as if they had never signed a prenup.

> ⚠ CAUTION
>
> **Be very careful when using a sunset clause to insulate marital property from premarital debts.** Fraudulent transfer laws might allow a creditor to reach property spouses declared "off limits" in a prenup if the court finds that the spouses used this clause to defraud the creditor. One court in California allowed a lawsuit against a couple to proceed where their retroactive sunset clause would be triggered after one spouse's premarital debts became unenforceable. (See *Sturm v. Moyer*, 32 Cal.App. 5th 299 (2019).) It's essential to work with a competent lawyer when you want to address protection from debts in your prenup.

Alternative 3: **Prenup Ends on a Specified Date (Not Retroactive)**

If you want a sunset clause, but you don't want it to retroactively cancel any property rights you've established while the prenup is in effect, you can use Alternative 3.

EXAMPLE: Alex and Randy live in California, a community property state. They are about to get married. Alex has eight years left to pay off the mortgage on his house. Under California law, if Alex uses his earnings during marriage to pay the mortgage, an increasing percentage of ownership in the house will be community property. Randy is writing a textbook, and he has a contract to write another one. Both books are scheduled to be finished in six years. California law states that any book royalties derived from Randy's writing efforts during marriage would be community property.

To avoid the effect of California law until after Alex has a chance to pay off the mortgage and Randy finishes the two books, they sign a prenup that states that all earnings and assets acquired during the first nine years of their marriage (including the house and the royalties) will be separate property and not community property. After that, they want to start building up community property together, but they don't want to undo the prenup's protection of their separate property ownership of the house and the royalties. So they include a nine-year sunset clause, using Alternative 3.

TIP

Using sunset clauses for individual provisions. You can adapt a sunset clause so that it applies only to specific issues in your prenup, rather than to the entire agreement. To do this you would insert into Alternative 2 or 3 a reference to the items affected by the sunset clause and then add the following sentence to the end of the clause: "All other provisions of This Agreement will remain in effect indefinitely, unless and until we sign a new agreement revoking or modifying This Agreement." For example, if Alex and Randy want everything in their agreement to continue during their marriage except the clauses that cover ownership of Alex's house and Randy's book royalties, they can modify Alternative 3 to refer only to the specific clauses rather than to the entire agreement and clarify that the rest of the agreement continues indefinitely.

Paragraph 3: Legal Representation

We've said it before and we'll say it again: If you go to all the trouble of preparing a premarital agreement, you should make sure that each of you works with a competent lawyer who can certify that you each have separate legal representation at the time you sign the agreement. This paragraph is where you indicate the names of your representatives. Alternatively, if one or both of you choose not to heed our advice, this is where you make it clear that you thought about getting a lawyer and voluntarily decided against it.

In addition, this paragraph is where you'll state who has drafted your prenup.

A and B. Representation of Each Party

Clauses A and B (one for each of you) state whether or not you are represented by lawyers. Each clause has two alternatives. You will most likely choose Alternative 1 for both clauses.

Alternative 1: **Full Representation**

Use this to show that you consulted a lawyer before signing your prenup. For example, Ted and Grace choose to be represented by lawyers. Clause A, designating Grace's lawyer, is reprinted below. This clause in their prenup is followed by a similar provision in Clause B naming Ted's lawyer.

Representation of Grace

Grace has been represented by Howard Greene in the negotiation and drafting of This Agreement. Grace has fully discussed the terms of This Agreement with her attorney and is voluntarily choosing to sign This Agreement.

Alternative 2: **Waiver of Independent Advice**

If you decide against using a lawyer, choose Alternative 2, showing you are waiving independent representation.

EXAMPLE: Monica is working with an attorney to make a prenup. Her fiancé Kai does not want to hire an attorney. This is how their agreement reads:

A. Representation of Monica

Monica has been represented by Marianne Keig in the negotiation and drafting of This Agreement. Monica has fully discussed the terms of This Agreement with her attorney and is voluntarily choosing to sign This Agreement.

B. Representation of Kai

Kai understands that he has a right to be represented by an independent attorney in the negotiation and drafting of This Agreement. Kai does not want to be represented by an independent attorney, even though he has had ample time and has sufficient funds to hire an attorney. Kai understands the terms of This Agreement and he is voluntarily choosing to sign This Agreement without obtaining independent legal representation.

CAUTION

Check state requirements before waiving representation. The waiver clause in your prenup might need to meet certain standards imposed by the laws of your state. In California, for instance, a person who is not represented when signing a premarital agreement can have it set aside by a court later on, unless that person signed a separate waiver and was given a prior explanation of the terms of the agreement, written in language they could easily understand. If either of you decides not to hire a lawyer, check the legal requirements in your state to make sure your agreement will hold up in court.

C. Drafting of Agreement

This clause affects the way a court might interpret your prenup if there is ever a legal dispute about the meaning of any provision in the agreement. If it is clear that you have drafted your agreement together, the court is less likely to slant its interpretation of a particular clause for or against either of you.

Alternative 1: Prenup Drafted Together

This alternative allows you to document the fact that you've worked on your prenup together, as Karen and Russ did:

> This Agreement was drafted through the joint efforts of Karen and Russ.

Alternative 2: Prenup Not Drafted Together

Just in case your agreement has been written exclusively by one of you (or one of your attorneys), we've given you an alternative clause that spells that out. But be aware that whoever writes up the agreement alone bears an extra responsibility for clear language. If there's a dispute and a court finds the language of a clause to be ambiguous, the confusion is likely to work against the person who wrote it.

Paragraph 4: Disclosures and Waiting Period

In this paragraph, you specify the extent and form of the financial disclosures included in your prenup and acknowledge that you've had a full opportunity to review the draft agreement. We'll start with the disclosures.

A and B. Disclosures

Virtually every state requires couples signing a premarital agreement to exchange full written disclosures of their finances or to sign a written waiver of the right to a formal written disclosure. If you are thinking of waiving disclosures, see Alternative 2, below, and check your state's requirements on the book's online companion page.

Alternative 1: Formal Written Disclosure

Choose your clauses from the following options if one or both of you will be making formal written disclosures to the other.

A. and B. Disclosures of Each Party

Disclosures usually consist of a complete list of assets and their values, the amount owed on any outstanding debts, and each person's annual or monthly income. You may also include a statement of each person's monthly or annual personal expenses, although this is less common. The disclosures themselves are usually listed on separate schedules attached to the end of the agreement. To avoid any question about whether each of you had enough time to consider the information in the disclosure before signing your prenup, we recommend that you exchange the disclosures in advance and date and initial each schedule. (For an example of how your schedules might actually look, see Steven and Freda's completed prenup at the end of Chapter 9. There is also a blank format for schedules in Appendix C and on the book's companion page.)

A common question at this stage is just how much detail is necessary in the written disclosure, especially when it comes to assets. For instance, if you have a household full of furniture, do you really have to list and value every item?

When answering this question, it helps to understand that the reason disclosures are required is not only to ensure that you are both fully informed before signing the agreement, but also to make a record of your premarital assets for future reference. Your lists of assets should be specific enough to allow you (or your inheritors) to sort out your separate assets from your marital or community property if it ever becomes necessary. If you own items that you feel are so insignificant in value that you don't need to keep track of them separately, just group them into one category.

For example, you can lump your household goods together as a group instead of separately listing them, except for pieces that are unique or especially valuable. Those items and their values can be listed separately. This is how Steven and Freda handle things in their prenup. (See the sample at the end of Chapter 9.)

Another approach is to set a minimum value for the assets included in the disclosure and ignore items that are worth less than that amount. If you opt for this method, you will need to pick a dollar amount low enough to include items the two of you consider significant. For example, Karen and Russ decide to include in their prenup only assets worth more than $2,500.

You can also combine these approaches. Ted and Grace take this route in their prenup. Ted attaches to his disclosure an itemization of his antiques and family furnishings (already prepared for insurance purposes) so those items can be easily identified and distributed among Grace and his children after his death. But for other assets, he and Grace decide not to include anything worth less than $5,000. Because neither of them has significant debts to disclose besides Ted's mortgages on commercial investment property, Grace's home mortgage, and one of Grace's credit cards, they don't bother with a minimum for their debts.

This is how the disclosures paragraph of Ted and Grace's prenup reads (the actual disclosures will be attached to the end of the document, on separate schedules):

Grace's Disclosures

All of Grace's assets having a value greater than $5,000 and all of her debts are listed on Schedule 1, attached to This Agreement. Grace's income for the calendar year 20xx is also listed on Schedule 1. Grace has provided the information on Schedule 1 in good faith. The values and other financial information on Schedule 1 are approximations and might not be exact, but they are intended to present a full, fair, and reasonable disclosure of Grace's assets, debts, income, and personal expenses as of the time they were presented to Ted.

Ted's Disclosures

All of Ted's antiques and family furnishings are listed on the appraisal dated June 16, 20xx, attached to Schedule 2. All of Ted's other assets having a value greater than $5,000 and all of his debts are listed on Schedule 2, attached to This Agreement. Ted's income for the calendar year 20xx is also listed on Schedule 2. Ted has provided the information on Schedule 2 in good faith. The values and other financial information on Schedule 2 are approximations and might not be exact, but they are intended to present a full, fair, and reasonable disclosure of Ted's assets, debts, income, and personal expenses as of the time they were presented to Grace.

C. Jointly Owned Premarital Assets and Jointly Owed Premarital Debts [OPTIONAL]

It's not always the case that all premarital assets belong to just one person. If you have been together for a while, you might already own property together. If that's the case, you may add this clause to refer to a third schedule of jointly owned assets. You can include jointly owed debts, too.

> EXAMPLE: Mae and Mert have lived together for five years and they are marrying in June. They have bought cars, an RV, and household furniture together, and they have a joint bank account. They also have joint debts. They list these items on Schedule 3, which is attached to their prenup, and the following clause appears in their agreement:

Be Specific When Listing Valuable Assets

List all assets of significant value with enough precision so that they could be clearly identified by a third party who has no prior knowledge about the asset. For example, Mary might list her "20xx Honda Accord," instead of the more generic "Mary's automobile." We recommend including at least the last four digits of bank account numbers, life insurance policies, or other assets that have account numbers.

For real estate, we recommend that in addition to listing the street address, you include or attach the legal description of the property. You can find it on the deed to the property; it consists of the county and state where the property is located, plus surveyor's language and any easements or restrictions relating to the property.

If you have retirement benefits, those should be listed by the official name of the retirement plan or account, such as "the ABC Brokerage Roth IRA, account number 555 1234," or "Retirement benefits with the Teachers' Retirement System of the State of Illinois."

> **Jointly Owned Premarital Assets and Jointly Owed Premarital Debts**
> Each jointly owned premarital asset having a value greater than $1,000, and all jointly owed premarital debts, are listed on Schedule 3, attached to This Agreement. The values stated on Schedule 3 are reasonably accurate as of April 20, 20xx.

Documents Provided [OPTIONAL]

Depending on how complex your finances are, you might also decide to include in your disclosure copies of tax returns, appraisals, financial statements, and other relevant documents. If you take this approach, it's a good idea to list the documents provided. For example, Ted's finances are complicated because he holds title to his commercial real estate investments through limited partnerships with others. He wants Grace and her lawyer to understand his situation in detail, so he gives Grace copies of numerous documents relating to the investments. Then he and Grace put the following clause in their prenup:

> In addition to the information listed on Schedule 1, Ted has given Grace copies of the following documents:
> - Federal and state individual income tax returns filed by Ted for the years 20xx through 20xx.
> - Tax returns for the years 20xx through 20xx for the following limited partnerships: Central 102, Blue Skies II, Park Place, and Boardwalk.
> - The following appraisals: 102 Central Avenue, September 3, 20xx, by Acme Appraisal Co.; Clearwater Resort, May 5, 20xx, by Appraisers Unlimited; Park Hotel, December 13, 20xx, by Appraisal Monopoly Co.; Boardwalk, July 27, 20xx, by Appraisal Monopoly Co.

Acknowledgment of Receipt of Disclosures

Some courts have thrown out prenups when the written disclosures were received too late—either too close to or after the agreement was signed. To avoid this issue, we recommend that you date and initial the disclosures when you prepare and receive them, and that you include this clause in your prenup. In fact, as we mention elsewhere in this book, it's a good idea to exchange disclosures—together with any additional documents mentioned in the preceding clause—several days, if not weeks, before you sign your prenup. For example, Ted and Grace sign their prenuptial agreement on April 20. They exchanged the written disclosures (and Ted's financial documents) about a month earlier. Their agreement contains this clause:

> Ted received a copy of Schedule 1 on March 15, 20xx. Ted reviewed this information before signing This Agreement.
>
> Grace received a copy of Schedule 2 and the documents described in Paragraph 4C on March 12, 20xx. Grace reviewed this information before signing This Agreement.

Mutual Waiver of Further Disclosure [OPTIONAL]

This clause might be called the "gilding-the-lily clause." It probably isn't necessary, but if your disclosure includes estimates and approximations, you can use this provision to ward off any arguments over whether your disclosures were complete and accurate enough. (Of course, a clause like this won't save a prenup based on false or deliberately misleading disclosures.)

This clause is mutual—that is, it applies to both of you, even if one of you provides more precise information than the other. For example, Karen decides to use her accountant's estimate of the value of her veterinary practice for the disclosure of her assets rather than pay for a formal appraisal. But both she and Russ use recent appraisals of their homes (and the office building housing Karen's business), because all three properties were appraised in connection with recent refinances. They include this mutual waiver of further disclosure in their agreement:

> Each of us understands that certain values and other information on Schedules 1 and 2 are approximate. We consider this information sufficient and each of us voluntarily waives the right to be given any additional information.

Alternative 2: Waiver of Formal Written Disclosure

Use the following clauses if one or both of you will waive the right to receive full written information about the other's finances.

A and B. Waiver of Each Party

Let's say one or both of you feel you know enough about the other person's finances and you've decided—after checking your state's legal requirements—that it's not necessary to receive a written disclosure. This pair of clauses gives you general language for waiving formal disclosure.

Note that this is not set up as a mutual waiver. Instead, there is a separate clause for each person. We've done it this way in case only one of you waives a written disclosure. And even if you both waive the disclosures, we recommend separate clauses to make it clear that this was a decision each of you considered carefully.

> EXAMPLE: Marisa and Alonso are marrying after living together for eight years. They both work for the same company. They own a house together, and they have other mutual assets, such as cars and bank accounts. Marisa owns some inherited property with her siblings. Marisa and Alonso decide to have a prenup to support Marisa's estate plan that leaves her share of the inherited property to her nieces and nephews. The prenup refers specifically to Marisa's inherited property, but she and Alonso decide they don't need to bother with formal disclosures. They include these clauses:

A. Marisa's Waiver of Formal Written Disclosure.

Marisa is aware of Alonso's financial circumstances. She voluntarily waives the right to be given a formal written disclosure or any other information about Alonso's finances.

B. Alonso's Waiver of Formal Written Disclosure.

Alonso is aware of Marisa's financial circumstances. He voluntarily waives the right to be given a formal written disclosure or any other information about Marisa's finances.

CAUTION

Think carefully before waiving disclosure. Formal disclosures create a record of what each of you knew about the other person's financial situation before signing the agreement. This could avoid a later disagreement about whether you did or didn't know what you were agreeing to. If you decide to go forward without formal disclosures, your prenup should at least clearly state that you concluded disclosures weren't needed after considering the issue carefully. Depending on your state's requirements, you might also need to certify that you had an opportunity to consult an independent attorney before waiving disclosure. You might even need to make the waiver a separate document instead of including it as a part of the prenup. Be sure to check your state's legal requirements. If necessary, consult a qualified lawyer about what goes into the waiver.

D. Waiting Period and Acknowledgment of Receipt

Some states require a waiting period between the date each person receives a draft premarital agreement and the date the person signs it. For example, under California law a premarital agreement can be invalidated if either party signed it less than seven days after receiving the draft agreement. Even if your state has no such requirement, observing and documenting a reasonable waiting period will help to show that the agreement was signed voluntarily. This clause will allow you to document your compliance with any applicable state waiting period. If there isn't a requirement, using this clause will demonstrate that you took plenty of time to consider it before signing.

For example, Russ and Karen are signing their agreement in California, so they need at least seven days between getting the draft agreement and signing. Although one court decision has held that the waiting period starts with presentation of the first draft, Karen and Russ allow for seven days between signing and the date they got the final version of their premarital agreement.

Again, there are two alternatives, depending on whether there were changes made in the agreement after the first draft was created.

Alternative 1:

Karen first received a draft of This Agreement on May 2, 20xx. This Agreement has been revised since that date, and Karen received the final draft of This Agreement on May 10, 20xx.

Russ first received a draft of This Agreement on May 2, 20xx. This Agreement has been revised since that date, and Russ received the final draft of This Agreement on May 10, 20xx.

Alternative 2:

Karen first received a draft of This Agreement on May 2, 20xx. This Agreement has not been revised since it was first presented to Karen.

Russ first received a draft of This Agreement on May 2, 20xx. This Agreement has not been revised since it was first presented to Russ.

Paragraph 5: Definitions

This paragraph defines some of the terms that will be used in your prenup. Including these definitions in your agreement will help avoid later misunderstandings. It will also save you the trouble of repeating the same definitions over and over in the document.

> **⊘ CAUTION**
>
> **Modify with care.** The defined terms in this paragraph are used in the rest of this book's prenup clauses. Therefore, use extreme caution if you decide to modify the definitions in any way. If you do make changes, you'll need to make sure your use of the defined terms in other parts of your prenup is consistent with your new definitions.

A. This Agreement

Your prenup will contain many references to "This Agreement." While this term obviously applies to the premarital agreement that you actually sign, the definition extends to any written modifications you make to the agreement later on.

> **This Agreement**
> The term "This Agreement" refers to the provisions of this document, once signed by us, as modified by any subsequent amendments in writing signed by us.

B. Separate Property

As we explain in Chapter 4, there are two basic property systems used in the United States: the "community property" system and the "equitable distribution" system. In a community property state, married people own certain assets (generally those acquired during marriage) jointly as community property and other assets individually as separate property, regardless of whose name is on the title document. In equitable distribution states, ownership is determined according to title, so any asset held in the name of one spouse alone is that person's separate property. However, equitable distribution states also treat some assets acquired during marriage as "marital property" no matter whose name is on the title. Marital property can be divided in a divorce or set aside for a surviving spouse after the other spouse dies.

Our definition of separate property assumes that your agreement will designate certain assets (such as items you own before you marry) as separate property that won't be divided between you in a divorce, but will instead belong to whichever spouse is the designated owner. This definition spells out that intention.

Because most states require a separate waiver of inheritance rights by a surviving spouse, our definition of separate property does not rule out a claim by a surviving spouse unless your prenup also includes the separate waiver. (See Optional Paragraph 1 on estate planning matters in Chapter 8.)

Separate Property

Any asset designated as one person's "Separate Property" in This Agreement belongs exclusively to that person. A spouse has the sole right to manage and dispose of their Separate Property assets. Separate Property is not subject to division between us if we divorce. However, if the owner of Separate Property dies, the surviving spouse might have a legal claim to it, unless they have signed a valid written waiver in This Agreement or in another document.

C. Marital Property or Community Property

In addition to the separate property definition, you should choose a definition for marital property or community property, depending on which system your state uses. (See Chapter 4 if you need help understanding your state's system. If you live in Alaska, South Dakota, Kentucky, Tennessee, Florida, or Wisconsin, see the end of this section for a note that applies to your choice.)

Alternative 1: Marital Property

If you are in an equitable distribution state, use the definition for marital property. It states that any asset designated as marital property in your prenup will be subject to division between you if you ever divorce. This form also includes an optional provision that spells out your rights to manage and control jointly and solely held marital property. For example, Ted and Grace live in New York, which is an equitable distribution state, so they choose the marital property definition, including the optional part about management and control.

Marital Property

An asset designated as "Marital Property" in This Agreement might be subject to division between us by a court if we divorce, unless we provide otherwise in This Agreement or in another document. Any asset designated as Marital Property might be subject to a claim by a surviving spouse, unless the surviving spouse has signed a valid written waiver of such claims in This Agreement or in another document.

We will both have equal rights to manage and dispose of any Marital Property held in our joint names. If an asset designated as Marital Property is held in only one of our names, the sole title holder will have the exclusive right to manage, control, transfer, or sell that property, to the extent allowed by state law.

Alternative 2: **Community Property**

Use the community property definition if you live in a community property state. Unlike marital property, community property is jointly owned by spouses. So the first part of the community property definition differs from the first part of the marital property definition.

Ownership of community property also includes the right to manage and control the property. We give you a couple of different options for specifying how you will share management of your community property. You can pick one of our options or insert your own if what we've written doesn't address your situation. Or you can research state laws regarding management and control of community property: If your state's law works for you, leave out this part of the definition. (To begin your research, see your state's summary on the book's online companion page.)

> **EXAMPLE:** Tara and Spike live in a community property state. Spike owns a restaurant that will remain his separate property. He and Tara plan to start up a new restaurant, "Tara's Bistro," after they marry, and they agree that it will be community property. However, Spike will run the restaurant. They insert this definition of community property in their prenup:

> **Community Property**
>
> Any asset designated as "Community Property" in This Agreement belongs to both of us equally. Our Community Property will be subject to division between us by a court if we divorce, taking into account any requirements for division spelled out in This Agreement.
>
> We will have equal rights to manage and control any Community Property, subject to any exceptions provided by state law. However, if an asset designated as Community Property is held in only one of our names, the sole title holder will have the exclusive right to manage, control, transfer, or sell that property, to the extent allowed by state law. In addition, Spike will have the exclusive right to manage and control the Community Property restaurant business known as Tara's Bistro; provided that he cannot sell the business or substantially all of its assets without Tara's consent.

CAUTION

Special note for Alaska, Florida, Kentucky, South Dakota, Tennessee, and Wisconsin readers.

Alaska: If you live in Alaska, you can make a written agreement or "community property trust" specifying that you want your property to be treated as community property. If that's what you prefer, you should check the legal requirements for making that election and modify the community property definition to reflect your choice. If you do not want to opt for community property, then you should use the marital property definition.

Florida, Kentucky, South Dakota, and Tennessee: These states allow spouses to transfer assets to a "community property trust." As long as the property is held in the trust, it is considered community property. You can't classify the property as community property in your prenup, because you must be married when you set up the trust. However, if you plan to use a community property trust, you might want to say so in your agreement and include clauses that are consistent with your plan. There are certain requirements you have to meet to create a community property trust, and having one affects your rights if you divorce or if one of you dies, so make sure you discuss it with your lawyer before you finalize your plan.

Wisconsin: Wisconsin residents face a different issue. Wisconsin's system is so similar to a community property system that it is considered a community property state. However, the term used in Wisconsin is "marital property." So if you're drafting a prenup in Wisconsin, you should use the community property definition, but substitute the word "marital" for the word "community," both in the definition and in references throughout the agreement. Wisconsin residents also have the option of using a form called the "Statutory Terminable Marital Property Classification Agreement Form." (You can find it in the Wisconsin Statutes at Section 766.588.) For couples that want to share everything 50/50, this form allows spouses (or future spouses) to have all of their existing solely owned property and their acquisitions during marriage treated as marital property.

The statutory agreement stays in effect for only three years unless the spouses provide each other with complete financial disclosures. In addition, either spouse can terminate the agreement at any time by giving 30 days' notice to the other spouse. (Terminating the agreement doesn't change the character of property already affected by the agreement; it affects only property acquired after the termination. Thus, ending the agreement probably won't amount to much of a change, since most property acquired after marriage in Wisconsin will be treated as marital property under the state's law.) If you think this type of agreement might be right for you, be sure to discuss it with your lawyer.

D. Divorce

Even if your prenup doesn't directly deal with divorce or separation issues, such as how your marital or community property will be divided or whether alimony will be paid, there are references to divorce in some of the standard clauses we've included, such as the definitions of marital property and community property discussed above. For that reason, you should include in your prenup a definition of divorce that covers the variety of legal names that could apply to a court proceeding that ends a marriage. You can also apply the term "Divorce" to annulment, if you want the same rules to apply in that context.

> **Divorce**
> The term "Divorce" in This Agreement refers to any legal proceeding to end or alter a marital relationship, including a proceeding for divorce, dissolution of marriage, total or absolute divorce, legal separation or separate maintenance, or annulment.

For more discussion of divorce-related clauses, see the optional paragraph, "Other Optional Provisions Related to Divorce," in Chapter 8, Optional Paragraph 3.

Next: Addressing Assets and Debts in Your Prenup

Once you've drafted the introductory paragraphs of your prenup, it's time to address how assets and debts will be handled during your marriage. Chapter 7 will walk you through paragraphs 6 through 8 of your draft prenup.

Paragraphs 6–8: Assets and Debts

Paragraphs 6, 7, and 8 address how you'll handle premarital assets, assets acquired during marriage, and debts acquired during marriage.

Paragraph 6: Ownership of Premarital Assets

The clauses contained in this paragraph deal with the property you own before you get married—your "premarital assets." Here, you'll specifically address issues such as:

- whether or not your premarital assets will continue to be separate property after you marry
- what happens if you sell your premarital assets or if they appreciate in value during your marriage, and
- what happens if you use marital funds to pay off the mortgage on separate property real estate.

A. Your General Rule for Premarital Assets

Every state recognizes premarital assets as separate property, unless there is a valid written agreement converting those assets to marital or community property. You should use one of the following three alternatives to state your general intentions regarding premarital assets:

- **Alternative 1** states that all premarital assets and any property traceable to those assets—that is, increases in their value or new assets exchanged for them—remain separate property.
- **Alternative 2** provides that all premarital assets remain separate property but any increases in value or new assets exchanged for them will be marital or community property.
- **Alternative 3** states simply that all premarital assets will be considered marital or community property.

After establishing your general rule, you'll have an opportunity to make exceptions to it for particular assets, if you choose to do so. Here's a little more detail about each of your choices.

Alternative 1: **All Premarital Assets and Property Traceable to Them Remain Separate Property**

This alternative states that premarital assets will remain each spouse's separate property after marriage. It also provides that any appreciation in value or sales proceeds of premarital assets will continue to be separate property.

As discussed in Chapter 4, state laws differ in how they treat increases in value of premarital separate property. Some states consider value increases to be property acquired during marriage and classify them as marital or community property. Other states say all property that's traceable to separate property remains separate.

To complicate the question, some states further differentiate value enhancement resulting from a spouse's efforts to build up the asset versus passive profits, such as market-driven increases in value. In those states, passive profits are separate property, but increased value due to spousal efforts is marital or community property. For example, in California, any profits or increase in the value of Karen's veterinary practice could be considered community property to the extent she devotes her time to the practice, unless Karen and Russ sign a prenup stating otherwise. Alternative 1 gives you the opportunity to address this issue by including—or omitting—in the definition of separate property any increases that result from spousal efforts.

CAUTION

Use Paragraph 7 to address income derived from separate property. The clauses in Paragraph 6 are designed to cover assets, not the income they might generate, such as interest or dividends. If your separate property will produce income after you are married, you can use Paragraph 7, below, to state whether that income will be separate property or whether you will share it as marital or community property.

Alternative 1 also states that any assets acquired with (or in exchange for) premarital assets will be separate property. You can limit separate property to only those new assets that are held in one spouse's sole name or you can include assets held in joint names.

To show you how the optional parts might play out, we provide three different examples of Alternative 1. There's one for each of our fictional couples: Steven and Freda, Karen and Russ, and Ted and Grace.

Steven and Freda's version of Alternative 1 states that enhancement in value resulting from a spouse's efforts during marriage are not included as separate property. Any asset acquired by selling a premarital asset will still be considered separate property, but only if the new asset is kept in the spouse's sole name.

All Premarital Assets and Property Traceable to Them Remain Separate Property

Except as specified elsewhere in This Agreement, Freda's premarital assets, which are listed on Schedule 1, and all property traceable to those assets, shall continue to be her Separate Property after we marry. "All property traceable to those assets" means any growth in value of those assets, not including growth in value arising as a direct or indirect result of the efforts of one or both of us during our marriage. It also means any sales proceeds of those assets, any asset purchased with the sales proceeds, or any asset(s) acquired in exchange for those assets, as long as the sales proceeds or any such new asset is held in the sole name of Freda.

Except as specified elsewhere in This Agreement, Steven's premarital assets, which are listed on Schedule 2, and all property traceable to those assets, shall continue to be his Separate Property after we marry. "All property traceable to those assets" means any growth in value of those assets, not including growth in value arising as a direct or indirect result of the efforts of one or both of us during our marriage. It also means any sales proceeds of those assets, any asset purchased with the sales proceeds, or any asset(s) acquired in exchange for those assets, as long as the sales proceeds or any such new asset is held in the sole name of Steven.

Karen and Russ come to a different conclusion. Their version of Alternative 1 provides for all increases in value to be separate property, even if they result from spousal efforts. The rest of their clause is the same as Steven and Freda's, including the requirement that any new asset derived from a premarital asset must be in the spouse's sole name in order to be considered separate. Later in Paragraph 6 of their prenup, they add clauses dealing with specific assets—their homes and Karen's veterinary practice—that customize the approach to appreciation and sales proceeds for those particular assets. (You can find the complete Paragraph 6 of their prenup with the sample documents at the end of Chapter 9.)

Ted and Grace, like Karen and Russ, decide that any increase in value from spousal efforts will be separate property, but they want new assets derived from premarital assets to be separate property even if held in joint names instead of the sole name of one spouse. Their version of Alternative 1 looks like this:

All Premarital Assets and Property Traceable to Them Remain Separate Property

Except as specified elsewhere in This Agreement, Grace's premarital assets, which are listed on Schedule 1, and all property traceable to those assets, shall continue to be her Separate Property after we marry. "All property traceable to those assets" means any growth in value of those assets, including growth in value arising as a direct or indirect result of the efforts of one or both of us during our marriage. It also means any sales proceeds of those assets, any asset purchased with the sales proceeds, or any asset(s) acquired in exchange for those assets, as long as the sales proceeds or any such new asset is held in the sole name of Grace, or if held in joint names, as long as it is traceable to the premarital asset.

Except as specified elsewhere in This Agreement, Ted's premarital assets, which are listed on Schedule 2, and all property traceable to those assets, shall continue to be his Separate Property after we marry. "All property traceable to those assets" means any growth in value of those assets, including growth in value arising as a direct or indirect result of the efforts of one or both of us during our marriage. It also means any sales proceeds of those assets, any asset purchased with the sales proceeds, or any asset(s) acquired in exchange for those assets, as long as the sales proceeds or any such new asset is held in the sole name of Ted, or if held in joint names, as long as it is traceable to the premarital asset.

> **CAUTION**
>
> **Tracing separate property through joint-title assets can be tricky.**
> Think carefully before agreeing that assets held in joint names can be treated as separate property. It might turn out to be quite difficult to identify the separate property portion of a jointly held asset. This is especially true if the asset in question is at all liquid, such as a bank account or a brokerage account, and if you combine separate and marital funds in the account. Unless you keep meticulous records of every transaction (as Ted and Grace plan to do), it can be nearly impossible to trace commingled separate property funds and marital property funds through years or even months of transactions. You'll make your lives easier if you agree up front that you will keep separate property assets in separate names and not try to trace them through jointly held assets. If on occasion you decide to contribute separate property to a joint-title asset, you can sign a separate agreement stating that a specified portion will be considered separate property, or that the spouse who contributed separate property will be entitled to reimbursement. You can even include a mechanism for this in Paragraph 7 of your prenup. (See the next section of this chapter for some examples.)

Alternative 2: All Premarital Assets Remain Separate Property but Not Property Traceable to Them

Alternative 2 for Clause A provides that—barring exceptions included later in the agreement—all premarital assets will continue to be a spouse's separate property. Unlike Alternative 1, however, this version designates as marital or community property all increases in value, together with sales proceeds or new assets derived from premarital assets. Use this alternative if you want to consider everything but the original premarital assets to be marital or community property. You can of course adapt this alternative to apply only to certain categories of gains if the blanket approach is too broad for your needs.

> **EXAMPLE:** Robyn and Marian each own rental property that they intend to keep separate after they marry. They decide that any profits from the rental properties, including rental income, will be marital property. (They take care of the income aspect in Paragraph 7.) To minimize accounting

and administrative burdens they also agree that if either of them sells their rental property during the marriage, they will throw the proceeds into the marital pot. (Their lawyers have advised them that if either of them decides to sell during marriage, and if they decide that they want to keep all or some of the sales proceeds separate, they will have to enter into a separate agreement at that time.) If they don't sell the property and later divorce— or if one of them dies—they want to be sure that the property, including any increase in the property's value, will be considered separate property. They adapt Alternative 2 in this way:

All Premarital Assets Remain Separate Property but Not Property Traceable to Them

Except as specified elsewhere in This Agreement, Marian's premarital assets, which are listed on Schedule 1, shall continue to be her Separate Property after we marry. However, all property traceable to those assets shall be considered Marital Property. "All property traceable to those assets" means any growth in value of those assets, including growth in value arising as a direct or indirect result of the efforts of one or both of us during our marriage. It also means any sales proceeds of those assets, any asset purchased with the sales proceeds, or any asset(s) acquired in exchange for those assets, even if the sales proceeds or any such new asset is held in the sole name of Marian. However, any increase in the value of Marian's premarital assets shall be her Separate Property.

Except as specified elsewhere in This Agreement, Robyn's premarital assets, which are listed on Schedule 2, shall continue to be her Separate Property after we marry. However, all property traceable to those assets shall be considered Marital Property. "All property traceable to those assets" means any growth in value of those assets, including growth in value arising as a direct or indirect result of the efforts of one or both of us during our marriage. It also means any sales proceeds of those assets, any asset purchased with the sales proceeds, or any asset(s) acquired in exchange for those assets, even if the sales proceeds or any such new asset is held in the sole name of Robyn. However, any increase in the value of Robyn's premarital assets shall be her Separate Property.

Alternative 3: **All Premarital Assets Will Be Considered Marital or Community Property**

If you want your premarital assets converted to marital property (if you are in an equitable distribution state) or to community property, use Alternative 3, inserting "marital" or "community" as applicable.

> EXAMPLE: Gail and Frank have lived together (in an equitable distribution state) for several years. When they first moved in together, neither of them had much property. They now own a house together and each of them has a car, some savings, and a small retirement plan. They have decided that once they marry, they want all of their assets to be considered marital property, as if they had been married the whole time. So they use this clause:

All Premarital Assets Will Be Considered Marital Property

Except as specified elsewhere in This Agreement, all of our premarital assets, which are listed on Schedules 1 and 2, and all property traceable to those assets, will be considered Marital Property as soon as we marry. "All property traceable to those assets" means any growth in value of those assets, including growth in value arising as a direct or indirect result of the efforts of one or both of us during our marriage. It also means any sales proceeds of those assets, any asset purchased with the sales proceeds, or any asset(s) acquired in exchange for those assets, even if the sales proceeds or any such new asset is held in the sole name of one of us.

> ⓘ **CAUTION**
>
> **Mind your As and Bs.** If you want all assets treated as you've described in Clause A, just above, you needn't bother with the following additional clauses. However, you will need to reformat your agreement to take out the "A," because you won't have a Clause B, Clause C, and so on. Leaving in the "A" could make it look like you accidentally forgot to include the subsequently lettered material. (For an example, see Steven and Freda's prenup at the end of Chapter 9.)

B. Other Clauses Affecting Specific Premarital Assets

In this section, we provide optional clauses dealing with jointly owned assets and with ownership of three types of premarital assets that tend to concern couples who make prenups: real estate, businesses, and retirement benefits.

We also offer a catchall clause you can use for other types of premarital assets. If none of the clauses in this section fit your situation exactly, feel free to modify them. But be sure to assign sequential letters to them if you add more than one clause. (To see how to do this, take a look at the excerpt from Karen and Russ's prenup at the end of Chapter 9.)

> **SKIP AHEAD**
>
> **When to skip this section.** If you want to treat all assets acquired during your marriage as you've specified in the clause just above, Paragraph 6 of your prenup is complete. Skip ahead to Paragraph 7.

Jointly Owned Premarital Property [OPTIONAL]

If you are attaching a schedule of jointly owned assets to your agreement, you will need to specify whether those assets will be considered jointly owned separate property or marital property once you marry. This optional clause allows you to do that.

> **EXAMPLE:** Mae and Mert (introduced in Chapter 6) lived together for four years before deciding to marry. During that time they bought cars, an RV, and household furniture together, and they also have a joint bank account. They have listed these items on Schedule 3, which is attached to their prenup. They want these assets to be considered marital property so they add the following clause to Paragraph 6 of their prenup:

Jointly Owned Premarital Assets Will Be Considered Marital Property
Except as specified elsewhere in This Agreement, all of our jointly
owned premarital assets, which are listed on Schedule 3, and all
property traceable to those assets, will be considered Marital
Property as soon as we marry. "All property traceable to those assets"
means any growth in value of those assets, including growth in value
arising as a direct or indirect result of the efforts of one or both of us
during our marriage. It also means any sales proceeds of those assets,
any asset purchased with the sales proceeds, or any asset(s) acquired
in exchange for those assets, even if the sales proceeds or any such
new asset is held in the sole name of one of us.

Premarital Real Estate [OPTIONAL]

If one or both of you own a home or other real estate when you marry,
you might want to include a specific clause spelling out your agreement
concerning the property. State marital property laws usually protect
a spouse's premarital interest in real estate, but if you make mortgage
payments with marital earnings, the property might someday be subject
to a marital property claim in an estate or a divorce proceeding—or
even in a debt collection action. To avoid any surprises, think through
what you want to have happen in these circumstances and include a
corresponding clause in your prenup.

We give you four alternatives to choose from:

- **Alternative 1** states that the real estate will remain entirely separate
  even if you use marital funds to make payments, repairs, or
  improvements to the property.
- **Alternative 2** allows you to specify a formula for apportioning
  the equity between separate property and marital or community
  property.

- **Alternative 3** provides for reimbursement of any marital or community property funds used for the property.
- **Alternative 4** makes the home or other real estate marital or community property after a certain date or event.

Alternative 1: **Real Estate Will Remain Separate Property**

Use this clause if you want the property to remain completely separate, even if you put marital funds into it. For example, Karen and Russ plan to live together in Karen's house. She will make the house payments from her community property earnings. Russ's condo will be rented out, and he will use the rent, supplemented by his earnings, to pay the mortgage and other expenses. They agree that each person's home—including any appreciation or sales proceeds—will remain entirely separate property without any reimbursement or community property claim, even if community property earnings are used for house payments, repairs, or improvements. (Again, see the end of Chapter 9 for an excerpt from their prenup.)

Alternative 2: **Real Estate Will Be Apportioned Between Separate Property and Marital or Community Property**

Use this clause if you want to apportion ownership between separate property and marital or community property according to a formula you've agreed on.

> EXAMPLE: Aaron and Laurie plan to live together and raise a family in Aaron's premarital home, which is located in a community property state. Aaron will make the house payments from his salary as an engineer, and Laurie will be a stay-at-home mom. They agree that an increasing percentage of equity will be considered community property, as follows:

**Equity in Aaron's Home Will Be Apportioned Between
Separate Property and Community Property**

The equity in Aaron's home located at 555 Serenity Lane will be apportioned between Aaron's Separate Property and Community Property as follows: Beginning on our first anniversary and on each subsequent anniversary during our marriage, 5% of the equity in the home will be converted to Community Property, up to a maximum of 90% total Community Property equity, and the balance of the equity will be Aaron's Separate Property. For example, at the end of one year of marriage, 5% of the equity will be Community Property. After five years, 25% of the equity will be Community Property, and so forth until the maximum of 90% Community Property is reached on our eighteenth anniversary. The above provisions will apply to any sales proceeds or assets acquired in exchange for the home during our marriage.

Alternative 3: Marital or Community Property Contributions to Real Estate Will Be Reimbursed

Instead of apportioning the equity, you might prefer to keep the equity separate but provide for reimbursement of any marital or community property funds used to pay for the mortgage, capital improvements, or other property-related expenses. If you use this clause, you must specify which types of payments qualify for reimbursement and under what circumstances the reimbursement becomes due and payable. Be sure to maintain detailed financial records related to the property.

EXAMPLE: Nadia and Sami intend to continue living together in Nadia's home after they marry. They will most likely use marital property funds for a kitchen remodel as well as for house payments. They agree the home will remain Nadia's separate property and that house payments won't be reimbursed. However, any marital funds used for capital improvements, such as the remodel, will be reimbursed and added to marital property funds if Nadia receives a gift or inheritance, or if they get divorced. This is the clause they add to their prenup:

Marital Property Contributions to Nadia's Home Will Be Reimbursed
If Marital Property funds are used to pay for certain expenses related
to Nadia's home located at 2020 Hindsight Avenue (referred to here
as "Hindsight"), Hindsight will remain Nadia's Separate Property, but
the Marital Property payments will be reimbursed as follows: if Nadia
receives a gift or inheritance of more than $10,000, or if we divorce,
Nadia shall reimburse to our Marital Property savings account the
total amount of Marital Property funds used, plus simple interest
of 3% per year, minus any amount already reimbursed. In the case
of a gift or inheritance, the reimbursement from any single gift or
inheritance shall not exceed the amount of the gift or inheritance,
less $10,000. The reimbursable expenses referred to in this clause
shall include only payments for costs and materials actually paid
with Marital Property funds for the improvement or remodeling
of Hindsight. Funds expended for ordinary maintenance, mortgage
payments, property taxes and assessments, casualty insurance, or
other incidental expenses not directly incurred in remodeling or
improving Hindsight shall not be reimbursed.

Alternative 4: Real Estate Will Become Marital or Community Property

If you want to convert premarital real estate to marital or community
property—perhaps in exchange for some other provision in the prenup
or after a specified length of time—you can use this clause.

EXAMPLE: Kim owns a townhouse. Her fiancé, Derek, owns a parcel of
undeveloped property in the mountains. Both properties are about equal
in value. They are planning to sell the townhouse. With the proceeds, they
will buy a bigger home that they will own together. Eventually, they will
build a cabin on the mountain lot. In their prenup, they include a clause
stating that once they get married, both the townhouse and the mountain
property will be converted to marital property.

> **Real Estate Will Become Marital Property**
>
> Kim's real estate located at 345 Towne Court will become Marital Property as soon as we marry. Derek's real estate (unimproved lot) located in Soda Springs will become Marital Property as soon as we marry.

Premarital Businesses [OPTIONAL]

If either of you owns all or a share of a business or a professional practice that you intend to operate while you are married, you might want to use your prenup to state whether the business will remain entirely separate property. If you don't address the issue, the business—or any increase in its value—could later be subject to a marital or community property claim because of the work devoted to the business during marriage. (Remember, any value resulting from the efforts of either spouse during marriage is generally considered marital or community property.)

In this section, we give you two clauses that address rights in a premarital business.

- **Alternative 1** provides that the business will remain separate property regardless of any time either spouse spends on the business after marriage.
- **Alternative 2** allows you to specify a formula for determining any marital or community property interest in the business.

Alternative 1: The Premarital Business or Professional Practice Will Remain Separate Property

Use this clause if you want a premarital business or professional practice to remain entirely the separate property of the spouse who owns it before marriage, regardless of how much time either one of you devotes to the business.

EXAMPLE: Nick and Susan are in their early 60s. Nick owns a printing business that he plans to continue to run after his marriage to Susan, a college professor. In a few years, Nick hopes to sell the printing business and retire on the proceeds. Susan will have a substantial monthly pension benefit when she retires from teaching. In their prenup, they insert the following clause regarding the printing business. (They also include a clause making Susan's pension—even the part earned during marriage—her separate property in a separate paragraph dealing with retirement benefits.)

Nick's Premarital Business Will Remain Separate Property

During our marriage, Nick plans to continue to operate his printing business, known as In the Nick of Time. The business shall continue to be Nick's Separate Property after we marry. Any increase in its value shall also be Nick's Separate Property, regardless of how we refer to it or how much time either of us devotes to it. If Nick sells the business or exchanges it for another asset, any sales proceeds or asset acquired in exchange will be his Separate Property.

Alternative 2: The Premarital Business or Professional Practice Will Be Subject to Apportionment Between Separate and Marital or Community Property

Some couples expect a premarital business to eventually have a marital property component to it, but they want to spell out an apportionment formula in their prenup to avoid any debate about how that component will be calculated.

This is what Russ and Karen decide to do. Since both Karen and Russ will be working in Karen's veterinary practice, they want a simple and fair way to calculate the marital property portion of any increase in the value of the practice if Karen were to die before Russ or if they divorce. You can read the clause in the excerpt from their prenup at the end of Chapter 9.

Premarital Retirement or Employee Benefits [OPTIONAL]

If you want your premarital retirement or other employee benefits to remain separate property and if you have already provided in Paragraph 6A that all premarital assets are to be separate property, you don't have to include a specific clause covering premarital retirement or employee benefits. However, if you want to make a point of excluding these benefits from marital or community property claims or if you want to treat them as marital or community property, you can use one of the following clauses.

Alternative 1: Premarital Retirement or Employee Benefits Will Be Separate Property

Use this alternative if you want to make it clear that each person's retirement or employee benefits—be they in the form of a pension, a 401(k), an IRA, stock options, or another type of retirement or employee benefit account—are to be that person's separate property, rather than marital or community property.

CAUTION

You must sign a waiver after you marry. Stating in your prenup that you want your retirement or employee benefits to be separate property is important, but it's not enough. For most retirement plans, the law requires a married person to obtain a spouse's written waiver of benefits. Usually, you must sign the waiver after you are married, not when you sign your prenup. This clause makes it clear that you agree to sign any needed documents, including written waivers, after you are married. To minimize problems that could arise if one of you dies before you sign the necessary waivers, we recommend that you list each retirement plan by its full name on the schedule of premarital assets attached to your prenup—for example, "John's benefits with the Acme Company Pension and Profit Sharing Plan," rather than "John's 401(k) plan." Then be sure to have your signatures on the prenup notarized. (This is discussed in Chapter 10, along with other suggestions for finalizing your prenup.) While there are no guarantees that this will suffice, some courts have approved waivers of retirement benefits in prenuptial agreements where the retirement plan was specifically listed and the parties' signatures were notarized.

Ted and Grace state (in Paragraph 6A of their prenuptial agreement) that all of their premarital property is to remain separate. Even so, their lawyers have suggested that they mention their retirement benefits specifically, to avoid any misunderstanding. They include this clause as well:

Premarital Retirement or Employee Benefits Will Be Separate Property

All retirement benefits earned by (or in the name of) one of us before we marry, as listed on Schedules 1 and 2, will be the Separate Property of the person who earned them or in whose name those benefits are vested. This applies to all benefits in all retirement, pension, deferred compensation, stock options, and other employee benefit or tax deferred plans, whether qualified according to IRS regulations or nonqualified.

Each of us hereby waives all present and future legal claims regarding the other person's premarital retirement or employee benefits referred to above. Each of us understands that this waiver might not be effective under applicable laws unless reaffirmed after we marry in a written waiver in a form approved by the retirement or employee benefit plan. Therefore we agree that after we marry, upon request by the other party, each of us will sign any document necessary to carry out the intent of this clause, including a written waiver in a form approved by the plan.

Alternative 2: Premarital Retirement or Employee Benefits Will Be Marital or Community Property

If you want to convert premarital retirement benefits to marital or community property, we recommend that you say so specifically. Then, after you marry, you might have to sign forms to change the way you own your retirement benefits. You'll need to check with your retirement plan administrator to find out whether there's something for you to sign. This clause includes a provision stating that you will follow through.

EXAMPLE: Michael began to accrue benefits in his company pension one year ago. Patrick has a small 401(k) retirement plan through his employer. They live in a community property state where retirement benefits earned during marriage are community property. They agree that the premarital portion of their retirement benefits will be considered community property, too, and they include this clause in their agreement:

**Premarital Retirement or Employee Benefits
Will Be Community Property**

All retirement or employee benefits earned by (or in the name of) one of us before we marry, as listed on Schedules 1 and 2, will be considered Community Property. This applies to all benefits in all retirement, pension, deferred compensation, stock options, and other employee benefit or tax deferred plans, whether qualified according to IRS regulations or nonqualified.

Each of us understands that under applicable laws, title to any retirement or employee account or benefit can be held in the name of only one person, and that the written consent of both spouses might be required prior to making any election of benefits under a retirement or employee benefit plan. We agree that after we marry, upon request by the other party, each of us will sign any document necessary to carry out the intent of this clause.

Other Premarital Assets [OPTIONAL]

If you want to include a specific provision relating to a premarital asset other than real estate, a business, or retirement plans, you can use or adapt one of the following alternatives:

- **Alternative 1** states that the assets you list will remain separate property.
- **Alternative 2** states that the listed assets will be apportioned between separate and marital or community property.
- **Alternative 3** states that the listed assets will become marital or community property.

Alternative 1: Certain Premarital Assets Will Remain Separate Property

Use this alternative if you state in Paragraph 6A that all premarital assets are to become marital or community property once you marry, but you want to make an exception for one or more specific assets.

> **EXAMPLE:** Paragraph 6A of Len and Donna's prenup states that all of their premarital assets will become community property as soon as they marry, except as otherwise specified in the prenup. They want Donna's heirloom art and jewelry to remain her separate property. They also want Len's baseball card collection to remain his separate property. They use Alternative 1 to accomplish this.

> **Certain Premarital Asset(s) Will Remain Separate Property**
> The following premarital assets will remain the Separate Property of the spouse who owns the assets prior to marriage and will not be converted to Community Property when we marry: Donna's heirloom art from her paternal grandparents and her heirloom jewelry from her maternal grandmother, as more specifically listed on Schedule 1, and Len's baseball card collection.

Alternative 2: Certain Premarital Assets Will Be Apportioned Between Separate and Marital or Community Property

This clause allows you to divide ownership of a particular premarital asset (other than real estate, a business, or retirement benefits) between separate and community property, according to whatever formula you choose. Be sure to specify when the apportionment is to occur.

> **EXAMPLE:** Dorian is a sculptor. At the time of his marriage to Rachel, he is about halfway through the process of completing a large sculpture. He and Rachel put this clause in their prenup:

> **Certain Premarital Asset(s) Will Be Apportioned Between Separate and Community Property**
>
> The following premarital asset will be apportioned between Dorian's Separate Property and Community Property as soon as we marry as follows: The unfinished sculpture tentatively titled "Postliteracy" will be 50% Dorian's Separate Property and 50% Community Property. If this sculpture is sold during our marriage, the above provisions will apply to apportionment of any sales proceeds

Alternative 3: Certain Premarital Assets Will Become Marital or Community Property

If you have stated in Paragraph 6A that your premarital assets will remain separate property, but you want a premarital asset (other than real estate, a business, or retirement benefits) to become marital or community property when you marry (or at some other time you specify), you can use this clause.

> **EXAMPLE:** Antonio and Lydia provide in their prenup that, except as otherwise stated, all premarital assets are to continue as separate property. Lydia and Antonio each own a share of a limited partnership that Antonio's brother manages. They want their shares of the partnership to be treated as marital property once they marry, so they use Alternative 3 to state their intentions.

> **Certain Premarital Assets Will Become Marital Property**
>
> The following premarital assets will become Marital Property as soon as we marry: Lydia's one-tenth interest in the limited partnership known as CDE Ltd. and Antonio's one-tenth interest in the limited partnership known as CDE Ltd.

Paragraph 7: Ownership of Assets Acquired During Marriage

Now that you've determined how you will handle property you each own before you get married, it's time to consider the assets you will acquire during your marriage. (To make the discussion simpler, we'll often call these "postmarital" acquisitions.) Will you keep new acquisitions entirely separate, as though you were not married? Will you pool everything, share and share alike? Will you let state laws determine your rights? The clauses in this paragraph are designed to give you some typical alternatives for answering these and other questions about postmarital acquisitions.

To help you choose the best clauses for your situation, let's review some basic marital property concepts. As we explain in Chapter 4, state laws dealing with married couples' rights in property acquired during marriage fall into two main categories: equitable distribution and community property.

In equitable distribution states, ownership of assets acquired during marriage is determined by who holds title. However, if a spouse dies, these states allow the surviving spouse to claim a certain percentage of the deceased spouse's property. And if a couple divorces in an equitable distribution state, much (if not all) of the assets acquired during the marriage will be considered marital property to be divided between the divorcing spouses, regardless of whose name appears on the title document.

In community property states, each spouse owns one-half of any asset acquired during marriage—even if the title is in the name of just one spouse. If one spouse dies, the survivor retains their half of the community property. In a divorce, the community property will be divided between the spouses.

You can use the clauses in this paragraph to confirm that your rights to assets acquired during marriage are to be determined by state law or to substitute your own rules for dealing with those assets.

A. Your General Rule for Assets Acquired During Marriage

This clause states your basic approach to dealing with acquisitions during marriage. You can choose from one of the following five alternatives:

- **Alternative 1** states that rights in assets acquired during marriage will be determined according to state law.
- **Alternative 2** provides that rights in assets acquired during marriage will be determined according to how title is held.
- **Alternative 3** allows you to keep all property separate—no marital or community property rights accrue.
- **Alternative 4** states that all assets acquired during marriage will be marital or community property.
- **Alternative 5** provides that all assets acquired during marriage will be owned proportionately, according to a formula you specify.

After selecting one of these alternatives, you'll be finished with Paragraph 7 unless you want to make an exception for a certain type of asset.

> CAUTION
>
> **Profits are included in this clause.** All of the alternatives for Clause A include profits received from assets acquired during marriage. If you want to treat ownership of profits differently from ownership of the assets themselves, you will need to modify the clause to make it clear that it doesn't apply to profits. Then adapt one of the alternative clauses relating to income (see Clause B, below) to spell out how profits will be owned.

Alternative 1: Rights in Assets Acquired During Marriage Will Be Determined According to State Law

If you like the approach to marital assets taken by your state's law, you can choose the default clause stating that your rights in any assets acquired during your marriage will be determined by that law. For an example of this alternative, take a look at Freda and Steven's prenup at the end of Chapter 9.

Alternative 2: Rights in Assets Acquired During Marriage Will Be Determined According to How Title Is Held

If you want your rights in postmarital acquisitions to be dictated by how you hold title rather than by state marital property laws, use this alternative.

> **EXAMPLE:** John and Carol live in California, a community property state. Since they are both retired, they do not expect to have any marital earnings that would be considered community property under California law. However, they want to leave open the possibility that they might buy property together and take title as community property for tax benefits available when one of them dies. This is what they put in their prenup:

Our Rights in Assets Acquired During Marriage Will Be Determined According to How Title Is Held

Except as specified elsewhere in This Agreement, every asset acquired after we marry, and any profits or growth in value or any sales proceeds or asset acquired in exchange for those assets, will be owned as specified in the document of title. If an asset is tangible personal property that does not have a document of title, the person who paid for the asset will be the owner.

Each of us understands that if it were not for This Agreement, certain assets acquired during our marriage might be considered Community Property despite the name in which title is held, and we knowingly agree to waive our Community Property rights in such assets and be bound by This Agreement instead, unless a Community Property form of ownership is specified in the title.

Alternative 3: All Property to Be Separate—No Marital or Community Property Rights Accrue

Use this alternative if you want the assets you acquire during your marriage, including any assets you purchase together in joint names, to be considered separate property. This clause is similar to Alternative 2 in that any asset held in one person's name will be that person's separate property. But this version states that any property in joint names will be co-owned by the spouses as if they were not married, whereas under Alternative 2 spouses could co-own joint title property either as separate property or as marital or community property, depending on how the title reads.

> EXAMPLE: Ryan comes from a wealthy family. He has built up an extensive investment portfolio from gifts and inheritances, and he is expecting to receive more gifts and inheritances as time goes on. His fiancée, Tricia, owns a duplex and she is planning to purchase another rental property shortly after the wedding. They might purchase a house together at some point in time. They agree that all assets they acquire during marriage, even assets they put in joint names, will be separate property, and not marital property, just as if they were not married. This is the clause in their prenup:

> **All Property to Be Separate—No Marital Property Rights Accrue**
> We intend to own every asset acquired during our marriage, including property acquired in joint names, and any profits or growth in value, or any sales proceeds or asset acquired in exchange for these assets as Separate Property and not as Marital Property, as if we were unmarried. Each of us understands that if it were not for This Agreement, certain assets acquired during our marriage might be considered Marital Property despite the name in which title is held, and we knowingly agree to be bound by This Agreement instead.

Alternative 4: Assets Acquired During Marriage Will Be Marital or Community Property

If you want every new asset you acquire during your marriage to be treated as marital or community property regardless of who acquires it or who holds title, use this clause.

EXAMPLE: Barrett is a real estate agent and Leilani manages a clothing store. Barrett sometimes buys "fixer-uppers," renovates them, and resells them for a profit. He and Leilani agree that everything they buy during their marriage, including the houses that Barrett purchases, will be marital property. They put this clause in their prenup:

Assets Acquired During Marriage Will Be Marital Property

Except as specified elsewhere in This Agreement, every asset acquired by one or both of us, and any profits or growth in value, or any sales proceeds or assets acquired in exchange for these assets after we marry will be considered Marital Property, regardless of how title is held. Each of us understands that if it were not for This Agreement, certain assets acquired in the name of only one person during our marriage might be considered Separate Property of the person in whose name it is held, and we knowingly agree to be bound by This Agreement instead.

Alternative 5: Assets Acquired During Marriage Will Be Apportioned

This clause allows you to specify certain percentages of each asset you acquire during your marriage as separate property or as marital or community property.

EXAMPLE: Suppose Barrett and Leilani, the couple described in the previous example, agree that instead of considering all of their new acquisitions marital property, they will divide ownership so that Barrett owns 30% as his separate property and the other 70% is marital property. They would insert this clause in their prenup:

Our Rights in Assets Acquired During Marriage Will Be Apportioned
Except as specified elsewhere in This Agreement, our rights in every
asset acquired during our marriage in the name of one or both of
us, and any profits or growth in value or any sales proceeds or asset
acquired in exchange for that asset, will be apportioned between us,
according to the following formula: 30% of each asset shall be Barrett's
Separate Property and the other 70% shall be Marital Property.

CAUTION

Mind your As and Bs. If you want all assets treated as you've described
in Clause A, just above, you needn't bother with the following additional clauses.
However, you will need to reformat your agreement to take out the "A," because
you won't have a Clause B, Clause C, and so on. Leaving in the "A" could make it
look like you accidentally forgot to include the subsequently lettered material.
(For an example, see Steven and Freda's prenup at the end of Chapter 9.)

B. Other Clauses Affecting Assets Acquired During Marriage [OPTIONAL]

If you want to single out certain assets or types of assets for special
provisions, you can include as many of the following clauses as apply.
The clauses discussed in this section cover:

- income
- inheritances
- gifts
- joint accounts
- retirement and employee benefits, and
- any other assets you want to treat differently than the ones
  described in Clause 7A, above.

If you choose more than one of the clauses in this section, be sure to
assign sequential letters to the remaining clauses, starting with "B" and

continuing alphabetically as necessary. If you want all assets treated as you've described in Clause 7A, above, you needn't bother with these additional clauses. However, as we explained for Clause 6, above, you will need to reformat your agreement to take out the "A," because you won't have any subsequent clauses.

⇨ SKIP AHEAD

When to skip this section. If you want to treat all assets acquired during your marriage as you've specified in the clause just above, Paragraph 7 of your prenup is complete. Skip ahead to Paragraph 8.

Income Earned or Received During Marriage [OPTIONAL]

State laws usually treat marital earnings as community or marital property. Depending on the state where you live, unearned income—that is, income from investments, interest, or other sources besides wages and other work (including income derived from separate property)—might also be considered marital or community property. If you want to ensure that your earnings or other income received during marriage will (or won't) be considered marital or community property, you can insert one of the following alternative clauses in your prenup.

Alternative 1: **All Income Will Be Marital or Community Property**

This alternative allows you to treat all income, whether earned or unearned, as marital or community property.

⚠ CAUTION

For income derived from separate property, be consistent with Paragraph 6. If you have separate property that will produce unearned income, you can use one of these alternatives to state whether that income will be treated as separate property or as marital or community property. Be sure that whatever you say is consistent with any provisions you included about this subject in Paragraph 6, above.

EXAMPLE: Alveno and Sabra live in a community property state. Under state law, their earnings will be community property, but unearned income (such as dividends or interest) from separate property would be considered separate property even if received during marriage. Alveno and Sabra want all income they receive or earn during their marriage to be community property. They insert this clause in their prenup:

All Income Will Be Community Property

Except as specified elsewhere in This Agreement, our wages and other earned or unearned income will be considered Community Property. This clause applies to wages or income earned during our marriage even if received at a later time. It also applies to unearned income such as dividends, interest, rents, and partnership distributions received during our marriage, regardless of whether it is derived from Separate Property or Community Property.

Alternative 2: **All Income Will Be Separate Property**

Use this alternative if you want all income, whether earned or unearned, to be considered the separate property of the person who receives it.

For example, Ted and Grace won't have much earned income, because Ted is retired and Grace will be quitting her job once they marry. They want all of their income, including any earnings and any unearned income from investments, to be separate property rather than marital property, so they use Alternative 2.

All Income Will Be Separate Property

Except as specified elsewhere in This Agreement, our wages or other earned or unearned income will be considered the Separate Property of the person who earned or received the income. This clause applies to wages or income earned during our marriage even if received at a later time. It also applies to all unearned income such as dividends, interest, rents, and partnership distributions received during our marriage.

Alternatives 3 and 4: **Earned and Unearned Income Will Be Treated Differently**

If you want to treat earned and unearned income differently, you can pick Alternative 3 or Alternative 4, depending on which type of income is to be separate property and which is to be marital or community property. Use Alternative 3 if earnings are to be marital or community property and unearned income will be separate property, adding the appropriate optional language about unearned income derived from marital property or jointly owned assets. Use Alternative 4 if earnings will be separate and unearned income will be marital or community property.

> **EXAMPLE:** Doreen and Tom want their earned income to be marital property and their unearned income to be separate property, except for unearned income derived from marital property or from assets held jointly, which will be considered marital property. They include Alternative 3 in their prenup:

> **Earned Income Will Be Marital Property; Unearned Income Will Be Separate Property**
> Except as specified elsewhere in This Agreement, our wages and other income earned during our marriage, even if received at a later time, will be considered Marital Property. Except as specified elsewhere in This Agreement, all unearned income such as dividends, interest, rents, and partnership distributions received during our marriage will be considered the Separate Property of the person who received the income, provided that any unearned income derived from Marital Property or an asset held in our joint names shall be considered Marital Property.

Inheritances Received During Marriage [OPTIONAL]

If the laws of your state dealing with ownership rights to inherited property don't work for you (see Chapter 4), we give you two alternatives.

- **Alternative 1** allows you to specify that inherited property will be separate property.
- **Alternative 2** makes inheritances marital or community property.

Alternative 1: Inheritances Received by One Party During Marriage Will Be Separate Property

Use this alternative if you want inherited assets to be the separate property of the person who receives the inheritance. You can choose to treat any profits, increase in value, sales proceeds, or assets received in exchange for inherited assets as separate property, or as community or marital property.

For example, Russ and Karen decide that all inherited property—and any property that can be traced to an inheritance—will be separate property. They use Alternative 1 to create the following clause:

> **Inheritances Received by One Party During Marriage Will Be Separate Property**
>
> If one of us receives an asset as an inheritance, bequest, trust distribution, or other death benefit during our marriage, that asset will be that individual's Separate Property. Any profits or growth in value or any sales proceeds or assets acquired in exchange for a Separate Property inheritance described above will also be Separate Property.

Alternative 2: Inheritances Received by One Party During Marriage Will Be Marital or Community Property

This alternative states that your inheritances will be treated as marital or community property. We presume here that you want any profits or other property traceable to inherited assets to also be treated as marital or community property. If you want to handle profits and other returns on inheritances differently, you will need to modify this clause.

EXAMPLE: Raj and Sasha live in a community property state where inheritances are separate property. But they prefer to treat any inheritances—as well as profits, growth in value, and sales or exchange proceeds—as community property, so they choose this alternative.

Inheritances Received by One Party During Marriage Will Be Community Property

If one of us receives an asset as an inheritance, bequest, trust distribution, or other death benefit during our marriage, that asset will be Community Property. Any profits or growth in value or any sales proceeds or assets acquired in exchange for that asset will also be Community Property.

Gifts Received During Marriage [OPTIONAL]

Gifts, like inheritances, often get special treatment under state laws. Many states treat gifts as separate property; some do not. If you don't want to follow your state's rule, you can select the clause in this section that most closely fits your situation and adapt it as needed.

The gift clauses work much the same way as those for inheritances, except that we've added two alternatives that allow you to have one rule for gifts you give to each other and a different rule for gifts from other people.

Alternative 1: Gifts Received During Marriage Will Be Separate Property

This one is straightforward: All gifts received during marriage are the separate property of the recipient. The only optional part concerns profits and other returns on gifts. You can treat those as separate property as well, or you can choose the option that makes any profits or increased value marital or community property.

Ted and Grace want to keep all gifts—and profits from gifts—separate. Here is the clause as it appears in their prenup:

Gifts Received During Marriage Will Be Separate Property

Except as specified elsewhere in This Agreement, any asset received by one us during our marriage as a gift from a third party or from the other spouse will be the Separate Property of the spouse who receives the gift. Any gift given to both of us jointly will be owned by us jointly in equal Separate Property shares unless at the time of making the gift the person making the gift specifies in writing a different percentage of ownership. Any profits or growth in value or any sales proceeds or assets acquired in exchange for a Separate Property gift described above will also be Separate Property.

Alternative 2: **Gifts Received During Marriage Will Be Marital or Community Property**

This alternative also takes a uniform approach to gifts, treating them all as marital or community property, regardless of whether they are given by a third party or a spouse. Notice that this alternative does not offer the option of treating profits of gifts as separate property; that would not ordinarily be something couples would want if they don't consider the gifts themselves separate property.

EXAMPLE: Drew and Amy decide that they are going to share all gifts as marital property. They use Alternative 2 to spell out their intentions.

Gifts Received During Marriage Will Be Marital Property

Except as specified elsewhere in This Agreement, any asset received by one of us during our marriage as a gift from a third party or from the other spouse, and any gift given to both of us jointly, will be Marital Property. Any profits or growth in value or any sales proceeds or assets acquired in exchange for that asset will also be Marital Property.

Alternative 3: Third-Party Gifts Will Be Separate Property; Interspousal Gifts Will Be Marital or Community Property

Use this alternative if you want gifts from third parties to be considered separate property while gifts between the two of you ("interspousal gifts") are marital property.

For example, Russ and Karen opt to make gifts from other people separate property, but not relatively expensive gifts they give each other, unless the one who makes the gift specifies in writing that the gift is intended to be the recipient's separate property. They also choose to treat the profits of any separate property gifts as separate property.

Third-Party Gifts Will Be Separate Property;
Interspousal Gifts Will Be Community Property

Except as specified elsewhere in This Agreement, any asset received by one of us during our marriage as a gift from a third party will be the Separate Property of the spouse who receives the gift. Any gift given to both of us jointly will be owned by us jointly in equal Separate Property shares unless at the time of the gift the person making the gift specifies in writing a different percentage of ownership.

Except as specified elsewhere in This Agreement, any asset received by one of us during our marriage as a gift from the other spouse will be Community Property if it has a value greater than $2,000 at the time of the gift, unless at the time of the gift, the spouse making the gift specifies in writing that the gift is intended to be the Separate Property of the receiving spouse.

Any profits or growth in value or any sales proceeds or assets acquired in exchange for a Separate Property gift described above will also be Separate Property.

Alternative 4: Third-Party Gifts Will Be Marital or Community Property; Interspousal Gifts Will Be Separate Property

This one's the reverse of Alternative 3: All gifts from other people are considered marital property, while gifts to each other are separate property. You also have a choice about how to treat profits of separate property gifts: as separate property or as marital or community property. As with the other alternatives, you can adapt this version to fit your particular situation.

> **EXAMPLE:** Julio and Carla decide that anything given to one or both of them by third parties (such as family members or friends) will be considered community property, unless the gift is clothing or jewelry. Gifts between them, and gifts of clothing or jewelry from other people, will be the separate property of the recipient. But profits or other returns on a separate property gift will be community property. This is what they put in their agreement:

Third-Party Gifts Will Be Community Property; Interspousal Gifts Will Be Separate Property

Except as specified elsewhere in This Agreement, any asset other than an article of clothing or jewelry received by one of us during our marriage as a gift from a third party, and any gift given to both of us jointly, will be Community Property. Any profits or growth in value or any sales proceeds or assets acquired in exchange for that asset will also be Community Property.

Except as specified elsewhere in This Agreement, any asset received by of one us during our marriage as a gift from the other spouse and any article of clothing or jewelry received from a third party will be the Separate Property of the spouse who receives the gift. However, any profits or growth in value or any sales proceeds or asset acquired in exchange for a Separate Property gift described above will be considered Community Property.

Joint Accounts [OPTIONAL]

Many couples like the convenience of having one or more joint bank accounts from which they pay household bills or other expenses, or into which they deposit wages or other funds. If one or both spouses deposit separate property funds into the joint account, questions can arise later about whether or not the separate funds should be repaid. And if an asset is purchased with the funds in the joint account, there might be a question about whether and to what extent the asset was purchased with separate property.

One solution to this problem is to avoid depositing separate funds into joint accounts—or to refrain from having joint accounts in the first place. But if you want the flexibility of maintaining joint accounts and perhaps putting separate funds into them, we suggest you use one of the two alternative clauses in this section to establish some simple guidelines for keeping track of who owns what.

- **Alternative 1** states that all money in a joint account will be marital or community property.
- **Alternative 2** says that joint accounts will be made up of separate property shares. Use the alternative that most closely matches what you have in mind and adapt the wording as needed.

Alternative 1: Joint Accounts Will Be Marital or Community Property

This alternative states that all funds in any joint account will be marital property—with or without potential reimbursement of separate property funds. If you opt for reimbursement, you will need spell out when and under what circumstances reimbursement will be due.

EXAMPLE: Marina and Anthony intend to open joint checking and savings accounts into which they plan to deposit only earnings. But because each of them has some separate property investments, they figure there might be times when they want to deposit separate funds into a joint account. So they decide that all funds in the joint accounts will be considered marital property, and that once a year they will review their bank records and reimburse any large deposits of separate property.

Joint Accounts Will Be Marital Property

Any funds deposited into a joint bank or other deposit account established by and between us will be considered Marital Property, even if one or both of us deposits Separate Property funds into the account. Whoever deposits $500 or more in a single deposit of Separate Property funds into a joint account will have a right of reimbursement for the amount of the funds contributed unless that person signs a written waiver of the right to be reimbursed. Any reimbursement owed shall be payable as follows: Between January 1 and January 31 of each year, we will review our records and determine whether either of us has made any Separate Property deposits of $500 or more into a joint account during the prior calendar year. If so, that person will be repaid from available Marital Property funds the total amount of those deposits, without interest. If we are both entitled to reimbursement and insufficient Marital Property funds are available to pay the full amount, each person shall receive a pro rata share from the available funds. Any reimbursement owed in excess of available Marital Property funds will be carried over to the following year.

Alternative 2: Joint Accounts Will Consist of Shares of Separate Property

This alternative provides that joint accounts will consist of specified percentage shares of separate property—with a choice about whether to require reimbursement of any marital funds deposited into the account. If you use this clause, you'll need to spell out the percentages of ownership or a formula for determining the percentages. If marital funds will be reimbursed, you'll need to say when and how the reimbursement is to be made.

Ted and Grace don't expect to have any marital property, but they might decide to open a joint checking or savings account after they're married. They agree that the funds in a joint account will retain their separate property character—proportionate to what each party deposits in the account—and if by chance any marital property funds get deposited in the account, each party will receive credit for half of the marital property funds when calculating their percentages. To make sure that they don't leave their heirs with a big accounting headache, they also agree that once a year they will review the account records and sign a memo specifying each person's share of the balance in the account at the end of the year. In case they don't get around to the annual review, they agree that the funds on deposit will be deemed to consist of equal shares of separate property. They adapt Alternative 2 as follows:

Joint Accounts Will Consist of Shares of Separate Property

If a bank or other deposit account is acquired by us jointly (in both of our names), each of us will own an undivided share of the funds in the account as Separate Property and not as Marital Property, as follows:

1. Each spouse's share of the funds on deposit at any date shall be in proportion to the total amount of Separate Property contributed by that spouse to the account during the calendar year in which the shares are determined.

2. Each spouse's contributions to a joint account in a given year shall consist of all Separate Property funds of that spouse plus one-half of any Marital Property funds deposited into the account during that year, plus that spouse's share of the balance in the account on December 31 of the preceding calendar year.

3. In January of each year, we will review the account records and determine each spouse's share of the funds on deposit in each joint account, and our determination shall be evidenced by a memorandum signed by both of us. If for any reason we do not complete this process in a given year, our respective Separate Property shares of the funds on deposit for the year-end in question shall be conclusively deemed to be equal.

This clause shall apply to any joint account, even if we deposit Marital Property funds into the account, unless we sign a separate written agreement expressly specifying a different form or percentage of ownership regarding a particular account. There will be no right of reimbursement for deposits of any Marital Property funds unless we expressly agree in writing to a right of reimbursement regarding a particular account or a specific deposit.

Retirement and Employee Benefits [OPTIONAL]

Use one of the following clauses to state your expectations regarding retirement or other employee benefits earned after you marry. You can specify that the general rule set out in Paragraph 7A of your agreement also applies to retirement benefits, or you can make an exception to that general rule.

Alternative 1: Retirement or Employee Benefits Earned During Marriage Will Be Separate Property

Select this alternative if you want to keep your retirement or other employee benefits separate—that is, not subject to marital or community property claims. As we explained in the above discussion of premarital retirement and employee benefits, you will need to sign waivers of spousal rights after you marry, so this clause requires each of you to sign any necessary documents later.

Ted and Grace provided in Paragraph 6 that their premarital retirement and employee benefits are separate property. Even though Ted is already retired and doesn't expect to build up additional retirement benefits, Grace will be earning retirement through her job until she resigns shortly after the wedding. They use the following clause to specify that any retirement or employee benefits earned after they marry will be separate property:

> **Retirement or Employee Benefits Earned During Marriage Will Be Separate Property**
>
> All retirement or employee benefits earned by (or in the name of) one of us during our marriage will be the Separate Property of the person in whose name those benefits are vested. This applies to all benefits in all retirement, pension, deferred compensation, stock options, and other employee benefit or tax deferred plans, whether qualified according to IRS regulations or nonqualified.

> Each of us hereby waives all legal claims to the other person's retirement or employee benefits referred to above. Each of us understands that this waiver might not be effective under applicable laws unless reaffirmed after we marry in a written waiver in a form approved by the employee benefit plan. We agree that after we marry, upon request by the other party, each of us will sign any document necessary to carry out the intent of this clause, including a written waiver in a form approved by the plan.

Alternative 2: Retirement or Employee Benefits Earned During Marriage Will Be Marital or Community Property

If you want to make it clear that you will treat any retirement benefits accumulated during marriage as marital or community property, you can insert this clause in your premarital agreement.

This is what Russ and Karen decide to do. There are so many specific clauses in their agreement about other assets that they want to spell out their agreement about postmarital retirement benefits just to avoid any possible confusion. This is the clause as it appears in their prenup:

> **Retirement or Employee Benefits Earned During Marriage Will Be Community Property**
>
> All retirement or employee benefits earned by (or in the name of) one of us during our marriage will be considered Community Property. This applies to all benefits in all retirement, pension, deferred compensation, stock options, and other employee benefit or tax deferred plans, whether qualified according to IRS regulations or nonqualified.
>
> Each of us understands that under applicable laws title to any retirement or employee account or benefit can be held in the name of only one person, and that the written consent of both spouses might be required prior to making any election of benefits under an employee benefit plan.
>
> We agree that after we marry, upon request by the other party, each of us will sign any document necessary to carry out the intent of this clause.

Other Assets Acquired During Marriage [OPTIONAL]

In Clause A of Paragraph 7, you specified the general rule regarding assets acquired during your marriage. If you want to make an exception for certain assets or categories of assets not covered in the clauses we've already discussed, such as specific investments you plan to purchase, you can use one of the next two alternatives to lay out your intentions for those specific assets.

- **Alternative 1** says the property you name will be kept separate.
- **Alternative 2** states that the assets will be marital or community property.

Alternative 1: Certain Assets Will Be Separate Property

You can use this alternative if you expect the assets you acquire during your marriage to be marital or community property but you want to carve out an exception for certain items.

For example, Karen knows another veterinarian who is talking about putting together a group practice emergency veterinary clinic. She and Russ agree that if Karen joins the group, her interest in the group practice (or in some other veterinary business venture that Karen might become involved in later) will be her separate property and not community property, and that if they divorce or if Karen predeceases Russ, he will receive a payment in lieu of his community property share using a formula as follows:

New Veterinary Business Ventures Will Be Separate Property

After we marry, Karen might acquire an interest in a group practice emergency veterinary clinic or other veterinary business venture. Any such veterinary business venture might otherwise be Community Property, but instead will be Karen's Separate Property. This also applies to any profits or increase in value or any sales proceeds or assets acquired in exchange for any such veterinary business venture. If Karen predeceases Russ or if we divorce, Russ shall be entitled to a payment equal to one-half of any Community Property funds invested in any such veterinary business venture, plus for each year of marriage, an amount equal to one percent of Karen's Separate Property investment in the business venture up to a maximum of $15,000 for the duration of the marriage.

Alternative 2: Certain Assets Will Be Marital or Community Property

If your prenup states that all assets acquired during your marriage will be separate property rather than marital or community property, this alternative allows you to make an exception for specific assets or categories of assets.

> EXAMPLE: Alina and George have agreed that each person's postmarital assets will be treated as separate property, not as marital property. But they plan to buy a house together. They agree to use separate property money to pay the down payment and to make house payments. All the equity in the house will be considered marital property. Their version of Alternative 2 reads like this:

> **Residence Will Be Marital Property**
>
> After we marry, we plan to acquire a residence in our joint names, using Separate Property funds for the down payment, mortgage payments, and all other expenses related to the residence. Under the terms of This Agreement, the residence would be Separate Property, but we agree instead that it will be considered equally owned Marital Property, even if the Separate Property contributions were unequal. This also applies to any profits or increase in value or any sales proceeds or assets acquired in exchange for the residence.

Contributions of Separate Property to Postmarital Acquisitions [OPTIONAL]

If one or both of you will use separate property funds to pay for the purchase or improvement of any marital or community property, you might want to spell out how the separate property will be treated. We give you three choices here:

- **Alternative 1** apportions the separate property contributions between marital or community property and separate property.
- **Alternative 2** provides that separate property funds will be reimbursed.

- **Alternative 3** treats the contribution as a gift and waives any right to apportionment or reimbursement the laws of your state might give you.

Alternative 1: Contributions of Separate Property to Marital or Community Assets: Ownership Will Be Apportioned

Use this alternative if you want to allocate separate property contributions between marital or community property and separate property. You will need to be clear about how you will determine the percentages. You will also need to decide whether or not to give credit to separate property funds spent on expenses other than direct purchase or improvement costs.

EXAMPLE: Salman and Jana want to be able to pool separate property and community property if an investment opportunity comes along. They settle on this version of Alternative 1:

Contributions of Separate Property to Community Property: Ownership Will Be Apportioned

During our marriage, one or both of us may contribute Separate Property funds to the acquisition or improvement of Community Property. If so, ownership of any such property will be apportioned between Separate Property and Community Property as follows: (1) If Separate Property is contributed to a purchase, ownership shall be apportioned between Separate Property and Community Property based on the ratio of Separate Property funds to Community Property funds contributed to the purchase price, with any financed funds credited to Community Property; (2) if Separate Property is contributed to an improvement, the Separate Property share will be a percentage based on the ratio of Separate Property funds to Community Property equity immediately prior to the improvement, as determined by deducting from the market value of the property the total balance then outstanding on any liens against the property. There will be no apportionment for Separate Property funds paid for expenses related to Community Property other than for acquisition or improvement of the property.

Alternative 2: Separate Property Contributions to Marital or Community Property Will Be Reimbursed

If separate property funds are to be reimbursed, you'll use this alternative. Be sure to specify the amount, timing, and other conditions that apply to the reimbursement, or refer to some other clause of your prenup where those particulars are set forth.

> EXAMPLE: Leila expects to receive a large distribution from a family trust during her marriage to Wendy. Leila might use some of these separate property funds for a down payment on a house for herself and Wendy, or to pay for fix-up or remodeling expenses. The house would be jointly owned marital property, but they agree that if they divorce, Leila would be reimbursed for any separate property funds used for the down payment, plus interest. They use Alternative 2 to state their intent to do this, and insert a cross-reference to a later section of their prenup, covering divorce, where the specifics are discussed.

Separate Property Contributions to Marital Property Residence Will Be Reimbursed

During our marriage, one or both of us may contribute Separate Property funds to acquire or improve a Marital Property residence. In the absence of a contrary written agreement, we will consider any such contribution to be subject to a right of reimbursement payable if we divorce as set forth in Paragraph XX of This Agreement. The reimbursable contributions referred to in this clause shall include only a down payment or other payments directly applied to the purchase of such a residence or payments for remodeling or other improvements to the residence, but not payment of any other expenses for the residence such as mortgage payments, property taxes, insurance, assessments, or ordinary repairs.

Alternative 3: **Waiver of Reimbursement for Separate Property Contributions**

If you simply want any separate property contributions to be considered a gift to your marital or community property holdings, use Alternative 3. You can also adapt this clause to apply only to certain contributions, using it in combination with Alternative 1 or 2.

> **EXAMPLE:** After Leila and Wendy use Alternative 2 to provide for reimbursement of Leila's separate property contributions to the purchase or improvement of a residence, they modify Alternative 3 to state that all other separate property contributions will be considered gifts and not apportioned or reimbursed.

Waiver of Reimbursement for Other Separate Property Contributions
During our marriage, one or both of us may contribute Separate Property funds to acquire or improve Marital Property or to pay other expenses related to Marital Property. Except for contributions to acquire or improve a residence as provided in Paragraphs XX and XX of This Agreement, and in the absence of a contrary written agreement, we will consider any such contribution to be a gift of Separate Property. Neither of us shall be entitled to reimbursement for any such contribution, and each of us hereby waives any right to reimbursement otherwise granted by law.

Paragraph 8: Responsibility for Debts and Expenses

This paragraph contains clauses that spell out each spouse's responsibility for debts—debts that predate the marriage and, if you choose to address them, debts and expenses that come up after the wedding day.

As we explain in Chapter 4, every state considers the premarital debts of a married person to be that spouse's primary responsibility. The other spouse won't be held liable for them, nor will a creditor be able to collect from the other spouse's separate property to pay the debt. State laws differ on whether creditors can go after marital or community property for premarital debts and on the treatment of debts incurred during marriage. It's a good idea to review the applicable sections of Chapter 4 and the summary of your state's laws on the book's online companion page before selecting the appropriate clauses for this paragraph. Then choose as many of the clauses as apply and adapt them as needed.

 CAUTION

The clauses in this section might not provide complete protection. Any agreement between just the two of you might not prevent a creditor from going after any available funds to collect a debt—even if your prenup states that the debt will be repaid from another source. In addition, any agreement to shift assets between you in order to avoid payment of debts could subject you to serious penalties. Take care when drafting any clauses relating to debts, and ask your lawyer for guidance before making a final decision.

A. Each Person Solely Responsible for Own Premarital Debts

This clause begins by stating the general rule that each person's premarital debts are their sole responsibility, and the other spouse will not be liable for those debts. You can also state your intent that the nondebtor spouse's share of marital or community property may not be used to pay a premarital debt, and you can add a requirement that each of you will pay the expenses of ("indemnify") the other spouse if a creditor nevertheless attempts to collect from the nondebtor spouse.

It's a good idea to include some form of this clause in your prenup, even if you don't select any of the optional clauses that follow.

Ted and Grace include this clause in their agreement. This is what it looks like:

Each Person Solely Responsible for Own Premarital Debts

Grace's debts listed on Schedule 1 are her sole and separate debts. Ted will not be responsible for them, nor may his Separate Property be used to pay them without his written consent. Grace will indemnify and hold Ted harmless from any proceeding to collect on Grace's debts from Ted's property, and she will be solely responsible for any expenses, including attorneys' fees, incurred by Ted in connection with such a proceeding.

Ted's debts listed on Schedule 2 are his sole and separate debts. Grace will not be responsible for them, nor may her Separate Property be used to pay them without her written consent. Ted will indemnify and hold Grace harmless from any proceeding to collect on Ted's debts from Grace's property, and he will be solely responsible for any expenses, including attorneys' fees, incurred by Grace in connection with such a proceeding.

CAUTION

Mind your As and Bs. If you want all debts treated as you've described in Clause A, just above, you needn't bother with the following additional clauses. However, you will need to reformat your agreement to take out the "A," because you won't have a Clause B, Clause C, and so on. Leaving in the "A" could make it look like you accidentally forgot to include the subsequently lettered material. (For an example, see Steven and Freda's prenup at the end of Chapter 9.)

B. Optional Clauses Related to Debts and Expenses Incurred During Marriage

The remaining clauses in this paragraph focus on responsibility for debts and expenses that arise after you marry. You can skip the rest of this section if you don't feel the need to pin down each person's responsibility for postmarital debts or if you are satisfied that the laws of your state provide adequate clarity and protection for each of you.

If you're not sure whether you need to include any of the optional clauses that follow, we suggest you peruse them, compare them to state law, and then decide whether you want to put any or all of them in your agreement. As with the other clauses in this book, adapt them to your particular circumstances as needed. And don't forget to use sequential letters for each clause if you decide to use more than one.

As in Paragraphs 6 and 7, if you don't include any optional clauses in Paragraph 8, you should remove the letter "A" from your first clause, above.

Each Spouse Solely Responsible for Debts Incurred by That Spouse During Marriage [OPTIONAL]

Include this clause if, as a general rule, you don't want either of you to be responsible for the other person's sole debts incurred during marriage. Bear in mind that you could still be jointly liable to a creditor for any debt you take on together—such as a credit card or promissory note in both names—no matter who runs up the actual charges or what you put in your agreement. Moreover, your community or marital property could be attached by the creditor even if the debt is only in one person's name. Nevertheless, a clause like this can be binding between the two of you unless the debt is one that the law of your state imposes on both of you, such as a debt for "necessaries of life," like food or medical bills.

EXAMPLE: Tkat and Han agree not to incur any joint debts. They plan to pay all household bills in cash or by separate payments, and they decide not to open any joint credit cards. They use this clause in their agreement:

Each Spouse Solely Responsible for Debts Incurred by That Spouse During Marriage

Except as specified elsewhere in This Agreement, all debts incurred by Han in her sole name during our marriage will be her sole and separate debts. Tkat will not be responsible for them, nor may his Separate Property or his share of any Community Property be used to pay them without his written consent. Han will indemnify and hold Tkat harmless from any proceeding to collect on Han's debts from Tkat's property, and she will be solely responsible for any expenses, including attorneys' fees, incurred by Tkat in connection with such a proceeding.

Except as specified elsewhere in This Agreement, all debts incurred by Tkat in his sole name during our marriage will be his sole and separate debts. Han will not be responsible for them, nor may her Separate Property or her share of any Community Property be used to pay them without her written consent. Tkat will indemnify and hold Han harmless from any proceeding to collect on Tkat's debts from Han's property, and he will be solely responsible for any expenses, including attorneys' fees, incurred by Han in connection with such a proceeding.

Debts Incurred During Marriage for Mutual Benefit Will Be Marital or Community Debts [OPTIONAL]

Even if you intend that each person will be responsible for their own postmarital debts—whether or not you use the clause above—you might want to make an exception for debts related to purchases that clearly benefit both of you, from basics such as groceries and utility bills to discretionary expenses like the cost of a romantic vacation together. If so, you can add this clause to your agreement.

EXAMPLE: After inserting in their prenup the general clause discussed in the preceding section, Han and Tkat add this clause to their agreement:

Debts Incurred During Marriage for Mutual Benefit Will Be Community Debts

Any debt incurred by either or both of us for our mutual benefit during our marriage will be considered a community debt and will be paid from Community Property funds. A debt will be considered incurred for our mutual benefit if it covers any of the following expenses: our necessaries of life (housing, utilities, telephone, automobile or other transportation, food, and medical and dental care), household furnishings and appliances, any joint entertainment or travel, and any jointly made gifts or contributions; but not the following expenses: clothing, cosmetics and personal hygiene, separate entertainment and travel, or separate gifts. If one of us uses Separate Property funds to pay all or part of the debt, they will not be entitled to be reimbursed from Community Property funds.

Taxes [OPTIONAL]

This optional clause is designed to establish some basic ground rules for deciding whether to file joint income tax returns, exchanging tax information, and allocating tax-related benefits and responsibilities—for example, joint income and deductions, tax liabilities, tax refunds, and expenses for preparing tax returns.

After you marry, you will have a choice of whether to file your federal income tax returns as married people filing jointly or married filing separately. (You might also have this choice for state income tax returns, depending on state tax laws.) There can be tax or other advantages to filing jointly or separately, depending on your circumstances during the year in question. You'll need to analyze your particular tax situation, possibly with the help of a competent tax adviser.

Once you decide whether to file jointly, you will need to decide how to share the taxes or refund on a joint return, or how to divide up joint income and deductions if you file separately.

Skip this clause if you plan to address these questions each year as they come up, or plan to file jointly every year and share all liability and refunds.

Grace and Ted have been advised by their accountant that there might be advantages to filing separately in some years, depending on Ted's investment income and deductions. They include this clause in their prenup:

Taxes

We agree to confer each year prior to the deadline for filing federal and state income tax returns for the preceding year in order to determine whether it is to our mutual advantage to file joint or separate returns. We will determine this by preparing draft joint and separate returns and then comparing the overall taxes that would be due on the joint and separate draft returns. Each of us will provide all information necessary to prepare the draft returns.

If we agree that it is to our mutual benefit to file joint returns, we will do so. Any taxes owed on joint returns, and any accountants' fees or other expenses incurred in preparing the draft and final returns, will be paid by Ted. Any refund received shall be paid to Ted.

If we file separately:

1. Our income and deductions will be allocated as follows:
   a. Any earned income will be allocated between us according to applicable tax laws;
   b. Any unearned income, gain, loss, or credit from any investment in joint names will be allocated between us according to our percentage of ownership;
   c. Any unearned income from Separate Property investments will be allocated to the person whose Separate Property investment produced the unearned income;
   d. Any deductible expense paid from joint funds will be allocated between us according to our percentage of ownership;
   e. Any deductible expense paid from Separate Property funds will be allocated to the person from whose funds they were paid.
2. Any taxes owed on any separate return will be paid by the person filing the separate return. Any refund on any separate return will be paid to the person filing the separate return. Any accountants' fees or other expenses incurred in preparing the draft and final returns will be paid by Ted.

Business Debts [OPTIONAL]

As with other debts incurred during marriage, state laws dictate who is responsible for business debts. And as with other debts, there are legal limits to your ability to change the rules when it comes to the rights of creditors who are not parties to your prenuptial agreement. But if you want to do what you can to limit your liability for each other's business debts, or if you want to spell out between the two of you who pays what, you can include a clause to that effect in your agreement.

The following clause is designed to apply to both of you—if you are both in business for yourselves—or to just one of you, if that's more appropriate.

For example, Russ and Karen are both self-employed, so they insert the necessary language to cover both of them. Here is what this clause looks like in their agreement:

Each Spouse Solely Responsible for Own Business Debts

All debts incurred by Karen in connection with her veterinary practice or related business before or during our marriage will be her sole and separate debts. Russ will not be responsible for them, nor may his Separate Property or his share of any Community Property be used to pay them without his written consent. Karen will indemnify and hold Russ harmless from any proceeding to collect on Karen's debts from Russ's property, and she will be solely responsible for any expenses, including attorneys' fees, incurred by Russ in connection with such a proceeding.

All debts incurred by Russ in connection with his bookkeeping business before or during our marriage will be his sole and separate debts. Karen will not be responsible for them, nor may her Separate Property or her share of any community property be used to pay them without her written consent. Russ will indemnify and hold Karen harmless from any proceeding to collect on Russ's debts from Karen's property, and he will be solely responsible for any expenses, including attorneys' fees, incurred by Karen in connection with such a proceeding.

Household Expenses [OPTIONAL]

The next two alternative clauses give you a chance to spell out any agreement you have about paying household expenses. They are set up to cover the most common aspects of such arrangements, including responsibility for children's expenses, if that's a concern. Pick one of the alternatives and adapt it as appropriate, or skip this clause altogether if you would rather not commit yourselves to a specific arrangement.

For each alternative, we give you a place to list the kinds of expenses that you want to include, such as housing costs, telephone, food, automobile expenses, and so forth, and to identify any expenses that are not covered, such as personal jewelry, separate hobbies, or other items you want to treat differently.

It's worth noting that most courts won't enforce clauses like this that deal with your day-to-day arrangements. The intent of this clause is to clarify your expectations rather than to create legally enforceable rights, so include it only if you find it helpful.

Alternative 1: Household Expenses Will Be Paid by One Spouse

Use this clause if only one of you will pay household expenses. Adapt it as necessary to fit your circumstances.

For example, Grace has been a little apprehensive about how to pay for her personal expenses after she and Ted marry, because she will be quitting her job. After talking things through, they agree that they will open a joint checking account into which Ted will deposit enough to cover all the household bills, including Grace's personal expenses and incidentals. They use this clause:

> **Household Expenses Will Be Paid by Ted**
> Ted will be responsible for paying all reasonable household expenses from his Separate Property funds. Household expenses will include all necessaries of life (housing, utilities, transportation, food, and medical and dental care), household furnishings and appliances, any entertainment or travel, any jointly made gifts, clothing, and personal hygiene and incidentals.

> For convenience, we will establish a joint checking account into which Ted will deposit sufficient funds per month to cover the regular household expenses, plus additional amounts as necessary to cover extraordinary household expenses. Either one of us may write checks on the joint account to pay for household expenses. Ted will be responsible for balancing and reconciling the joint account on a regular basis.

Alternative 2: Household Expenses Will Be Shared

Use this alternative to lay out a plan for sharing responsibility for household bills.

Russ and Karen choose this option. Because they both have children who occasionally will be in their home, they include language about covering the children's expenses.

> **Household Expenses Will Be Shared**
>
> We will be responsible for paying all reasonable household expenses on an equal basis, using Community Property earnings. Household expenses will include all ordinary living expenses and any necessary extraordinary expenses incurred in furnishing and maintaining our home and our joint lifestyle, but will not include expenses incurred in maintaining either party's Separate Property.
>
> For convenience, we will establish a joint checking account into which we will each deposit our earnings plus additional equal amounts of Separate Property if necessary to cover household expenses. Either one of us may write checks or use a debit card connected to the joint account to pay for household expenses. Russ will be responsible for balancing and reconciling the joint account on a regular basis.
>
> The household expenses listed above include reasonable living expenses for Karen's children, Shawn and Kyle, and for Russ's child, Tiffany, while they are living with us. Each of us will deposit all of any child support payments received into the account established for payment of household expenses.

Next: Optional Paragraphs for Your Prenup

To help you further personalize your prenup, in the next chapter we suggest some optional paragraphs you might consider adding to your prenup. If you choose to use any of these optional paragraphs, you'll want to insert them after Paragraph 8, then renumber the subsequent closing paragraphs we address in Chapter 9.

Additional Provisions for Your Prenup

I n the previous chapter, you drafted the basic paragraphs and clauses for your prenuptial agreement.

If you want to go beyond those fundamentals, you can use some or all of the additional paragraphs and clauses we provide here that address topics such as:

- whether you will retain your rights to inherit property from one another
- whether you will leave specific gifts to one another when you die
- whether either of you will transfer property to the other, either after or at the time of your marriage
- whether either of you will purchase an annuity or a new life insurance policy for the other person's benefit
- how you want property, debts, and alimony to be handled in the event of a divorce, and
- any other matters you consider important.

As with the basic provisions discussed in the previous chapters, all of the paragraphs and clauses in this chapter are available in Appendix C and on the book's companion page.

If you decide to use any of the paragraphs from this chapter, you should insert them into your draft agreement before Paragraph 9: Interpretation, Modification, Review, and Enforcement of This Agreement. Then be sure to renumber the paragraphs so they remain in sequence. If you need more help, "Working on Your Prenup," in Chapter 5, provides general instructions on how to fill in clauses and add them to your agreement, either by hand or using a computer.

When your draft is complete, turn to Chapter 10 to learn how to finalize your prenup.

Optional Paragraph 1: **Estate Planning Matters**

This paragraph contains clauses that address what happens if one of you dies while the prenup is in effect. These clauses are intended to support and supplement your estate plans. As we've stressed, your prenup is not a substitute for a good estate plan. After you get married, it is important to update and complete your wills and other estate planning documents. (Chapter 12 gives you some suggestions for this.)

Waiver of Inheritance Rights

The clauses in this section ensure that state laws regarding spousal inheritance rights won't interfere with your estate plans. It's especially important to include one of these clauses if you expect to provide for someone other than—or in addition to—each other in your will or other estate planning documents. For example, you might want to make sure that your children from a prior marriage receive the inheritance you intend or that certain property stays in your family when you die. As we discuss in Chapters 2 and 4, without a prenup and some basic estate planning documents such as a will or trust, it's possible that the application of state law could result in an outcome different from what you want.

The clauses below allow you to waive some or all of your inheritance rights as a surviving spouse. Choose:
- **Alternative 1** to waive all surviving spouse rights, or
- **Alternative 2** to waive only some of them.

In most states, a surviving spouse has some or all of these rights:
- to claim a portion of the deceased spouse's estate under dower or curtesy laws or any similar state laws (see "Property Rights at Death" in Chapter 4, for a definition of dower and curtesy)
- to take property of the deceased spouse other than what is left under a will or another estate planning document

- to claim a share of the separate property of a deceased spouse who dies without a will
- to act as administrator or executor of the deceased spouse's estate
- to claim a homestead allowance, and
- to claim a family allowance or personal property allowance.

The first three of these rights are "election" rights. All states ordinarily guarantee a surviving spouse an inheritance when the other spouse dies. These laws are often called "election" laws because under them, the surviving spouse elects to take property—often as much as one-third to one-half of the deceased spouse's estate—instead of what was left under the deceased spouse's will or other property transfer documents. In community property states, a surviving spouse already owns half of the community property. Even so, a few community property states give a surviving spouse the right to take a portion of the deceased spouse's community or separate property, in some circumstances.

In addition to election rights, a surviving spouse can ask to be appointed executor (or administrator) of the deceased spouse's estate and can request "allowances." Allowances typically fall into three categories: homestead, personal property, and family allowances (though individual states might use different names). An allowance might give the surviving spouse the right to stay in the family home, to receive support payments from the estate, or to claim a certain amount of the household goods and other personal property that belonged to the deceased spouse.

Depending on your situation, it might make sense to waive some or all of these additional rights. Waiving all inheritance rights is an extreme measure. Carefully read the rest of this section—and consult your lawyer, if one is helping you with the prenup—before you make this important decision.

One final note: These clauses are set up to be mutual—that is, both of you waive and retain the same rights. If you want your choices about waivers to be different, you'll need to adapt the appropriate clause to apply to only one of you at a time.

CAUTION

Think carefully before waiving surviving spouse rights. Waiving your legal right to something is a big step. Be sure you understand what you might be entitled to and think through whether you really need a waiver to help you carry out your estate plans. For a more thorough explanation of your rights, see "Property Rights at Death" in Chapter 4. Then check the summary of your state's laws on the book's companion page. If you are at all in doubt about what's involved, get some advice on the subject from a qualified lawyer. Finally, make sure you follow your state's legal requirements for a waiver: As we note in Chapter 4, state requirements can be quite complex. While we've tried to give you a comprehensive waiver clause, it might need some tweaking to pass muster in your state.

Alternative 1: Mutual Waiver of Rights in Each Other's Estate—Complete Waiver

Use this clause if you want to waive all of your surviving spouse rights. Typically, you would use a complete waiver if your estate plans cover everything that needs to be addressed if one of you dies and if you want to be sure there won't be a glitch in those plans due to the spousal rights conferred by state law.

Ted and Grace, for example, choose this alternative. They already have written estate plans that they will sign as soon as they marry. Ted's plan leaves the bulk of his estate, including family heirlooms, to his children, and also makes provisions for Grace, since she will be giving up her job to marry Ted. Grace's estate, which is much smaller and includes a share of a family farm, will go to Grace's sister. Ted is naming one of his adult children as executor of his estate. Grace's sister is designated to handle her estate. The couple decides that a complete waiver is the best way to ensure that their plans will be carried out and that state spousal protection laws won't interfere with settling their estates. This is the clause they put in their prenuptial agreement:

Mutual Waiver of Rights in Each Other's Estate—Complete Waiver

Each of us waives and forever gives up any and all rights and claims to the Separate Property of the other person due to our marriage, including but not limited to:

1. Rights or claims of dower, curtesy, or any substitute for those rights or claims provided by any applicable state statute at the time of the other person's death;

2. The right of election to take against the will of the other;

3. The right to a share in the Separate Property estate of the other person if the other person dies without a will;

4. The right to act as administrator of the estate of the other;

5. The right to a probate homestead or homestead allowance;

6. The right to a family allowance and to a personal property allowance.

Nothing in This Agreement shall be deemed to constitute a waiver by either of us of any gift one of us might choose to make to the other by will or other estate planning document, or to act as executor designated in the will of the other. However, we acknowledge that no promises of any kind have been made by either of us to the other person regarding any such gift or designation, except for any specific provisions included in This Agreement.

Alternative 2: Mutual Waiver of Rights in Each Other's Estate—Partial Waiver

This clause allows you to waive only the surviving spouse rights that you specify in the prenup. For example, Karen and Russ want to waive their rights to claim a share of each other's property when one of them dies so that property earmarked for their respective children will go to the children without a hitch. But they decide not to waive the right to be executors of each other's estates or to request allowances. Russ in particular decides against waiving allowances, because he and Karen plan to live in Karen's home. He wants to be sure he can ask for the right to stay in the home if Karen dies and for an allowance to help with the mortgage if necessary. So they opt for a partial waiver:

Mutual Waiver of Rights in Each Other's Estate—Partial Waiver

Each of us waives and forever gives up the following rights or claims that we might acquire in the Separate Property of the other person due to our marriage:

1. Rights or claims of dower, curtesy, or any substitute for those rights or claims provided by any applicable state statute at the time of the other person's death;

2. The right of election to take against the will of the other;

3. The right to a share in the Separate Property estate of the other person if the other person dies without a will.

Nothing in This Agreement shall be deemed to constitute a waiver by either of us of any gift one of us might choose to make to the other by will or other estate planning document, or to act as executor designated in the will of the other. However, we acknowledge that no promises of any kind have been made by either of us to the other person regarding any such gift or designation, except for any specific provisions included in This Agreement.

Leaving Property to Each Other at Death

This clause is for couples who want to make a binding agreement to provide for each other in their estate plans. In general, state laws allow you to change your will whenever you feel like it. In fact, you are not legally required to have a will (or any other estate planning document) at all. And other than legal protections for surviving spouses and children, you are free to leave your estate to anyone you choose.

In most states, however, you can voluntarily sign a written agreement to bind yourself to include certain provisions in a will or other estate planning document. This is what is often referred to as an "agreement to make a will" or a "contract to make a will." The clause below is intended to constitute such an agreement. It is binding unless you are in the process of legally separating, divorcing, or getting an annulment when one of you dies. Ted and Grace choose this clause for their prenup. Ted is confident he will be financially sound even if Grace predeceases him. Grace, on the other hand, expects to need some support from Ted's estate, especially since her retirement benefits from the county will be less as a result of her decision to stop working after she and Ted marry. If Ted dies, Grace also wants to be able to stay for a while in Ted's house (where she and Ted plan to live) before moving back into her own house (which will be rented out while they are married). After talking about various options, they decide that Ted should include in his estate plan a provision that gives Grace the right to stay in Ted's house rent-free for up to one year, plus $5,000 per month for her living expenses for one year, and a distribution of $500,000 from Ted's estate. Here's the clause they agreed on:

Provision for Grace Upon Ted's Death

Upon Ted's death, if no proceeding for Divorce, dissolution, legal separation, or annulment is pending at the date of death, Grace shall be entitled to receive the following distribution from Ted's estate:

A lump sum payment of $500,000.

In addition, Grace shall be entitled to occupy (rent-free) the residence in which we have been residing at the date of Ted's death, for a period of up to one year after Ted's death, and she shall be entitled to receive the monthly sum of $5,000, payable from Ted's estate for a period of one year after Ted's death.

At all times during our marriage, Ted shall maintain in effect a valid will, trust, or other estate planning document that includes the foregoing provisions.

CAUTION
State laws might differ. The requirements for an agreement to make a will can vary from state to state, so you'll need to check the laws of your state before including a clause like this in your prenup. You should also be sure to coordinate what you say here with your actual estate plan. Be sure to have your draft of this clause reviewed by your lawyer.

Making Consistent Estate Plans

If you're waiving some or all of your surviving spouse rights or if you've agreed to provide for each other after death, it's especially important to make a binding commitment to follow through with your estate plans as soon as you marry. This clause does that. Here is how this commitment was made in Ted and Grace's agreement:

Estate Plans to Be Consistent With This Agreement
We acknowledge the importance of making valid estate plans that are consistent with This Agreement. Therefore, as soon as possible after our marriage, each of us will establish and maintain in effect a valid will, trust, and/or other estate planning document or combination of documents that will be consistent with, and carry out the terms of, This Agreement. We further agree to review our estate plans periodically to ensure that our estate planning documents remain consistent with This Agreement and to modify our estate planning documents if necessary to keep them consistent with This Agreement.

Optional Paragraph 2: Property Transfers or Purchases of Insurance Upon Marriage

Use one or more of the clauses in this paragraph to agree to:
- give property or cash to the other person after you are married, or
- set up a life insurance policy or an annuity for the benefit of the other person.

We give you several common scenarios to choose from. If none of them fits exactly, pick the one that's closest and adapt it to your situation.

CAUTION
Be aware of possible tax consequences. Gifts between spouses are usually exempt from gift taxes, while gifts between unmarried people might not be. Making the transfer after marriage might make the transfer a nontaxable gift between married people, even though a prenup signed before marriage requires the transfer. However, the tax consequences can differ, depending on the circumstances. Avoid unpleasant surprises by familiarizing yourself with the tax rules that will apply to your agreement; ask your tax adviser or lawyer if you need help.

Transferring Real Estate

Use this clause to set forth an agreement to transfer ownership of real estate following your wedding.

EXAMPLE: Rodney owns land where he and Tony plan to build a house together. They agree that after three months of marriage, Rodney will transfer a one-half interest in the land to Tony. The title will be in joint tenancy with right of survivorship, which means that if one of them dies after the transfer, the surviving spouse will own the entire property. This is the clause as it appears in their prenup:

Transfer of Real Estate
Within 90 days after our marriage, Rodney will sign, deliver, and record a deed granting to Tony a 50% interest, as joint tenants with right of survivorship, in the following real estate: unimproved real property located in the state of Maine, more specifically described on Schedule 1 attached to This Agreement. Each of us will pay for one-half of any expenses related to the transfer, including the cost of obtaining title insurance on the property.

Transferring Cash, Securities, or Other Personal Property

This clause provides for the payment of cash or transfer of property other than real estate following marriage. As with the other clauses in this section, it is worded to provide for a one-time payment or transfer, but you can adapt it to provide for multiple transfers.

> EXAMPLE: Olga and Jorge are in their mid-20s. Olga owns extensive investments inherited from her grandparents, plus her car and household goods. Jorge has only a small savings account, a car, and household goods. They want to be able to save and invest for their joint future on more equal footing. They agree that each year on their anniversary, Olga will transfer a share of her investments to a joint account so that over time, they will have more and more joint investments. This is how they adapt this clause:

> **Transfer of Cash, Securities, or Other Personal Property**
> Within 30 days after our marriage, and each year within 30 days after our wedding anniversary for nine additional years, Olga will deliver and assign to a joint securities account to be established by us, ownership of the following property: $20,000 in funds and/or investments selected by Olga, for a total of $200,000 over the first ten years of our marriage. Olga will pay all expenses related to each transfer.

Assigning Life Insurance

Use this clause if one of you has agreed to transfer ("assign") ownership of a life insurance policy to the other person after marriage. Assigning ownership of life insurance is usually done by people whose estates might be subject to estate taxes in order to reduce the overall value of their estate and therefore avoid taxes. Typically, the insured person is also the "owner" of the life insurance policy, meaning that the insured person has the right to designate beneficiaries and to control all other aspects of the policy. If the insured person dies, the proceeds of the life insurance policy will be counted as part of the estate that is subject to estate tax. But if the insured person assigned ownership of the policy to someone else and therefore did not own it at the time of death, the proceeds won't be subject to tax. (For a further explanation of estate taxes and ways to reduce or avoid them, see the estate planning resources listed in Chapter 12.)

Changing ownership of life insurance is normally part of an overall estate plan. It gives complete control of the policy to the new owner. If you transfer ownership of a life insurance policy to your spouse and you later divorce, you can't cancel the policy or get it back without your spouse's consent. So be sure to consider your plans carefully before including this clause. If you decide that it meets your needs, you can go ahead and use it.

> **EXAMPLE:** Michael and Evelyn are in their late 40s and marrying, each for the second time. Michael owns a home, business investments, retirement accounts, and miscellaneous other assets. Evelyn is much less wealthy. Michael owns life insurance on his life with a death benefit of $1.5 million. He and Evelyn agree that she should be designated the beneficiary of the policy; they also want to get the policy out of his taxable estate. They decide to use this clause to transfer ownership of the policy to Evelyn. She can then designate herself as beneficiary.

Assignment of Life Insurance

Within 15 days after our marriage, Michael will deliver and assign to Evelyn ownership of the following fully paid life insurance policy on Michael's life: XYZ Insurance Company policy number 222333, face amount $1,500,000. Michael will pay any expenses related to the assignment.

Purchasing an Annuity or Life Insurance

Some people include in their prenups a clause requiring one of them to buy an annuity or life insurance policy for the benefit of the other person. To decide whether to include such a clause, you'll need to know something about the potential benefits and costs of annuities and life insurance. A comprehensive analysis of these matters is beyond the scope of this book, but here are some basic considerations to keep in mind.

Typically, you purchase an annuity by paying a certain amount of money up front or at regular intervals. In exchange, the annuity provider agrees to make specified monthly, quarterly, or annual payments to a beneficiary that you designate. Payments begin at a specified time and continue for the beneficiary's lifetime. An annuity is used to provide cash flow for the beneficiary, and there can be income tax benefits involved in setting up some types of annuities.

Life insurance is similar to an annuity, except that the payments to the beneficiary don't begin until the death of the insured person, and then the payment is usually a lump sum. Obviously, the main purpose of life insurance is to provide cash when the insured person dies. As noted above, the proceeds might be subject to estate tax.

As with all of the clauses in this paragraph, you should be sure to think through all the implications—including tax consequences—before using one or both of the following clauses in your agreement.

Here are two examples of the completed clauses, one involving an annuity and one providing for life insurance.

> **EXAMPLE:** Beatriz and Arnolfo plan to have children after they marry. They agree that Beatriz will take time off from her job until their children reach school age. To make up for any reduction in Beatriz's retirement benefits, they agree that Arnolfo will buy an annuity that Beatriz can start to draw on after age 50.

Purchase of Annuity

Within 60 days after our marriage, Arnolfo will purchase and maintain in effect during our marriage an annuity contract that will pay at least $30,000 per year beginning on Beatriz's 50th birthday, and continuing until the death of Beatriz, who shall be designated as sole primary beneficiary of the annuity.

Arnolfo will pay all of the costs of purchasing and maintaining the annuity.

EXAMPLE: Dirk is quitting his job and relocating in order to marry Maxine. Maxine plans to support the two of them until Dirk reestablishes himself in a new job. Dirk is concerned about how he will pay his expenses if something happens to Maxine before he is fully self-supporting again. They agree to take out life insurance on Maxine's life for Dirk's benefit, so that Dirk will have funds to live on if Maxine dies unexpectedly.

Purchase of Life Insurance Policy

Within 30 days after our marriage, Maxine will purchase and maintain in effect for a period of ten years a life insurance policy that will pay at least $300,000 upon her death. Dirk shall be designated as sole primary beneficiary of the policy. Maxine and Dirk will each pay one-half of the costs of purchasing and maintaining the policy.

Optional Paragraph 3: Provisions Applicable to Divorce

This paragraph contains clauses that allow you to spell out in advance how various financial and property matters will be handled if you divorce. (If in Paragraph 5 of your prenup you have defined the term

"Divorce" to include other legal proceedings, such as legal separation or annulment, this paragraph will apply to those events too.)

Before you decide whether or not to include a paragraph on divorce matters, we suggest that you review the general information on divorce in Chapter 4. Conduct follow-up research or contact a local attorney so that you clearly understand what's likely to happen to your property and finances if you say nothing about divorce in your prenup.

You might conclude that you don't need to include this paragraph at all. If you've specified what is separate property and what is marital or community property in the preceding paragraphs of your prenup, you can leave the details of how the marital assets and debts get allocated to later negotiation or court decision. But if you want to ensure a specific outcome, this is where you should do that.

> CAUTION
> **A court might not enforce some terms regarding divorce.** All states allow you to make a binding agreement about how some financial matters will be handled if you divorce. However, there can be exceptions, especially when it comes to child support and alimony. For example, no state will allow you to waive child support in advance. Some states don't allow advance waivers of alimony, either, while others impose certain requirements for a valid alimony waiver. Even some property division agreements won't be enforced if a court finds that the provisions violate public policy or are egregiously unfair. Read "Property Rights If You Divorce" in Chapter 4 for more information. Be sure you understand any legal limits on what you can include in this paragraph before using any of the clauses that follow.

Making Sure Your Prenup Applies If You Divorce

If you decide to include a paragraph dealing with divorce matters, you should start with this clause. It requires you to file your prenup with the divorce court at the beginning of the case and directs that any dispute about the prenup be resolved before any decisions about property or other financial matters can be made.

Karen and Russ include a paragraph about divorce in their prenup, so they start the paragraph with this clause:

Terms of This Agreement to Control

In the unhappy event that our marriage ends in Divorce, as that term is defined in Paragraph 5 of This Agreement, we want to resolve all issues as amicably and efficiently as possible. Therefore, if we divorce, we agree to the following:

1. This Agreement will control all issues addressed by This Agreement.
2. As soon as possible after the Divorce is filed, we will file This Agreement (or a true copy of it) in court and we will sign and file a stipulation acknowledging the validity of This Agreement.
3. Any dispute about the validity or interpretation of This Agreement will be separated from all other issues in the Divorce and submitted to the court for determination before any issues addressed in This Agreement are decided.

Dividing and Distributing Property

Chances are good that your paragraph addressing divorce will include one or more of the optional clauses in this section. We'll discuss them separately, so that you can decide which of them are right for your situation. If you don't see exactly what you need, pick one that's close and adapt it to your requirements.

Distribution of Separate Property Assets

This clause ensures that each spouse ends up with their separate property in a divorce. If you'd like, you can also include language providing for any separate property held in joint names to be divided into two shares (if possible) or sold, with the proceeds divided according to each person's ownership share.

Russ and Karen add this clause to their prenup. Even though they live in California (a community property state) they include the optional part about dividing any separate property assets that they hold in a form of joint ownership, such as joint tenancy. Though California law presumes that any joint ownership property acquired during marriage is community property, they could opt out of the community property system for a particular asset by making a written agreement to hold it as separate property in a joint ownership form. They include the full clause because they want to keep all of their options open.

Distribution of Separate Property Assets

In any Divorce proceeding, our Separate Property assets will be distributed as follows:

1. Each party's Separate Property assets, as defined in This Agreement, shall be confirmed to that party absolutely, without being included in any division of Community Property.

2. Each jointly owned Separate Property asset shall be divided between us in proportion to our respective ownership interests in the asset ("in kind"), if that is possible without making us co-owners of the same asset after the asset is divided. If an in-kind division of any asset is not possible, the asset shall be sold and the net proceeds divided in proportion to our respective ownership interests in the asset.

Distribution of Marital or Community Property Assets

All marital or community property—regardless of whether your prenup addresses it—must be divided between you and your spouse if you divorce. If you don't spell out in your prenup how you want the property divvied up, either you'll have to negotiate the division later, or a judge will divide the property for you according to the laws of the state where you divorce. To limit uncertainty or to divide the marital or community property in a way that differs from state law, address the issue in your prenup.

We give you two alternative clauses:

- **Alternative 1** requires an equal division of the assets, and
- **Alternative 2** allows for an "equitable" (not necessarily equal) division.

There are many other possibilities. For example, you might want the property to be divided in some specified proportion (such as 60/40 or 70/30), or you might want to exclude certain categories of assets. Pick one of the alternatives we give you as a starting point and adapt it to meet your needs.

If you want to provide for special treatment of a particular asset, there's a place to do that further on in this paragraph.

Alternative 1: Equal Distribution of Marital or Community Property Assets

This clause assumes that the marital or community property assets will be divided so that you each wind up with assets of equal value. Your options are to:

- literally divide individual assets in half—for example, split up the money in bank accounts
- sell assets and divide the proceeds, or
- agree to give certain assets to one person and other assets to the other.

This alternative also allows for exceptions, so you can use this clause to set out a general approach and then insert a separate clause to designate any assets you'd like to treat differently. And it provides that you can agree later to divide your assets in a different manner, as long as you put your new agreement in writing.

In most states, judges have the power to divide marital property unequally unless the divorcing spouses make their own settlement agreement stating otherwise. This is true in all equitable distribution states and a number of community property states. If you live in an equitable distribution state, but you want your property to be divided equally (even if you don't reach a settlement), then consider including this clause (or some variation of it that accomplishes what you have in mind).

EXAMPLE: Chan and Mara live in New Jersey, an equitable distribution state. They didn't want to leave open the possibility that a judge might order an unequal division of their property in a divorce, so they added the following clause to their prenup:

> **Equal Distribution of Marital Property Assets**
>
> In any Divorce proceeding, except as provided elsewhere in This Agreement or in a written agreement signed by both of us at the time of the Divorce, any Community Property assets shall be distributed between us in such a way as to achieve a monetarily equal division of the aggregate net value of the Community Property assets.

Even if you live in a state where the law requires a judge to divide the property equally, unless you reach a settlement agreeing to an unequal division (this is the case in a few community property states), you could still use this clause to specify how the equal division of the property will be accomplished or to confirm your intent to divide things equally. For example, Russ and Karen live in California, a state where equal division of property is almost always required unless a couple agrees otherwise. They use this alternative to state their general intent that their community property will be divided equally, but they don't include any details of how that will be accomplished. This is the clause as it appears in their agreement:

> **Equal Distribution of Community Property Assets**
>
> In any Divorce proceeding, except as provided elsewhere in This Agreement or in a written agreement signed by both of us at the time of the Divorce, any Community Property assets shall be distributed between us in such a way as to achieve a monetarily equal division of the aggregate net value of the Community Property assets.

Alternative 2: Equitable Distribution of Marital or Community Property Assets

As mentioned just above, most states don't require that marital or community property be divided equally at the time of divorce. Unless a couple agrees otherwise, the divorce judge can divide the assets in whatever proportion seems fair ("equitable") to the judge.

If you are in one of the few states that require equal division of community property and you prefer the equitable distribution approach, you can use this clause to say so.

If you live in a state where community or marital assets will be divided equitably and you are comfortable with that approach, you can use this clause to confirm your position or you can skip it and allow property to be divided according to a settlement agreement or state law.

Note that this alternative, like the first one, allows you to create exceptions for specific assets and to make a later agreement that divides your community or marital property in some other way.

> **EXAMPLE:** Lupe and Ike live in an equitable distribution state. They might someday move to a community property state where equal division is required. They like the equitable distribution concept, but they want to provide some guidelines. They decide to include this version of Alternative 2 in their prenup:

Equitable Distribution of Marital or Community Property Assets
In any Divorce proceeding, except as provided elsewhere in This Agreement or in a written agreement signed by both of us at the time of the Divorce, any Marital or Community Property assets shall be distributed between us in such a way as to achieve an equitable division of the aggregate net value of the Marital or Community Property assets, as determined by written agreement signed by both of us or by the court in the Divorce case. If we so agree, certain assets may be distributed to one of us in exchange for a distribution of offsetting assets to the other. Otherwise, each asset will be divided between us ("in kind"), if that is possible without making us co-owners of the same asset after the asset is divided. If an asset cannot be divided in kind and there is no agreement to assign the asset to one party, it shall be sold and the net proceeds divided so as to accomplish an equitable division of all the assets. In determining whether the assets have been equitably divided, any asset not sold will be valued at its fair market value as of the date the assets are divided.

Dividing Retirement or Other Employee Benefits

If you want to spell out what will happen to any marital or community property share of retirement or other employee benefits in the event of a divorce, you can include one of the following alternatives:

- **Alternative 1** states that the benefits are allocated to the person whose name is on them. The other spouse gets some other property or a payout in exchange (as part of either an equal division or an equitable distribution, depending on which general approach you are using).
- **Alternative 2** provides that any marital or community property interest in the benefits will be divided up, with each spouse getting a percentage of the benefits.
- **Alternative 3** states that each person keeps his or her own benefits, without including them in any division of marital or community property.
- **Alternative 4** states that you will decide how to distribute any marital or community property share of a spouse's benefits if and when you divorce.

Pick the one that most closely fits the way you want to handle employee benefits. As always, adapt a clause if necessary.

Alternative 1: Benefits Are Divided by the Offset Method

Use this alternative if you want to make sure that any retirement accounts or other employee benefits will be assigned to the person who earned or accumulated them, with some other asset or payment given to the other party in exchange. This is called the "offset method" because what one spouse gives up is "offset" (compensated) by an award of other property.

> EXAMPLE: Kyle and Hannah both have retirement plans through their jobs. Both of them have been working only a short time, so most of their retirement benefits will be considered marital property because they will have been earned while they are married. They agree that if they ever divorce, each of them will keep his or her own benefits. If one person's benefits are worth more, the other will receive some other property to even things up. They use this clause in their prenup:

Retirement or Employee Benefits to Be Divided—Offset Method

If we divorce, the terms of the Divorce decree or judgment shall provide that any Marital Property interest in retirement, pension, deferred compensation, stock options, and other employee benefit or tax deferred plans, whether qualified according to IRS regulations or nonqualified, shall be divided so that the person who earned the benefits or in whose name those benefits are held receives all of the benefits and the other person receives other property or funds as an offset in the equitable division of the Marital Property.

Alternative 2: Benefits Are Divided in Kind

This alternative provides that any marital or community property share of retirement or other employee benefits will be divided between you, regardless of whose name they are in. This is usually called an "in kind" division.

Dividing a retirement or employee benefit in kind during a divorce is often accomplished through a qualified domestic relations order ("QDRO"), under which each spouse receives a share of the benefits directly from the retirement or other employee benefit plan. The clause states that the spouses will cooperate in preparing the necessary order.

EXAMPLE: Bal expects to make major contributions to his 401(k) plan during his marriage to Xenia. They hope to have a family together, and the plan is for Xenia to be a stay-at-home mom. They agree that if there is a divorce, the community property share of Bal's 401(k) will be divided in kind between them. This is the clause they use:

Retirement or Employee Benefits to Be Divided—In-Kind Method

If we divorce, the terms of the Divorce decree or judgment shall provide that any Community Property interest in retirement, pension, deferred compensation, stock options, and other employee benefit or tax deferred plans, whether qualified according to IRS regulations or nonqualified, shall be divided so that each of us receives a share of the benefits payable, with each person's share calculated in a manner consistent with equitable division of the Community Property. Each of us will cooperate in preparing any court order for division of the benefits required by the plan or as provided by applicable law.

Alternative 3: **Benefits Are Not Divided**

You should use this alternative if each spouse wants to keep their own retirement or other employee benefits, without including them in the division of other marital or community property assets.

EXAMPLE: Maxine and Delia want any employee benefits they earn while they're married to be considered community property if one of them dies. If they divorce, however, they want to keep their benefits completely separate. They decide to accomplish this by including the following clause in their prenup:

No Division of Retirement or Employee Benefits

If we divorce, the terms of the Divorce decree or judgment shall provide that any Community Property interest in retirement, pension, deferred compensation, stock options, and other employee benefit or tax deferred plans, whether qualified according to IRS regulations or nonqualified, shall be confirmed to the person who earned the benefits or in whose name those benefits are vested and shall not be included in the equal division of the Community Property.

Alternative 4: **Method of Dividing Benefits to Be Determined at Time of Divorce**

Most people who want to defer the question of how to divide up retirement benefits won't need to add this clause; anything left out of the prenup will be decided at the time of a divorce anyway. But if you're including specific instructions on everything else and the issue of retirement benefits is the only issue you haven't addressed, you can use this alternative.

EXAMPLE: Andres and Lara are providing in their prenup for equal division of their personal property and any liquid assets if they divorce. They aren't sure what to do with their employee benefits, so they decide to make it clear that this issue will be decided when and if they divorce. They use this clause:

Retirement or Employee Benefits to Be Divided—Method to Be Determined

If we divorce, the terms of the Divorce decree or judgment shall provide that any Marital Property interest in retirement, pension, deferred compensation, stock options, and other employee benefit or tax deferred plans, whether qualified according to IRS regulations or nonqualified, shall be divided in a manner consistent with the equitable division of the Marital Property, as determined by a written agreement signed by both of us or by the court in the Divorce case.

Dividing Other Assets

Once you've laid out your general approach to dividing your marital or community property assets and dealt with any issue relating to retirement benefits, you might still have one or more assets that require special treatment. For example, you might be planning to buy a house together and want to allow one of you to buy out the other person's share if you divorce. Or you might have a similar agreement regarding a business you plan to start up.

This is where you would address those lingering assets. Use the same format we've given you for other clauses, give your clause a title, and insert it in your prenup.

> **EXAMPLE:** Kamlesh and Bhavana plan to buy a house together after they marry. They agree that if they ever divorce, Kamlesh can buy out Bhavana's share on certain prearranged terms. Here's what they put in their prenuptial agreement:

Right to Purchase Residence

We plan to purchase a residence in which we will live together during our marriage. The residence will be considered Marital Property. If we ever divorce, Kamlesh will have the right to buy out Bhavana's share of the equity in the residence as follows: The fair market value of the residence shall be determined by a mutually approved appraiser. If we cannot agree on an appraiser, each of us will select a licensed appraiser, and those appraisers shall select a licensed appraiser to perform the appraisal. The amount owing on any mortgages or liens shall then be deducted from the fair market value to determine the equity in the residence. Kamlesh shall pay Bhavana cash in the amount equal to one-half of the equity. Kamlesh may refinance the property to obtain the funds for the buyout, and Bhavana agrees to cooperate with such a refinance. The buyout must be completed within 90 days after the Divorce decree or judgment, unless we agree in writing to extend the time. If Kamlesh does not buy Bhavana out by that time, Bhavana shall have 60 days to buy out Kamlesh on the same terms and conditions. If neither of us buys out the other person's share, the house shall be listed for sale and sold as soon as possible, and the net proceeds shall be divided equally between us.

Responsibility for Outstanding Debts

The next few clauses contain provisions for dealing with outstanding debts in the event of a divorce. Ordinarily, state laws give divorce judges the power to divide up responsibility for debts incurred by one or both spouses during marriage. (See "Property Rights If You Divorce," in Chapter 4, for a review of this issue.) Often, a judge will have fairly broad discretion to allocate debts, depending on the circumstances at the time of the divorce. If you want to provide a more predictable outcome, you can use one or more of these clauses to do so.

Premarital Debts

Even though the law in most states is that one spouse is not responsible for the other's premarital debts, you can ensure this result by writing it into your prenup.

Here's the clause that Karen and Russ add to their agreement:

Responsibility for Premarital Debts

If we divorce, the terms of the Divorce decree or judgment shall provide that any outstanding premarital debt will be allocated to the person who incurred the debt, and the person who incurred the debt shall be required to pay the debt and to indemnify and hold the other person harmless from the debt and all costs related to it.

Debts Incurred During Marriage—General Rule

In the absence of an agreement between the spouses, state law gives divorce judges a lot of latitude to divide debts incurred during marriage. You can eliminate this uncertainty by establishing your own arrangement. We give you a couple of alternatives to select or adapt as needed. Alternative 1 requires that debts be divided equally between you. Alternative 2 allows debts to be divided in a manner that's fair at the time you divorce, either by agreement or, if you can't agree, according to the divorce judge's decision.

Alternative 1: Equal Responsibility for Debts Incurred During Marriage

You'll probably want to use this clause if you stated that you want your assets to be divided equally in the event of a divorce. You'll want to make sure that provision is not undermined by an unequal division of debts. Because it's not always practical to equally divide debts—for example, one spouse might be a homemaker and not able to make debt payments—this clause allows for an unequal division of debts to be balanced out in the division of property. Note that this clause states a general rule, leaving room for exceptions to be addressed in other clauses of the prenup.

> EXAMPLE: Chan and Mara, who opted for an equal division of their marital property in a previous clause of their agreement, include this clause requiring equal division of any mutual debts:

Equal Responsibility for Debts Incurred During Marriage—General Rule

Except as provided elsewhere in This Agreement, if we divorce, the terms of the Divorce decree or judgment shall provide that any outstanding debts incurred by one or both of us during our marriage will be paid and allocated between us equally, to the extent an equal allocation is practical, as specifically determined by written agreement signed by both of us, or by the court in the Divorce case. If the allocation is unequal, there shall be a corresponding offset in the division of our Marital Property assets, in order to equalize the overall division of assets and debts.

If a debt is allocated to one of us in accordance with this clause, the person to whom it is allocated shall be required to indemnify and hold the other person harmless from the debt and all costs related to it.

Alternative 2: Equitable Allocation of Responsibility for Debts Incurred During Marriage

This alternative says that debts incurred while you are married will be divided between you if you divorce, but leaves the exact method of division to be determined according to a flexible "equitable" standard. If you have opted for equitable division of your property, you will probably want to stick with an equitable division of debts, too. As with Alternative 1, this clause allows for exceptions to the general rule.

EXAMPLE: Ike and Lupe have opted for equitable division of their marital property, so they include this clause to deal with debts incurred while they are married:

Equitable Allocation of Responsibility for Debts Incurred During Marriage—General Rule

Except as provided elsewhere in This Agreement, if we divorce, the terms of the Divorce decree or judgment shall provide that any outstanding debt incurred by one or both of us during our marriage will be paid and allocated between us equitably, as determined by written agreement signed by both of us or by the court in the Divorce case.

If a debt is allocated to one of us in accordance with this clause, the person to whom it is allocated shall be required to indemnify and hold the other person harmless from the debt and all costs related to it.

Student Loans

If one of you takes out a student loan while you are married and you get divorced before it's completely paid back, will the debt be the sole responsibility of the person who got the education or can it be allocated between you in the divorce? State laws vary on this point, so you might want to include your own clause here. We give you two alternatives to choose from. **Alternative 1** makes student loans the sole responsibility of the student, while **Alternative 2** allows them to be shared between the spouses.

Alternative 1: **Sole Responsibility for Student Loans**

This clause makes any balance due on a student loan the sole responsibility of the spouse who was the student.

> EXAMPLE: Lamont plans to finish his bachelor's degree and get a teaching credential after he and Jetta marry. Lamont will take out student loans to cover his educational expenses. He and Jetta agree that the student loans will be their joint responsibility while they are married. But if they ever get divorced, Lamont will be solely responsible for anything still owing on the loans. Although it is unlikely that Jetta will go back to school, if she does, the same rules will apply to any student loans she takes out. They use this clause in their prenup:

> **Sole Responsibility for Student Loans**
>
> If we divorce, the terms of the Divorce decree or judgment shall provide that any outstanding student loan debt will be allocated to the person whose education was financed by the loan, who shall be required to pay the debt and to indemnify and hold the other person harmless from the debt and all costs related to it.

Alternative 2: **Shared Responsibility for Student Loans**

Use this alternative if you want to treat student loans as a shared responsibility.

> EXAMPLE: Ty plans to attend graduate school after he and Jen marry. Jen is already in medical school. Both of them will use student loans to help pay for their tuition and expenses. They agree that the loans will be their mutual responsibility while they are married and if they ever divorce. They insert this clause in their agreement:

> **Shared Responsibility for Student Loans**
>
> If we divorce, the terms of the Divorce decree or judgment shall provide that any outstanding student loan debt will be allocated between us in the same manner as any other debts incurred during our marriage for which we are mutually responsible, and not solely to the person whose education was financed by the loan.

Sole Responsibility for Certain Debts Incurred by One Spouse During Marriage

During marriage, you might incur other types of debts that you'd want just one spouse to pay back post-divorce. Or perhaps one of you might borrow money for an expensive hobby, and you both agree that only the spouse who takes on the debt should have to pay it back if you get divorced.

You might also want to provide for general contingencies, such as the possibility that one of you might run up a debt without the other person's consent. If you want to provide this type of exception to the general approach used for allocating debts incurred during your marriage, this is the place to do it.

For example, Karen and Russ are both self-employed. If they divorce, they agree that each of them will be solely responsible for business debts they each incurred during their marriage.

> **Sole Responsibility for Certain Debts Incurred by One Party During Marriage**
>
> If we divorce, the terms of the Divorce decree or judgment shall provide that any of the following outstanding debts incurred by one of us during our marriage will be allocated solely to the person who incurred the debt: (1) debts incurred by Karen in the course of engaging in the practice of veterinary medicine or in any other business; (2) debts incurred by Russ in the course of operating his bookkeeping business or any other business.
>
> If a debt is allocated to one of us in accordance with this clause, the person to whom it is allocated shall be required to indemnify and hold the other person harmless from the debt and all costs related to it.

Reimbursement for Debts or Expenses Paid

This clause addresses whether either of you will be reimbursed, if you divorce, for certain debts or expenses you paid for during marriage. **Alternative 1** lists particular types of payments that will be reimbursed. **Alternative 2** provides for no reimbursement.

Alternative 1: Reimbursement for Debts or Expenses Paid

This alternative provides for reimbursement to a spouse who pays certain expenses of the other party. You can modify and add to the suggested list of expenses provided as necessary. At the end, decide whether you want to limit possible reimbursement to just the items you list. If so, include the optional sentence providing for no reimbursement other than what you specify.

If you use this clause, be sure to keep good records of the reimbursable expenditures.

> **EXAMPLE:** You might remember our discussion of Jetta and Lamont, who agree that each of them will be responsible for his or her own student loans if they divorce. They use this clause to require reimbursement for money spent on premarital debts and student loans during their marriage:

Reimbursement for Debts or Expenses Paid

In any Divorce proceeding, each of us will be entitled to reimbursement from the other for:

1. Payments made during our marriage from Separate Property funds of one of us for premarital debts owed by the other;

2. One-half of payments made during our marriage from Marital Property funds for premarital debts owed by the other;

3. Payments made from Separate Property funds of one of us for necessary expenses incurred by the other in connection with attendance at an accredited educational institution (including tuition, fees, books, and supplies but not including living expenses), whether paid directly or by payments on student loans incurred for those expenses;

4. One-half of payments made during our marriage from Marital Property funds for necessary expenses incurred by the other in connection with attendance at an accredited educational institution (including tuition, fees, books, and supplies but not including living expenses), whether paid directly or by payments on student loans incurred for those expenses, and

5. Any other amounts expressly agreed to be reimbursable as provided elsewhere in This Agreement.

Neither of us will be entitled to any reimbursement from the other for paying any debts or expenses except those listed above, whether paid from Separate Property funds or Marital Property funds or both.

Alternative 2: **No Reimbursement for Debts or Expenses Paid**

Use this clause if you don't want to reimburse each other for payment of debts or expenses in the event you divorce. This is what Karen and Russ do. They both have children that they expect to spend money on while they are married, and they don't want to go to the trouble of keeping track of those or other personal expenditures during their marriage. They use this clause:

No Reimbursement for Debts or Expenses Paid

In any Divorce proceeding, neither of us will be entitled to any reimbursement from the other for paying the debts or expenses of the other during our marriage except as might be provided elsewhere in This Agreement, whether paid from Separate Property funds or Community Property funds or both.

Alimony

As you might recall from Chapter 2, there are some subjects that are considered off-limits for premarital agreements. For example, all states prohibit agreements waiving the right to receive child support.

Similarly, state laws vary on the question of whether you can use a prenup to waive the right to receive alimony (called "spousal support" or "spousal maintenance" in some states). Some states forbid waivers of alimony. Some allow waiver of permanent alimony, but not of temporary alimony. Other states allow waivers, but provide an exception when waiving alimony means the waiving spouse will become eligible for welfare. Still others allow a judge to set the waiver aside if it was "unconscionable" (extremely unfair) when the agreement was signed or (in some states) at the time of the divorce. Some states also require the parties to a waiver to have independent attorney representation and sign separate waivers.

Because of the many possible restrictions, you should check out the laws of your state very carefully before including an alimony clause in your prenup. This is one area where independent attorney representation in the making of your prenup is especially important. Your attorneys might have suggestions for adapting one of the clauses we give you so that it meets the legal requirements in your state.

We give you two alternatives for this clause: **Alternative 1** is a complete waiver of alimony, and **Alternative 2** places limits on the amount of or duration of alimony payments. If it suits your situation, you can use a different alternative for each of you. For example, you might agree that one of you will waive the right to alimony using Alternative 1, while the other is entitled to alimony payments as specified using Alternative 2.

If your state uses a different term, such as "spousal support" or "spousal maintenance," substitute that term for the word "alimony" in the clause you select.

> CAUTION
>
> **Consider carefully before waiving alimony.** There is a reason state laws are tough on alimony waivers. Unless you are already established in a secure career or retired with a sure and steady source of support for your lifetime, your economic future might be hard to predict. You might find yourself needing some help from your spouse in order to make ends meet.

Alternative 1: Waiver of Alimony

Use this alternative if you want to completely waive the right to ask for alimony if you divorce. If the laws of your state don't allow for a total waiver, you can change the clause to waive what you can. If both of you will waive alimony, include a separate clause for each of you.

For example, Karen and Russ both have established careers, Karen as a veterinarian and Russ as a bookkeeper. Neither of them wants to be in a position of paying or receiving alimony (called "spousal support" in California, where they live). They check California law and discover that in order to include a valid waiver of spousal support in their premarital agreement, each of them must be represented by an independent attorney (they are) and the waiver cannot be "unconscionable" at the time of a divorce. To minimize the chance that the waiver will be considered unconscionable later, they include a limited exception for spousal support payments if one of them becomes disabled and can't support himself or herself. Following is the clause in which Russ waives spousal support. (The agreement contains an identical clause for Karen.)

Waiver of Spousal Support by Russ

Russ expects to have sufficient earning capacity, income, and assets to provide for his reasonable needs if we divorce. Therefore, Russ hereby waives absolutely any and all rights to request temporary and permanent spousal support from Karen, except in the following limited circumstances only: If at the time we divorce, Russ is disabled and unable to fully provide for his own support, he may request and receive temporary or permanent spousal support in a reasonable amount determined by taking into consideration all relevant circumstances, including Karen's reasonable ability to pay without impairing her own standard of living, for a period not to exceed one-half the length of our marriage. Russ understands that this waiver could later result in a hardship, and has taken that risk into account in making this waiver.

Alternative 2: **Specified Alimony Payments**

This clause allows you to place a cap on payment amounts or limit the duration of alimony. Be sure to check on any legal limitations in your state before using this alternative.

Because Grace is giving up her job as a social worker when she marries Ted, Ted and Grace use this clause to allow for limited alimony payments to Grace. (Ted waives his right to alimony because his assets and income ensure he won't have a need.) This is the clause that applies to Grace:

Specified Alimony to Grace

If we divorce, Grace shall be entitled to temporary or permanent alimony payments of $5,000 per month from Ted, beginning on the date when we stop living together and ending absolutely on the date of Grace's remarriage, the death of either party, or when Grace reaches the age of 65, whichever occurs first. This clause may not be modified except by a written agreement signed by both of us. Grace hereby waives absolutely any and all rights to request temporary and permanent alimony from Ted except as provided in this clause. Grace understands that this waiver could later result in a hardship, and has taken that risk into account in making this waiver.

Other Optional Provisions Related to Divorce

This is a place for you to insert any other provisions that will apply if you divorce. The possible topics are numerous, depending on your circumstances. For example, you might agree that:

- one of you will have the right to occupy the family residence during any separation
- one or both of you will make contributions to a college education fund, or
- you will share custody of (and financial responsibility for) your pets.

Agreements in prenups that involve custody of children, such as where the children will live or how much child support you will pay, are generally prohibited by state law. However, agreements about some parenting issues, such as whether to educate children in certain schools or to provide lessons in certain activities, might be okay to include. Below are a couple of examples.

EXAMPLE: After they marry, Enrique and Lashana will move into the house leased by Enrique. There are three years left on the lease. They decide that if they divorce before the lease is up, Enrique will have the right to stay in the house and Lashana will move out. This is the clause they put in their agreement:

Occupancy of Rental
We plan to reside together in a home leased by Enrique. If, during the remaining lease term, we separate and divorce, Lashana will move from the home within 60 days after the filing and service of a complaint for Divorce, and from that date on Enrique shall have the sole right to occupy the home, the sole obligation to pay all expenses related to the home, including lease payments, and the sole right to receive any refund of the security deposit paid to the landlord.

EXAMPLE: Diane and Brad share a love of purebred Chesapeake Retriever dogs. They are planning to breed and show Chesapeake Retrievers together after they marry. They agree on the following arrangement for sharing their dogs if they ever get divorced. This is what they include in their prenup:

Agreement Regarding Dogs

If we divorce, we agree to share custody and responsibility for any dogs we own as follows: We will share custody of our dogs on an alternating weekly basis. The dogs shall be kept together and not separated from each other. Each of us will be responsible for one-half of any expenses for the dogs, including food and veterinary expenses. We will equally share any profits from breeding the dogs. Any dispute about the welfare of a dog will be submitted for binding decision to the dog's veterinarian. In addition, each of us shall have the sole rights to up to two of the next available purebred puppies born to or sired by the dogs. We will flip a coin to determine who has first pick of the puppies and then alternate between us.

Optional Paragraph 4: **Other Matters**

If there are other issues you want to address in your prenup and they don't fit in any of the other paragraphs, you can use this paragraph for those matters. For example, if you've agreed to put each other through graduate school, you might insert a clause on that subject here.

You might be tempted to include nonmonetary provisions in this paragraph, such as responsibility for household chores or upbringing of children. As we caution you in Chapter 2, however, agreements on such subjects probably aren't enforceable, and they might cause a judge to take the rest of your prenup less seriously. Our advice is to leave those subjects out of your official prenup. You can include them in a separate and nonbinding private agreement, if you find that helpful.

You might also be thinking of including a so-called "bad-boy" (or "-girl") clause in your agreement. This is a provision that imposes a financial penalty on a spouse who is caught being unfaithful. Such a clause is problematic at best. Aside from the effect on a marriage of planning for infidelity in this way, the clause might be unenforceable, especially in states where there is no-fault divorce. Fully consider the legal—and emotional—consequences of a clause like this before you include it in your prenup.

The following examples demonstrate appropriate topics to address in this paragraph. One is a couple's agreement to support each other through graduate school; the other lays out a couple's plans to save money.

> EXAMPLE: Neal and Jana are both college graduates. They plan to buy a house together, using equal amounts of premarital savings for the down payment. Neal plans to attend a two-year master's program in business administration. Jana will work to support them during that time, and then she hopes to attend architecture school. Neal will support her while she is in school. They also agree to take out a home equity loan to pay the tuition for both of them. They include this clause in their agreement:

Graduate Education

After we marry, Jana's employment will support us for two years while Neal obtains a master's degree in business administration at Temple University. After Neal completes the program, he will support us through employment while Jana attends an accredited program leading to a degree in architecture, for up to two years. The tuition and fees for both programs shall be paid from a home equity loan to be obtained by us after we marry and purchase the home we plan to acquire together. The home equity loan will not be used for any other purpose without our joint written approval. The terms of this clause shall apply even if we divorce.

EXAMPLE: Antoine and Natasha agree that they will each contribute a percentage of their monthly earnings to a savings account earmarked for a down payment on a house or for other joint investments. This is what they put in their prenup:

Contributions to Savings

During our marriage, each of us will deposit each month an amount equal to 2.5% of his or her gross monthly income into a savings account in our joint names. The account shall require two signatures for any withdrawal and the funds deposited shall be used for only a down payment on a residence in our joint names or for other investments we both agree upon.

Next Steps

Congratulations! You've now worked through all the clauses you need for your draft prenup. If you need help putting together your draft, "Working on Your Prenup" in Chapter 5 provides general instructions on how to assemble your agreement by hand or computer.

When your draft is complete, turn to the next chapter to learn how to finalize your agreement.

Closing Paragraphs and Sample Prenups

Now that you've drafted Paragraphs 1 through 8 and possibly added some of the optional paragraphs discussed in Chapter 8, it's time to draft the closing paragraphs of your prenup. Although these paragraphs are somewhat "boilerplate," you'll want to read and understand the terms and make any adjustments to suit your circumstances. If you added optional paragraphs after Paragraph 8, don't forget to renumber these final paragraphs accordingly.

After the discussion of the final two paragraphs, you'll find some sample prenups to compare your drafts against.

Paragraph 9: Interpretation, Modification, Review, and Enforcement of Your Agreement

This is the next-to-last paragraph of your prenup. If you decided to include any of the optional paragraphs discussed in Chapter 8, you should insert them before this paragraph and renumber it so it remains in sequence (just before the signatures).

This paragraph includes all the standard provisions that make for a clear and enforceable agreement. We also give you some options for setting up periodic reviews of the agreement and providing a mechanism for resolving any future disagreements about the prenup.

Because the clauses in this agreement are standard to most agreements, we will focus our discussion on those aspects of the clauses that either require some explanation or present you with choices.

A. Entire Agreement

This clause (sometimes referred to by lawyers as an "integration clause") provides that all aspects of your agreements with each other have been included in the prenup. By requiring everything to be in one written document, it prevents confusion down the road.

If you live together before you marry, it's a good idea to include in your prenup any matters you agreed on previously that you want to carry forward into your marriage. Then, include language that makes it clear that any prior agreements between you are replaced by the terms in the prenup ("superseded") unless specifically excluded.

> **EXAMPLE:** Trevor and Rebecca have lived together for five years. They put this clause in their agreement:

Entire Agreement

This Agreement contains our entire agreement on the matters covered. Any oral representations made concerning This Agreement shall be of no force or effect. This Agreement supersedes any written or oral agreements or understandings between us prior to the date of This Agreement. Each of us hereby waives any and all claims we might have against the other arising out of our cohabitation prior to the date of our marriage.

B. Binding Effect of Agreement

This clause makes it clear that you expect your premarital agreement—after you sign it—to be legally binding on you and on anyone benefiting from or carrying out your estate plan.

Once we sign This Agreement, it shall be binding on us and our respective inheritors and estate representatives.

C. Commitment to Carry Out This Agreement

After you marry, you will probably need to take some steps to fulfill the terms of your prenup. For example, if you have agreed to set up a joint bank account for paying bills, you'll need to go to the bank and open up the account. Or if your prenup says you'll transfer property into both of your names, or that one of you will be added as a beneficiary of life insurance or retirement benefits, you'll have to take care of those things.

This clause makes it clear that you expect to do what is necessary to implement the agreement once you are married.

> Each of us shall take any steps that are reasonably necessary to carry out the terms and intent of This Agreement, including signing, notarizing, and delivering any necessary documents, upon request by the other party.

D. Modification of This Agreement

To make it less likely that something you do or say could be interpreted incorrectly as modifying your agreement, we recommend including this clause:

> This Agreement may be modified only by a subsequent written agreement signed by both of us. Any oral or written statements made by us (other than express representations in a subsequent written agreement), including but not limited to statements referring to Separate Property as "ours" or to Marital Property as "mine," "yours," "his," or "hers" (or another possessive) will be only for convenience and will not be deemed to modify This Agreement in any way. The filing of joint or separate tax returns during our marriage will not be deemed to modify This Agreement in any way.

E. Voluntary Transfers and Restoration of Rights

This clause is intended to prevent an inadvertent modification of your agreement by providing that either of you can be more generous to the other than the prenup requires, without changing the agreement. We recommend that you include it.

Nothing in This Agreement prevents either of us from making a voluntary transfer of an interest in property to the other party, and any such transfer, once completed, shall be deemed a gift, unless This Agreement or a subsequent written agreement provides otherwise.

During our marriage, or upon death, either of us is free to restore to the other party any legal right waived in This Agreement.

Absent an express written agreement modifying This Agreement, any voluntary transfer or restoration of a right will not be deemed an amendment of This Agreement nor a waiver of the terms of This Agreement.

F. Interpretation and Choice of Law

This clause accomplishes three things. First, it states your intent to have your agreement interpreted in a fair and straightforward manner. Second, it points to the state law to be followed when interpreting or enforcing your agreement. In our mobile society, it's wise to specify that the laws you consider applicable when you make your agreement are the laws that apply no matter where you end up living. Third, it provides that you can use a copy of the signed agreement to establish the terms of the agreement in any future legal proceeding. Hopefully, you won't misplace the signed original of your prenup, but in case you do, this allows you to use a copy in court without jumping through a lot of legal hoops.

This Agreement has been drafted and entered into in the State of California. It shall be interpreted fairly and simply, and enforced according to the laws of California. A copy of This Agreement may be submitted to the court and admitted into evidence in place of the original in any proceeding to enforce or interpret This Agreement.

G. Severability

To prevent a court from tossing out your whole agreement if one clause is found unenforceable, we recommend that you include this clause:

> If any part of This Agreement is determined by a court to be invalid, illegal, or unenforceable, the validity and enforceability of the remaining parts of This Agreement shall not be affected.

H. Attorneys' Fees

We hope, as you do, that you never get near a courthouse with your agreement, and that it happily gathers dust among your important papers. But if you do end up in a legal dispute over the matters covered by your prenuptial agreement, this clause can discourage ill-founded legal arguments by requiring the losing party to pay the winning party's legal expenses.

> In any proceeding to enforce or interpret the terms of This Agreement, the prevailing party shall be entitled to recover their reasonable expenses incurred in connection with the proceeding, including reasonable attorneys' fees.

Optional Clauses Regarding Periodic Reviews and Dispute Resolution

Here, we give you three optional clauses: one requiring regular reviews of the agreement, and two containing provisions for resolving future disagreements. We suggest you read through them and then pick any or all that suit you, adapting them as you see fit. If you use one or more of these clauses, remember to assign them sequential letters in your agreement.

Periodic Reviews [OPTIONAL]

The future is bound to bring changes, and it's smart to review your premarital agreement from time to time. You'll want to make sure the provisions still make sense to you and tweak any clauses that might need updating.

While you don't have to include a requirement that you review your prenup, doing so might make it more likely you'll actually get to it. If you add this clause to your agreement, be sure to specify a reasonable time frame for the reviews. Somewhere between every other year to every seven years is probably right. For example, Karen and Russ agree to look over their prenup every five years.

> We agree to review the terms of This Agreement every five years during the month of January, beginning in January 20xx.

Mediation of Disputes [OPTIONAL]

Mediation is a private, voluntary way to work through a disagreement. In mediation, you and your spouse would meet with a mediator, a neutral third party whose job is to help you reach an agreement. The mediator has no authority to impose a decision, but is there to facilitate a productive, solution-oriented conversation. The goal is to resolve disagreements between spouses without court intervention. Of course, there's no guarantee that mediation will be successful. Still, because it's both private and informal, it's almost always worth a try. If you want to commit to giving mediation a try, you can include this clause in your prenup.

> If any dispute arises between us concerning any terms of This Agreement, we will first try to resolve the dispute in mediation with a qualified mediator acceptable to both of us.
>
> We will share the expenses of mediation equally. The mediation sessions shall be confidential, and neither of us may subpoena the records of the mediator or call the mediator as a witness in any arbitration or other legal proceeding between us.

Arbitration of Disputes [OPTIONAL]

Use this clause if you want to submit any dispute over your prenup to private arbitration, either instead of mediation or in the event a mediation is unsuccessful. There are pros and cons to arbitration.

Submitting a disagreement to arbitration is much like having it decided by a judge: In both instances, the case is heard by a neutral third party who listens to the evidence and the arguments and then decides the case. However, an arbitrator is selected and paid by the disputing parties, whereas a judge is paid and appointed by the state.

Arbitration gives you more choice over who decides your case, but it can also make it more expensive, because you are footing the bill. Arbitration is usually (but not always) a faster process than trial in a court. Arbitration is also private, so you might be able to protect sensitive information from becoming public record. In most states, the decision of an arbitrator can be appealed only in very limited circumstances. Although this more private process has the benefit of providing quick closure, overturning the arbitrator's decision—even if it's clearly wrong—can be difficult.

In short, requiring arbitration won't be right for every couple. Consider getting some good legal advice before deciding whether to include this provision in your premarital agreement.

For example, Karen and Russ decide that arbitration makes sense for them because it is private. They hope not to have any dispute that would need to be decided by a third party, but if it happens, they would prefer to avoid any gossip that could affect their business reputations. So they include the arbitration clause in their prenup:

> If a dispute between us concerning This Agreement cannot be resolved in mediation, then we agree to submit the dispute to binding arbitration within thirty (30) days after either of us makes a written demand. If we cannot agree on an arbitrator, each of us shall appoint one person and the persons so appointed shall select the arbitrator. Participation in arbitration, or a waiver of arbitration by both of us, is required before either of us brings any legal action concerning the matters covered by This Agreement, unless the law prohibits arbitration of the disputed issue(s).

Paragraph 10: Signatures, Acknowledgments, and Attorneys' Certifications

You and your lawyers sign and date the agreement in this final paragraph of your prenup. Its contents are simple and essential.

We start with a place for the date and your signatures. This is followed by a page in which each lawyer certifies that they have thoroughly reviewed the agreement with you. You have two options: The first alternative is more detailed and attests that you are signing the agreement freely and voluntarily.

However, because some lawyers are reluctant to sign a certificate that could put the lawyer in the position of being called as a witness if the agreement is challenged in court, we give you a second alternative that is much more basic. Your lawyers might want to modify or replace this part with their own forms. (See Chapter 10 for more on working with lawyers.) If you've decided against using lawyers, you should delete this page.

The next page contains notary certificates. Many states require prenups to be notarized. Legalities aside, it's a good idea to ensure the authenticity of your signatures by notarizing them. The form we've given you is just an example. Some states have specific requirements for the notary form; the notary should be able to provide what you need.

You can find more information about signing your agreement in Chapter 10. For an example of Paragraph 10 as it would appear in an agreement, see Steven and Freda's prenup at the end of this chapter.

Assembling the Pages of Your Draft

After you have selected the clauses that go in each paragraph of your draft prenup—including any of the optional paragraphs discussed in Chapter 8—you should put them in order and attach to them copies of the schedules containing your written disclosures. A suggested format for the disclosure schedules is included in Appendix C and on the book's companion page. You can find an example of the completed schedules in Steven and Freda's agreement at the end of this chapter.

Make one copy of the whole packet for each of you. You now have a draft that you can turn into a binding agreement—with help from your lawyers, if you are working with lawyers. Congratulate yourselves on a job well done. When you're ready, continue on to Chapter 10.

Sample Prenups

To give you an idea of what your completed prenup might look like, here are some samples. The first is an excerpt from Karen and Russ's agreement, showing in detail how they decided to handle property they each owned before their marriage. That's followed by the complete, simple prenup made by Steven and Freda.

Excerpt from Karen and Russ's Prenup

Paragraph 6: Ownership of Premarital Assets

A. All Premarital Assets and Property Traceable to Them Remain Separate Property

Except as specified elsewhere in This Agreement, Karen's premarital assets, which are listed on Schedule 1, and all property traceable to those assets, shall continue to be her Separate Property after we marry. "All property traceable to those assets" means any growth in value of those assets, including growth in value arising as a direct or indirect result of the efforts of one or both of us during our marriage. It also means any sales proceeds of those assets, any asset purchased with the sales proceeds, or any asset(s) acquired in exchange for those assets, as long as the sales proceeds or any such new asset is held in the sole name of Karen.

Except as specified elsewhere in This Agreement, Russ's premarital assets, which are listed on Schedule 2, and all property traceable to those assets, shall continue to be his Separate Property after we marry. "All property traceable to those assets" means any growth in value of those assets, including growth in value arising as a direct or indirect result of the efforts of one or both of us during our marriage. It also means any sales proceeds of those assets, any asset purchased with the sales proceeds, or any asset(s) acquired in exchange for those assets, as long as the sales proceeds or any such new asset is held in the sole name of Russ.

B. Real Estate Will Remain Separate Property

During our marriage, we plan to reside in Karen's home located at 56 Bell Street, Sacramento, California. The home shall continue to be Karen's Separate Property after we marry, regardless of how we refer to it or how long we live there. Use of Community Property funds to pay any mortgage payments, property taxes, insurance, improvements, repairs, or other expenses for the property or time spent by one or both of us fixing it up will not alter the Separate Property nature of the home. Such payments will not be reimbursable to the Community Property estate unless we sign a written agreement expressly providing otherwise. Any increase in the home's value shall also be Karen's Separate Property. If Karen sells the home or exchanges it for another asset, any sales proceeds or asset acquired in exchange will be her Separate Property.

Excerpt from Karen and Russ's Prenup (continued)

Russ plans to rent out his home at 247 Stone Creek Drive, Sacramento, California, after we marry. The home shall continue to be Russ's Separate Property after we marry, regardless of how we refer to it or whether we ever live there. Use of Community Property funds to pay any mortgage payments, property taxes, insurance, improvements, repairs, or other expenses for the property or time spent by one or both of us fixing it up will not alter the Separate Property nature of the home. Such payments will not be reimbursable to the Community Property estate unless we sign a written agreement expressly providing otherwise. Any increase in the home's value shall also be Russ's Separate Property. If Russ sells the home or exchanges it for another asset, any sales proceeds or asset acquired in exchange will be his Separate Property.

C. Premarital Professional Practice Will Be Subject to Apportionment Between Separate and Community Property

During our marriage, Karen plans to continue to operate the veterinary practice known as Valley Pet Hospital, and Russ will provide bookkeeping services to the practice. After we marry, the practice will be subject to apportionment between Karen's Separate Property and our Community Property as follows.

If Russ predeceases Karen, the practice, including any increase in its value during our marriage, will be entirely Karen's Separate Property.

If Karen predeceases Russ, or if we divorce, the practice shall be appraised as of the date of Karen's death or the date of our separation (whichever is applicable). The appraisal shall be performed by Faultless Business Appraisal Co., or by another appraiser jointly selected by us. From the appraised value, an amount equal to the value of the practice as of the date of our marriage (as set forth on Schedule 1, attached to This Agreement), plus $10,000 for each of the first five years of our marriage, shall be apportioned to Karen's Separate Property. The excess value, if any, shall be apportioned to Community Property.

If the practice is sold during our marriage, the above provisions will apply to apportionment of the sales proceeds. However, instead of appraising the practice, the value at sale will be equal to the net sales proceeds after deducting costs of sale and any taxes due on the sale.

Freda and Steven's Prenup

Prenuptial Agreement
of
Freda Hoyle and Steven Kawamoto

Paragraph 1: Introductory Facts

A. Parties

This Agreement is between Freda Hoyle and Steven Kawamoto. We refer to ourselves by our first names in This Agreement.

B. Purpose of Agreement

We plan to marry on June 5, 20xx. The purpose of This Agreement is to identify our premarital assets and debts and to define our mutual rights and obligations regarding property and finances after we marry.

C. Current Circumstances

Freda currently resides at 123 Hightower Street, Chicago, Illinois. Her occupation is teacher. She has no children.

Steven currently resides at 6578 Maplethorne Avenue, Des Plaines, Illinois. His occupation is sales manager. He has no children.

Paragraph 2: Effective Date and Term

A. Effective Date of Agreement

This Agreement will be effective on the day we marry. If we do not marry, This Agreement will be null and void.

B. Term of Agreement

After we marry, This Agreement will remain in full force and effect indefinitely, unless and until we sign a new written agreement revoking or modifying This Agreement.

Paragraph 3: Legal Representation

A. Representation of Freda

Freda has been represented by Pat McNight, Esq., in the negotiation and drafting of This Agreement. Freda has fully discussed the terms of This Agreement with her attorney and is voluntarily choosing to sign This Agreement.

Freda and Steven's Prenup (continued)

B. Representation of Steven

Steven has been represented by Martine Neilsen, Esq., in the negotiation and drafting of This Agreement. Steven has fully discussed the terms of This Agreement with his attorney and is voluntarily choosing to sign This Agreement.

C. Drafting of Agreement

This Agreement was drafted through the joint efforts of Steven and Freda and their attorneys.

Paragraph 4: Disclosures

A. Freda's Disclosures

All of Freda's assets and all of her debts are listed on Schedule 1, attached to This Agreement. Freda's income for the calendar year 20xx is also listed on Schedule 1. Freda has provided the information on Schedule 1 in good faith. The values and other financial information on Schedule 1 are approximations and might not be exact, but they are intended to present a full, fair, and reasonable disclosure of Freda's assets, debts, income, and personal expenses as of the time they were presented to Steven.

B. Steven's Disclosures

All of Steven's assets and all of his debts are listed on Schedule 2, attached to This Agreement. Steven's income for the calendar year 20xx is also listed on Schedule 2. Steven has provided the information on Schedule 2 in good faith. The values and other financial information on Schedule 2 are approximations and might not be exact, but they are intended to present a full, fair, and reasonable disclosure of Steven's assets, debts, income, and personal expenses as of the time they were presented to Freda.

C. Acknowledgment of Receipt of Disclosures

Freda received a copy of Schedule 2 on February 22, 20xx. Freda reviewed this information before signing This Agreement.

Steven received a copy of Schedule 1 on February 25, 20xx. Steven reviewed this information before signing This Agreement.

Freda first received a draft of This Agreement on February 22, 20xx. This Agreement has been revised since that date, and Freda received the final draft of This Agreement on March 2, 20xx.

Freda and Steven's Prenup (continued)

Steven first received a draft of This Agreement on February 22, 20xx. This Agreement has been revised since that date, and Steven received the final draft of This Agreement on March 2, 20xx.

Paragraph 5: Definitions

A. This Agreement

The term "This Agreement" refers to the provisions of this document, once signed by us, as modified by any subsequent amendments in writing signed by us.

B. Separate Property

Any asset designated as one person's "Separate Property" in This Agreement belongs exclusively to that person. A spouse has the sole right to manage and dispose of their Separate Property assets. Separate Property is not subject to division between us if we divorce. However, if the owner of Separate Property dies, the surviving spouse might have a legal claim to it, unless they have signed a valid written waiver in This Agreement or in another document.

C. Marital Property

An asset designated as "Marital Property" in This Agreement might be subject to division between us by a court if we divorce, and the surviving spouse might have a legal claim to it, unless the surviving spouse has signed a valid written waiver in This Agreement or in another document.

D. Divorce

The term "Divorce" in This Agreement refers to any legal proceeding to end or alter our marital relationship, including a proceeding for divorce, dissolution of marriage, total or absolute divorce, legal separation, or separate maintenance.

Paragraph 6: Ownership of Premarital Assets

All Premarital Assets and Property Traceable to Them Remain Separate Property
Except as specified elsewhere in This Agreement, Freda's premarital assets (which are listed on Schedule 1), and all property traceable to those assets, shall continue to be her Separate Property after we marry. "All property traceable to those assets" means any growth in value of those assets, not including growth in value arising as

Prenuptial Agreement—Page 3

Freda and Steven's Prenup (continued)

a direct or indirect result of the efforts of one or both of us during our marriage. It also means any sales proceeds of those assets, any asset purchased with the sales proceeds, or any asset(s) acquired in exchange for those assets, as long as the sales proceeds or any such new asset is held in the sole name of Freda.

Except as specified elsewhere in This Agreement, Steven's premarital assets (which are listed on Schedule 2), and all property traceable to those assets, shall continue to be his Separate Property after we marry. "All property traceable to those assets" means any growth in value of those assets, not including growth in value arising as a direct or indirect result of the efforts of one or both of us during our marriage. It also means any sales proceeds of those assets, any asset purchased with the sales proceeds, or any asset(s) acquired in exchange for those assets, as long as the sales proceeds or any such new asset is held in the sole name of Steven.

Paragraph 7: Ownership of Assets Acquired During Marriage

**Ownership of Assets Acquired During Marriage Will
Be Determined According to State Law**

Except as specified elsewhere in This Agreement, our rights in every asset acquired after we marry and in any profits or growth in value or any sales proceeds or asset acquired in exchange for those assets, will be determined in accordance with the laws of Illinois.

Paragraph 8: Responsibility for Debts and Expenses

Each Person Solely Responsible for Own Premarital Debts

Freda's debts listed on Schedule 1 are her sole and separate debts. Steven will not be responsible for them, nor may his Separate Property or his share of any Marital Property be used to pay them without his written consent. Freda will indemnify and hold Steven harmless from any proceeding to collect on Freda's debts from Steven's Separate Property, and she will be solely responsible for any expenses, including attorneys' fees, incurred by Steven in connection with such a proceeding.

Steven's debts listed on Schedule 2 are his sole and separate debts. Freda will not be responsible for them, nor may her Separate Property or her share of any Marital Property be used to pay them without her written consent. Steven will indemnify and hold Freda harmless from any proceeding to collect on Steven's debts

Freda and Steven's Prenup (continued)

from Freda's Separate Property, and he will be solely responsible for any expenses, including attorneys' fees, incurred by Freda in connection with such a proceeding.

Paragraph 9: Interpretation, Modification, Review, and Enforcement of This Agreement

A. Entire Agreement

This Agreement contains our entire agreement on the matters covered. Any oral representations made concerning This Agreement shall be of no force or effect.

B. Binding Effect of Agreement

Once we sign This Agreement, it shall be binding on us and our respective inheritors and estate representatives.

C. Commitment to Carry Out This Agreement

Each of us shall take any steps that are reasonably necessary to carry out the terms and intent of This Agreement, including signing, notarizing, and delivering any necessary documents, upon request by the other party.

D. Modification of This Agreement

This Agreement may be modified only by a subsequent written agreement signed by both of us. Any oral or written statements made by us (other than express representations in a subsequent written agreement), including but not limited to statements referring to Separate Property as "ours" or to Marital Property as "mine," "yours," "his," or "hers" (or another possessive) will be only for convenience and will not be deemed to modify This Agreement in any way. The filing of joint or separate tax returns during our marriage will not be deemed to modify This Agreement in any way.

E. Voluntary Transfers and Restoration of Rights

Nothing in This Agreement prevents either of us from making a voluntary transfer of an interest in property to the other party, and any such transfer, once completed, shall be deemed a gift, unless This Agreement or a subsequent written agreement provides otherwise.

During our marriage, or upon death, either of us is free to restore to the other party any legal right waived in This Agreement.

Prenuptial Agreement—Page 5

Freda and Steven's Prenup (continued)

Absent an express written agreement, any voluntary transfer or restoration of a right will not be deemed an amendment of This Agreement nor a waiver of the terms of This Agreement.

F. Interpretation and Choice of Law

This Agreement has been drafted and entered into in the State of Illinois. It shall be interpreted fairly and simply, and enforced according to the laws of Illinois. A copy of This Agreement may be submitted to the court and admitted into evidence in place of the original in any proceeding to enforce or interpret This Agreement.

G. Severability

If any part of This Agreement is determined by a court to be invalid, illegal, or unenforceable, the validity and enforceability of the remaining parts of This Agreement shall not be affected.

H. Attorneys' Fees

In any proceeding to enforce or interpret the terms of This Agreement, the prevailing party shall be entitled to recover his or her reasonable expenses incurred in connection with the proceeding, including reasonable attorneys' fees.

Paragraph 10: Signatures, Acknowledgments, and Attorneys' Certifications

Each of us has read This Agreement carefully and is signing it freely after obtaining all advice he or she considers appropriate.

Dated: _March 30, 20xx_   _Freda Hoyle_ _____
Freda Hoyle

Dated: _March 30, 20xx_   _Steven Kawamoto_ _____
Steven Kawamoto

Freda and Steven's Prenup (continued)

Certificate of Attorney for Freda Hoyle

I certify, as attorney for Freda Hoyle only, that she has freely and voluntarily signed the attached premarital agreement. I have advised Freda Hoyle about the legal effects of the terms of This Agreement, and she has had a full opportunity to discuss it with me and with any other advisers of her own choosing. I believe that she has been fully advised and that she is aware of all the legal effects of This Agreement. This certificate does not constitute a waiver of attorney-client privilege.

Dated: _March 30, 20xx_   _Pat McNight_
                                  Pat McNight

Certificate of Attorney for Steven Kawamoto

I certify, as attorney for Steven Kawamoto only, that he has freely and voluntarily signed the attached premarital agreement. I have advised Steven Kawamoto about the legal effects of the terms of This Agreement, and he has had a full opportunity to discuss it with me and with any other advisers of his own choosing. I believe that he has been fully advised and that he is aware of all the legal effects of This Agreement. This certificate does not constitute a waiver of attorneyclient privilege.

Dated: _March 30, 20xx_   _Martine Neilsen_
                                  Martine Neilsen

Prenuptial Agreement—Page 7

Freda and Steven's Prenup (continued)

Certificate of Acknowledgment of Notary Public

State of Illinois } ss
County of Cook }

On <u>March 30, 20xx</u> , before me, <u>Roger Glenfield</u> , personally appeared <u>Freda Hoyle</u> , who proved to me on the basis of satisfactory evidence to be the person whose name is subscribed to the within instrument, and acknowledged to me that she executed the same and that by her signature on the instrument she executed the instrument.

WITNESS my hand and official seal.

I certify under PENALTY OF PERJURY under the laws of the state of Illinois that the foregoing paragraph is true and correct.

[NOTARIAL SEAL]   *Roger Glenfield*
Notary Public

My commission expires <u>April 20xx</u>

Certificate of Acknowledgment of Notary Public

State of Illinois } ss
County of Cook }

On <u>March 30, 20xx</u> , before me, <u>Roger Glenfield</u> , personally appeared <u>Steven Kawamoto</u> , who proved to me on the basis of satisfactory evidence to be the person whose name is subscribed to the within instrument, and acknowledged to me that he executed the same and that by his signature on the instrument he executed the instrument.

I certify under PENALTY OF PERJURY under the laws of the state of Illinois that the foregoing paragraph is true and correct.

WITNESS my hand and official seal.

[NOTARIAL SEAL]   *Roger Glenfield*
Notary Public

My commission expires <u>April 20xx</u>

Prenuptial Agreement—Page 8

Freda and Steven's Prenup (continued)

Schedule 1—Freda's Disclosures

Premarital Assets

Description	Approximate Value
Household furnishings	$ 3,500
Personal computer & software	$ 5,000
Diamond ring and other jewelry	$ 6,000
20xx Honda Accord Sedan LX	$ 22,000
Retirement benefits with the Teachers' Retirement System of the State of Illinois	$ 70,000
ABC Brokerage, Account # xxx 3492	$ 50,000

Premarital Debts

To Whom Owed	Approximate Balance
None	

Freda's Annual Income (Calendar Year 20xx): $45,000

February 17, 20xx	*FH*
Date Prepared	Initials
February 17, 20xx	*SK*
Date Prepared	Initials

Schedule 1—Page 1

Freda and Steven's Prenup (continued)

Schedule 2—Steven's Disclosures

Premarital Assets

Description	Approximate Value
Furnishings	$ 4,000
Entertainment Center	$ 5,000
Bluemeadow Tennis Club Membership	$ 21,000
20xx Toyota RAV4	$ 19,250
Benefits with the Employee Profit Sharing Plan and Trust of XYZ Sales, Inc.	$130,000

Premarital Debts

To Whom Owed	Approximate Balance
Bank of Illinois Visa, Account # xxxx xxxx xxxx 1234	$ 1,800

Steven's Annual Income (Calendar Year 20xx): $45,000

February 17, 20xx   *SK*
Date Prepared   Initials

February 17, 20xx   *FH*
Date Prepared   Initials

Schedule 2—Page 1

Turning Your Draft Into a Binding Agreement

After you select the clauses for your prenup and assemble them in a draft, you're ready to turn the draft into a legally binding document. To begin, you'll take the draft to separate lawyers (unless you've decided to throw caution to the wind and proceed without them). Then you or your lawyers will make any final changes to the draft to ensure that it is clear and legally sound. Finally, you'll arrange for one last review of the written agreement before signing it and tucking it safely away prior to the big day.

Finishing Up: A Checklist

This chapter walks you through each of the following steps:
- interviewing and selecting lawyers
- giving your draft prenup to the lawyers for review
- making any changes necessary to finalize your document
- reviewing your prenup one last time to be sure it says exactly what you want it to say and that you understand every part of it, and
- signing the final agreement in the manner required by the laws of your state.

Planning Ahead

As we discussed in Chapter 1, you should give yourselves at least three months to complete your premarital agreement. Unless you've already hired lawyers, finding and selecting a good representative for each of you might take some time. It's not uncommon to be told that you'll have to wait several weeks for an initial appointment with a lawyer. And after you choose lawyers, you'll need enough time to discuss any changes they suggest, plus time to prepare and review the final document. Realistically, this means that you should start the process of contacting and meeting with lawyers several months prior to the wedding.

Finding Good Lawyers

We cannot emphasize strongly enough how important it is that each of you finds a competent lawyer who will carefully review your prenup and sign it to indicate that they've advised you about the document.

> **SKIP AHEAD**
>
> **When to skip this section.** If you both are already working with good lawyers, you can skip ahead to "Preparing the Formal Agreement." But if you need help selecting a lawyer or if you want tips for dealing with lawyers, read on.

The ideal lawyer to consult in connection with a prenup is one who is experienced in preparing prenuptial agreements and who has expertise in the area of family law, including property issues and divorce. It's a plus, although less common, to find a lawyer who also has some experience with estate planning issues. You want a lawyer who has good communication skills and who can advise each of you about your best interests while working with the other person's lawyer collaboratively— that is, without becoming adversarial in the process.

It might be difficult to find one lawyer who has the expertise to address all facets of your situation. For this reason, some experts recommend having a team of professionals help you craft your prenup. Typically, the team includes a family lawyer, an estate planning lawyer, and a tax lawyer or CPA. If your prenup involves complex estate planning, tax, and property issues—and if you can afford the additional lawyers' fees—you might want to consider the team approach. Start by finding one key professional who can assemble the rest of the "team."

> **TIP**
>
> **Be prepared.** Using this book to write out the basics of your prenup before asking your lawyers to draft or finalize the specifics can help you save money and avoid conflict. Stick with what you've agreed on unless there's a really good reason to make a change.

Consider a Collaborative Approach

One way to avoid having the process become adversarial is to use a "collaborative law" process. In collaborative law, the lawyers and their clients make a commitment to work together, usually in "four-way" meetings, to come up with an agreement that meets the needs of both parties. This nonadversarial approach began as a way to minimize acrimony in divorce cases, but it is catching on in the prenup arena, too. Consider asking about this option as you look for lawyers to represent you.

A Note About Lawyers' Fees

Many lawyers charge by the hour and often ask for a significant payment in advance—called a "retainer." Be prepared for the hourly fee to range as high as $250 to $500, especially in major metropolitan areas.

Some attorneys use a mixed flat/hourly fee structure, in which you pay a set amount for the draft, and then pay hourly for revisions and negotiations with your fiancée's attorney. Whatever fee structure you agree to, be sure to get it in writing.

Make a List of Lawyers to Interview

You and your fiancé can start your search for the right lawyers together by making a list of candidates—at least three or four—to interview and choose from.

Get Referrals

The best way to find names for your list is through referrals. Here are some possible sources of good referrals:

- a lawyer that one of you is already working with—whether it's on the prenup or another legal matter

- a priest, rabbi, minister, or other officiant you've hired to perform your marriage
- a marriage counselor
- a financial adviser or personal banker
- friends, family, and acquaintances
- your local bar association
- group legal services benefits provided through employment or membership in an organization, or
- online lawyer directories, such as Martindale-Hubbell (www.martindale.com).

Coordinate Your Lists

When you have a list of names to choose from, the two of you should divide the list so that you don't create a conflict of interest for any of the lawyers. (This could happen if both of you call the same lawyer—or even lawyers at the same firm, because conflict of interest rules prevent lawyers in the same firm from representing both sides to a contract or a dispute.) If one of you already has a lawyer, then the other person can select names from the entire list.

If there's enough time, you can take turns finding a lawyer: After one of you finds a good lawyer, asking that lawyer for a referral might be the best way to locate a lawyer for the other person. If there's not enough time, both of you will be interviewing lawyers at the same time. In that case, you might want to compare notes as you go.

It's also a good idea to decide in advance which person's lawyer will take the lead in preparing the final document. As a matter of logistics and cost savings, it usually makes more sense to have all drafts prepared by one office, even when both sides are contributing ideas and wording. It doesn't really matter whose lawyer will take the lead—you can even flip a coin to decide. The key is to avoid costly duplication of efforts. Be open to a different arrangement if your lawyers suggest it; there might be reasons why your situation calls for a different approach.

Interview and Select a Lawyer

After dividing the list of potential lawyers between you, you're ready to set up interviews and select the lawyers who will represent each of you. This is something you'll do separately.

Make Appointments

With your list in front of you, decide how many appointments you will start with. The number of initial appointments you make might be influenced by what you can afford. Many lawyers—especially experienced ones—charge for initial consultations, so be prepared to pay for the lawyer's time.

If your budget allows, consider making appointments with two or three candidates before making your selection. Or simply start at the top of the list and make one appointment at a time until you meet someone who seems like a good fit.

When you make an appointment, be prepared to give some basic information, including your name and the name of your fiancé (for conflict of interest screening), your address, your phone number, and so forth. Be sure to let the office know that you want an appointment to discuss possible representation regarding a prenuptial agreement. Your initial contact with the office will likely be with a receptionist or secretary, who will schedule you for an in-person appointment.

Remember to ask about the lawyer's fee for the initial appointment so there will be no surprises later on.

Interview Prospective Lawyers

Your initial appointment is an opportunity to find out whether you are comfortable with the lawyer. Take some time to prepare for the appointment. You might want to make a list of questions about the lawyer's experience and qualifications. (See "Questions to Ask a Prospective Prenup Lawyer," below.) Then review your draft prenup and any notes you've made. Jot down any questions you have so you can make the appointment as efficient as possible.

Take your notes and draft prenup with you to the appointment. Tell the lawyer a little about yourself and your situation. Then let the lawyer know you have some questions. Start with any questions about the lawyer's qualifications and approach; then, if you still feel comfortable, show the lawyer your draft and move on to your questions about it. Refer to your notes as you go along and make sure you've covered everything before you leave the office.

You should receive direct answers to your questions about the lawyer's qualifications and experience. You probably won't get answers to all your questions about the specifics of your prenup until you've officially hired the attorney and they've had a chance to review your draft. But bringing up your questions at the first appointment will make for a more meaningful conversation during your initial meeting and give the lawyer a focus for reviewing your draft prenup later.

Questions to Ask a Prospective Prenup Lawyer

You can ask some or all of the following questions to ascertain the lawyer's qualifications and basic approach to writing up a prenup.

- What is your experience and expertise in:
  - advising clients who want prenups
  - drafting prenups
  - divorce and separation issues, and
  - estate planning?
- If the lawyer does not have divorce or estate planning expertise: How do you handle divorce or estate planning issues that come up in prenups?
- What is your attitude toward prenups? Do you think they are a good idea or not?
- Are you willing to take the draft we've worked out together and help us turn it into a binding agreement?
- If so, how would you go about this?
- How long do you think it will take to review and finalize the agreement?
- How much do you think it will cost, and what would be the arrangement for payment?

After the appointment, reflect on your experience. Were your questions answered clearly? Were you treated respectfully? Do you feel that the lawyer understood your concerns? If you can answer yes to these questions, and if you are satisfied with the lawyer's qualifications and pricing, you might not need to look any further. If you are uncertain or uncomfortable with how things went in the appointment, interview other candidates. It's important to find someone you feel good about: You'll be spending both money and time on a lawyer—not to mention the fact that your future happiness and security might be affected by the lawyer's advice.

Preparing the Formal Agreement

After you choose the lawyers who will help you finish your prenuptial agreement, the process of drawing up the formal document begins in earnest. The lawyers will probably start by thoroughly reviewing your draft. What happens next depends on how the lawyers divide up the job of preparing the formal agreement, and on whether any new provisions or changes need to be worked out. Here's how to work with your lawyers to make this part of the experience as constructive and efficient as possible.

Provide a Written Draft or an Outline

Providing your lawyer with a carefully considered and thorough draft prenup will help you make the best use of your lawyer's time. A written plan—whether it's a draft containing actual clauses or a detailed written outline—will streamline the process and help avoid miscommunications. (Even if one lawyer is designated to prepare the formal draft, it is a good idea to provide both lawyers with a draft or an outline of what you've agreed to. This will give your lawyer a sense of what to expect from the other lawyer and it will help your lawyer alert you to potential problems so you can deal with them before the formal agreement is prepared.)

When reviewing your draft or outline, your lawyer might ask why you chose certain clauses and request additional information about your financial situation. Normally, the lawyer will meet with you after reviewing the draft to make suggestions, express any concerns, and answer any questions you might have.

Be Flexible

Every lawyer has an individual approach to advising clients and drafting legal documents, so what happens in your case depends to some extent on your lawyer's process. And your situation is even more unique because you will be dealing with the styles of two different lawyers. Not to worry. Good lawyers are used to working with other lawyers and their clients on collaborative drafting projects, so the whole process should go smoothly. Just know that not every step can be predicted in advance, and be ready to adapt as needed.

For example, be prepared for your draft to undergo a significant transformation before you sign it. Most lawyers have their own forms containing standard clauses drafted with state law in mind. The lawyer preparing the formal agreement might be reluctant to use the organization and clauses contained in your draft if they vary too greatly from the lawyer's preferred format.

It's also possible that it will be more cost effective for the lawyer to use their own form rather than take the time to revise your draft to conform to state law. As long as the agreement still says what you intend it to say, be open to a document that looks quite different from what you started with.

Keep the Lines of Communication Open

Even though each of you will work with your own lawyer, it's important to keep each other abreast of the discussions you are having with your lawyers. Keep the process moving by asking your lawyer to give you an estimated date for completion of each step. Then note the date in your calendar and follow up if the date passes without any word from your lawyer. Let your partner know the projected timeline and advise each other of any changes or delays.

If your lawyer tells you that something you've already agreed upon should be changed, make sure you understand the advice and the reasons for it. Then talk with your fiancé about it. See if the proposed change makes sense to the two of you. Have your fiancé run the idea by their lawyer. If either of you still has questions about the proposed change, consider scheduling a four-way meeting with the two of you and your lawyers present.

Successfully finalizing a prenup is a joint effort. Whatever you do, keep each other informed about what you're hearing from your lawyers. (If you get stuck and need help communicating with each other about your prenup, see Chapter 11.)

> **CAUTION**
>
> **Keeping things confidential.** Conversations between you and your lawyer are usually private; your lawyer can't disclose the details later—even if asked to testify in court—unless you consent. But if you tell someone else (even your fiancé) about what was said, the rule of confidentiality no longer applies to that conversation. We think the value of staying in close communication about your prenup outweighs the loss of confidentiality. But if you find yourself in a special situation where you need to insulate sensitive information from potential disclosure to others, talk to your lawyer about how to proceed without losing the legal protection afforded by lawyer-client confidentiality rules.

Read Each Version Carefully

Be sure to read each version of the proposed final agreement carefully and thoroughly. This is especially important if each lawyer is making revisions as the document goes back and forth, but it's good practice even when just one office is implementing all the changes.

Make your own copy of each draft as you receive it, and write the date you receive it on your copy. If you get a later version, you can compare the two to look for any changes that were supposed to be made and to check for typographical errors. (You can also ask the lawyers to prepare "red-lined" versions that track any changes made. Word processing programs make this easy to do.) Let your lawyer (and each other) know if you find anything amiss.

Guidelines for Working With Your Lawyer

Beyond the specific steps outlined above, here are some general points to keep in mind. Most important is to remember that, like all relationships, your relationship with your lawyer is a two-way street: There are some basic things you can expect from your lawyer and some actions you can take to make the most of both your time and your money.

Communication

Your lawyer should communicate with you clearly and in plain language. By the same token, you'll need to take responsibility for your end of the communication. If you don't understand something, say so. Be persistent. Ask questions until you're sure you get it. Your lawyer should be open to your questions.

Responsiveness

Expect your lawyer to respond to your telephone calls or letters within a reasonable time, usually two or three days for nonurgent phone messages and emails and a week or so for letters. You are not the lawyer's only client, so there will be times when you can't reach your lawyer right away. You can and should expect to hear back soon, however. If there is special urgency, be sure to say so when you leave a message. If you don't get a return call or email within the times we've suggested, call and find out the reason for the delay.

Questions

Every time before you meet with your lawyer, write down your questions and concerns. Leave room to jot down your lawyer's answers and notes about what you plan to do next.

Bring your list with you to the appointment. Tell your lawyer that you have a list of questions and double-check the list at the end of the meeting. Write down notes of your lawyer's answers as you go along. Go as slowly as you need to.

Support People

If you're having trouble focusing and find it difficult to remember your questions or the answers, consider bringing along a support person—a friend or family member—when you meet with the lawyer. Be sure to clear this with your lawyer ahead of time, and consider whether there is any need to maintain the legal privilege of lawyer-client confidentiality. As we mention above, the rule of confidentiality no longer applies if another person learns the details of a conversation with a lawyer. Normally, this won't be a concern. If it is, discuss with your lawyer how to best handle the situation. For example, you might decide to have a support person present for some but not all of the discussions with your lawyer.

If you bring a support person, ask them to take notes for you during the meeting. Some people also find it helpful to tape-record their meetings with their lawyer. If you think this would be useful, be sure to discuss it with your lawyer in advance.

Summing Up Meetings

Before you end a meeting with your lawyer, review what's been discussed and ask your lawyer to summarize the next steps to be taken and to give a time frame for each one. Make notes of the steps and the timetable.

Using the Lawyer's Advice

Take seriously the advice you get. Lawyers who work on prenups are sometimes frustrated by clients who just want a lawyer to "sign off" on the agreement and who aren't interested in having a meaningful discussion about its contents.

You are paying a professional to give you advice you wouldn't think of on your own. Make sure you understand the advice and the reasons for it. Consider it carefully before accepting or rejecting it.

If Problems Arise

Hopefully, completing the formal agreement will go smoothly and you won't need to refer to this next section at all. If you do hit a snag, chances are it will fall into one of two categories:

- You have a problem with your lawyer.
- There's trouble between you and your fiancé.

We'll address each of those situations in turn.

Problems With Your Lawyer

Three of the most common problems that can arise when working with a lawyer are:

- communication problems
- unhappiness with the lawyer's work, or
- fee disputes.

Communication Problems

A communication problem between you and your lawyer might be solved with a little constructive attention. If the problem is a lack of responsiveness—for example, your lawyer isn't returning your phone calls or emails, or hasn't communicated with you for an extended period of time—try sending a polite letter setting out your concerns.

In your letter, ask for an appointment to go over your questions and concerns. Let your lawyer know you'll be calling for an appointment, then follow up.

If the problem lies in the actual communications—your lawyer says things you don't understand or doesn't seem to get what you are talking about—start by letting your lawyer know there's a problem. Say you're having trouble following what you're being told and ask your lawyer to rephrase the information. Or explain that you aren't sure your questions or concerns are being heard. Your lawyer might not even know there's a problem. Once you bring it up, your lawyer will probably work harder to communicate well.

If these approaches don't work, consider whether you can continue despite the poor communication. A bad deskside manner doesn't mean that the lawyer doesn't do excellent legal work. But if all else fails, you can look for a new lawyer whose style of communication is more consistent with your own.

Unhappiness With the Lawyer's Work

You might find yourself unhappy with the advice you receive from your lawyer, or you might be dissatisfied with the format or content of the documents your lawyer prepares.

If you're confused by or disagree with the advice you're getting, talk with your lawyer. Ask why the lawyer is advising a certain course of action and what other options might be available to you. Then decide for yourself whether you want to follow the advice, disregard it, or get a second opinion.

A different but related problem arises if your lawyer tells you something about the law that seems to contradict the legal advice your fiancé is getting. Ask your lawyer to help you sort out the reason for the discrepancy. You can always ask the two lawyers to talk to each other and determine whether the issue is a difference of opinion or whether the law itself is not as black and white as it seems. If all else fails, consider getting another lawyer's opinion.

EXAMPLE: Simon's lawyer tells him that his separate property investment in real estate would remain entirely his separate property if he and Elena divorce, even without a prenup to spell that out. Elena's lawyer tells her that the investment would be partly community property in a divorce, unless the prenup makes it separate property. What's going on? Perhaps the legal guidelines aren't clear and the two lawyers interpret them differently. Maybe they're using different factual information in forming their opinions. Or one of them might be wrong about the law.

Simon and Elena ask their lawyers to talk about the problem. As a result, the lawyers learn that they agree on the general legal principles, but each has been making a different factual assumption about the extent of Simon's involvement in managing the asset. After talking, the lawyers agree that it would be impossible to say whether a divorce court would find a partial community property interest in the investment. Based on that conclusion and their lawyers' advice, Simon and Elena then insert a specific provision on the subject in their prenup so that there will be no uncertainty if they divorce later on.

If you find what you think is a mistake in a document your lawyer prepares, bring this to the lawyer's attention. Give the lawyer a copy of the document with the mistakes noted and keep a copy for yourself so you can double-check that the errors have been fixed. Keep a sense of perspective when it comes to typographical errors. Lawyers and their staff are only human; a typo here and there shouldn't be cause for concern if steps are taken to correct them. Repeated or multiple errors, though, might be indications of a bigger problem, and at some point you might decide to take your business elsewhere.

Unhappiness with the actual terms of a document drafted by your lawyer probably derives from a communication problem: You weren't clear about what you intended, your lawyer misunderstood what you meant, or perhaps a bit of both. Talking it through with your lawyer will usually take care of the problem.

Fee Disputes

Avoid problems about fees at the outset by making sure you have a written agreement with your lawyer covering how fees will be charged, when you will be billed, and other details. If you don't pay as you go (at the time of each meeting with your lawyer), ask for a detailed monthly bill and address any problems as soon as they arise.

Maintain your perspective when it comes to fees. Many a great working relationship has been poisoned by disagreements over relatively minor fee amounts. If you are otherwise pleased with your lawyer's performance, consider cutting your lawyer some slack when it comes to the fees. If the fees truly are more than you anticipated, see if your lawyer will agree to a payment plan.

If you end up with a significant dispute about fees and if talking about it doesn't resolve the problem, you might be able to get help from your local or state bar association. Often there is a panel of volunteer lawyers available to review the situation and give an advisory opinion about the fee dispute.

Problems Between the Two of You

If a difficulty arises between you and your fiancé while you're finalizing your agreement, try to figure out what's at the bottom of it. Consider first whether you're reacting to the stress of getting ready for the big day. If that's the case, maybe you need to take a vacation from the whole topic for a day or two, or even longer. Do something fun and relaxing together. The whole situation might look different after you've had a break from it.

If what's going on between you is not just a reaction to pressure, and if you seem to be communicating reasonably well about the subject, you might have a real disagreement about some provision of the prenup. In that case, you'll need to find a way to resolve the disagreement before you can move on—either on your own or with the help of your lawyers or another qualified person (such as a counselor or a mediator). For more on how to deal with disagreements, see Chapter 11.

Preparing an Abstract of the Agreement

In some states, a married person who wants to sell, lease, or borrow against their separate property must have their spouse sign a written consent each time. If you are in this situation and you want to be able to carry out these transactions without obtaining your spouse's consent each time, you can prepare what's called an "abstract" of your prenup and put it on file in the local land records office, to confirm that the property is your separate property and that your spouse has no rights in it. In some places, the abstract is called a "memorandum."

The abstract summarizes the parts of your prenup that contain your agreements about the real estate. You both must sign it in front of a notary public after you are married. Then, you can record the abstract in the county where the real estate is located so that it becomes part of the official county records, just as a deed would be. You could always record your entire prenup as proof of your ownership agreements, but then your prenup would be a public record, available for anyone to see. The advantage of recording an abstract instead of the whole agreement is that you can keep the other parts of your agreement private.

It's convenient to prepare the abstract when the prenup is prepared, but you don't have to do them together. If you're not sure whether you'll need an abstract, you can always prepare and record one later on.

FORM
Check out the sample abstract. If you have any lingering questions about what an abstract should contain and how to format one, check out our sample abstract included at the end of Appendix C and on the book's online companion page.

Signing the Agreement: Formalities and Fun

When the final version of your premarital agreement has been read, reread, and approved, it's time for you and your lawyers to sign it. You can make separate trips to your respective lawyers' offices and sign the agreement there. Logistically, this might be the simplest way to get the necessary signatures, because you'll need to coordinate the schedules of only two people at a time.

If you want to make more of an occasion out of signing the agreement, consider asking for an appointment when the two of you—and both lawyers—can all meet and sign at one time. Or you could have a private signing ceremony of your own, just the two of you, either before or after the lawyers sign their part of the agreement. If you like the idea of signing without your lawyers present, be sure to clear this with your lawyers. They might have reservations about this approach, because there would be no witnesses to call if a question later arises about whether you voluntarily signed the document. Some lawyers even like to videotape the signing as additional insurance against a claim that one of you did not sign voluntarily. (If so, you might want to dress up for the occasion, even though the video might not be one you'll keep on the shelf next to your wedding album.)

Another potential barrier to a completely private signing ceremony is that state law might require you to sign the document in front of others. Although some states simply require that your signatures be acknowledged—that is, authenticated—by a notary public (not necessarily at the time you sign), other states require that you sign in front of the notary or other witnesses. If witnesses other than a notary are required, ask if signing in the presence of your lawyers will do. (See the state summaries on the book's companion page for the requirements in your state; be sure to confirm these with your lawyer.)

If your state law doesn't require witnesses, it's still a good idea to have your signatures notarized to head off any doubt about the fact that you actually signed the agreement. If your agreement will be notarized, ask ahead of time whether your lawyer will provide the notary.

TIP

A note for New Yorkers. If you live in New York, you'll see from your state's information sheet that your agreement must be notarized. But New York allows anyone who is authorized to conduct a marriage ceremony to acknowledge a prenup. (N.Y. Dom. Rel. Law § 236(B)(3).) We're not suggesting that you sign your agreement at the altar, but you might feel more comfortable asking the person who will solemnize the marriage, rather than a notary public, to be present when you sign the agreement and to acknowledge your signatures.

Even if you decide not to make an event out of the signing, consider making a point of acknowledging together the completion of this big and important project. It could be a toast over dinner at your favorite restaurant, a weekend trip to a favorite getaway, or maybe something as simple as a high five or a handshake. Whatever you do, think of some way to congratulate yourselves and to mark this accomplishment before you put the signed agreement away in a safe place and turn your attention to the other details of preparing for your wedding.

Working Together

deally, working together on your prenup will be a positive and constructive experience. But any couple can run into some difficulties when discussing property and money matters. This chapter contains ideas and suggestions to help the process go smoothly.

Because every stage of putting together a prenup involves working together, you might find yourselves referring to this chapter more than once as you go along. Read it the first time to get a general understanding of ways to avoid problems, then turn to it as needed for tips to help you deal with any challenges that arise.

Five Keys to Working Together Successfully

If you keep the following tips in mind, you'll probably find it easier to work together and negotiate at every step of the process. You might even be able to head off problems before they come up.

Know Yourself

Understanding yourself—including your financial goals, your general attitude toward money, your spending and saving habits, and your approach to communicating about those issues—is essential to a healthy and productive partnership in the making of your prenup. If both of you maintain self-awareness as you go, each will always know where the other stands.

The steps outlined in Chapter 3 give you a chance to better understand how you approach financial issues. If you want to expand your self-knowledge beyond the financial realm, consider doing an inventory of your individual approach to a variety of life experiences. (See "Using a Premarital Inventory," just below.) Regardless of whether you limit your self-examination to financial issues or broaden your inquiry, the key is to hone your self-knowledge so that you can deal with each other more clearly.

Using a Premarital Inventory

A premarital inventory helps you investigate what makes you tick—your strengths and weaknesses, your likes and dislikes, your preferences and pet peeves. Many premarital counseling programs offered by religious communities include this kind of inventory. You can also do this work with the help of a licensed counselor.

If you prefer to work on your own, you can research premarital inventories online or take a more general personality inventory using one of the many books available on the market. A classic is *Please Understand Me: Character and Temperament Types*, by David Keirsey and Marilyn Bates (Prometheus Nemesis Book Co.), which offers a simplified version of the Myers-Briggs personality inventory. Other choices include *Discovering Your Personality Type: The Essential Introduction to the Enneagram, Revised and Expanded*, by Don Richard Riso and Russ Hudson (Houghton-Mifflin Co.), and *The 16 Personality Types: Descriptions for Self-Discovery*, by Linda V. Berens and Dario Nardi (Telos Publications).

As long as you don't take tests like these too seriously, they can be a useful, informative, and often entertaining way to focus on some of the differences and similarities between the two of you.

Accept Your Differences

Being able to accept and appreciate the ways in which the two of you are different is the second key to successfully negotiating and drafting your prenup. It's pretty easy to agree on terms when you see eye to eye. The challenge is in finding ways to accommodate your differences. Start with the premise that differences can be a good thing in a relationship—in moderation, of course. Then be prepared to learn about and accept the ways in which you see things differently. You can practice doing this as you work through the material in Chapter 3.

Communicate Effectively

Creating a prenup that works for both of you depends on clear communication. There's a lot more to say about how to communicate effectively. For now, take our word for it that good communication is a key ingredient.

Negotiate Lovingly

It's unlikely that you'll agree on every detail of your prenup, at least in the beginning. You are two different people, with different financial circumstances and backgrounds, and there are bound to be some issues that you'll need to negotiate to a satisfactory conclusion. This doesn't mean that the negotiation needs to be adversarial. On the contrary—your mutual love and respect will give you a foundation from which to negotiate with each other's best interests at heart. We call this negotiating lovingly, and this chapter offers more suggestions on how to proceed.

Accentuate the Positive

Last, but not least, maintaining a positive outlook is key. The whole point of your prenup is to support each other and your relationship by agreeing to clear financial guidelines that will carry you for many years to come. Experts who study marriage conclude that maintaining a positive attitude toward each other and the relationship is a critical factor in the health of a marriage.

By maintaining an open and constructive outlook toward the experience of making your prenup, you'll not only enhance the chances of ending up with a solid agreement, you'll also practice a life skill that will support your marriage.

A Suggested Approach to Working Together

Here are some simple points to remember each time you work together on your prenup.

Before You Begin

- **Think through your concerns.** Be aware not just of what you want, but why you want it.
- **Prepare to listen.** As you decide what goes into your prenup, try to hear and really understand each other's concerns. What seems like a disagreement might actually be a simple miscommunication.
- **Be open to new ideas.** It often happens that the solution that best addresses your mutual concerns is different from what was first proposed. Being ready to accept fresh ideas will enhance your chances of finding the right approach for your prenup.
- **Set the stage.** Pay attention to when and how you discuss your prenup. Pick a time and place that are conducive to a thoughtful conversation about your agreement. Consider setting a reasonable time limit in advance so that you aren't tempted to bite off more than you can chew at one time.

While You Are Talking

- **Ask for what you want.** Tell your future spouse what you want and why.
- **Speak clearly.** Say what you mean. Communicate what's on your mind specifically and accurately.
- **Listen to understand.** Pay attention to what you are being told, and check to be sure you've heard correctly.
- **Don't interrupt.** Let your fiancé finish their thought before you respond.

If You Run Into Trouble

- **Check your communications so far.** Have you said something unclear? Did you misunderstand each other? (See "Communicating Effectively," below, for suggestions on resolving miscommunications.)
- **Look for options that work for both of you.** If you seem to disagree about some aspect of the prenup, think about whether you're considering both sides. Try to come up with a solution that takes each person's needs into account. (For more on how to do this, see "Negotiating Lovingly," below.)
- **Get help if you need it.** There are times when you're just too close to a situation to understand exactly what's going on, and you're at a loss how to move things forward. If you've tried the suggestions in this chapter and are still having trouble working through an issue, maybe a little help from an outsider—your clergyperson, a wise elder, or a qualified counselor—is what you need. (For tips on finding the right help, see "Work With Advisers," below.)

Communicating Effectively

To create a successful premarital agreement, you'll need to be able to communicate clearly and effectively with each other, with your lawyers, and perhaps with interested family members throughout the process. Understanding what effective communication is—and how to do it—is key.

What Is Communication?

There are undoubtedly many ways to define communication. Because we are talking here about how to craft the terms of a legally binding agreement, we define communication as a statement made by one person (the speaker) that imparts information to another person (the listener). Usually, this type of communication is spoken rather than written, but written communications also follow the same general patterns discussed here.

Using this definition, here are three examples of communication:

"Waiter, there's a fly in my soup."

"Dave, we're giving you a raise of 50 cents an hour starting the first of next month."

"I can't come to your party because I'll be out of town that day."

In each of these examples, the speaker makes a statement containing information for the listener. Our everyday lives are made up of hundreds of communications like these. For a communication to go smoothly, the speaker's statement needs to be clear and the listener must hear what is actually being said. In most of our daily communications, the information is accurately expressed by the speaker and understood by the listener. The waiter now knows that there is a fly in the customer's soup, Dave has learned that he will get a raise next month, and the party host knows not to expect the friend who will be out of town.

Tips for Speakers

The first part of any communication is the speaker's statement. When you are the one speaking, your job is to clearly and accurately convey the information you want to get across. Remember to:

- **Be clear about what you want to say.** Ask yourself what you intend to communicate. Are you expecting to impart factual information? Do you want to convey your opinion or your feelings? Is it your intention to state a preference for one option over others? Are you making a proposal? Knowing what you want to say will help you figure out the best way to say it.

- **Say what you mean.** Once you're sure about what you want to say, put your statement in words that will be easy for your listener to understand. When conveying factual information, be as specific and accurate as possible. If you have a purpose beyond imparting factual information, begin with a phrase that will clue your listener in to your purpose. For example, "I think we should do x, y, or z" or "What I want is thus and such."

Tips for Listeners

The listener's attitude and approach have as much to do with quality of the communication as does the speaker's delivery.

- **Listen attentively.** When you're the one listening, pay attention to what the speaker is saying. Listen to the whole statement and don't interrupt. This sounds simple, but we all know how difficult it can be. Try to avoid being distracted by your own thoughts. Maintain eye contact with the speaker until they finish. This will help focus your attention on what's being said. (If direct eye contact is considered rude and inappropriate in your culture, adapt your behavior to maintain a respectful listening posture.)

   Pay attention to your body language. If you're fidgeting with papers, looking away, or frowning, you probably aren't listening—and you might even be distracting the speaker. Whether you intend to or not, you're also conveying a lack of interest in what the speaker is saying, which can stop any conversation in its tracks.

- **Confirm the communication.** Avoid misunderstanding by confirming the communication using a simple feedback technique: State your understanding of the speaker's statement, in your own words.

   Even if you're sure you know what the speaker means, you can put your feedback into the form of a question by starting with something like "Are you saying …?" or "Do you mean …?" You might be surprised to discover you missed something, and even if you got it right, you'll send the message that you're listening and sincerely wanting to understand.

Steven and Freda
Steven says to Freda, "I'll meet you at Starbucks at 8 a.m. tomorrow morning." Freda assumes Steven is referring to the Starbucks across from Steven's office, whereas Steven is thinking of the one down

the street from the art museum. If they don't clear this up, they'll be waiting in different cafes at opposite ends of town the following morning. But if Freda responds, "So I'll see you at 8 a.m. tomorrow morning at the Starbucks across from your office, right?" Steven can say, "No, I meant the one next to the art museum." By using feedback, Freda has averted a potential mishap.

Pay Attention to Emotions

Make sure the emotions accompanying a communication don't derail your efforts. Not every communication includes an emotional component. When emotions run high, however, it's important to recognize the emotion to avoid getting thrown off course.

The emotional content of a communication is like an ocean current at the beach. If it is recognized and well marked, swimmers can safely enjoy the surf. They can even use the current to swim farther and faster. But if the emotion in the communication is ignored, it can be like an undertow pulling unwitting swimmers out to sea.

Depending on whether you are the speaker or the listener, you can "swim" with the emotional currents in the communication by following these guidelines.

When you're speaking, alert your listener to your emotional state. If you feel strongly enough about something, you will probably express how you feel nonverbally. If your words don't include some acknowledgment of your emotional state, you risk confusing or alarming your listener into a reaction that prevents true listening. So take a moment to tune in to how you are feeling before speaking. Check for physical signs. Is your jaw clenched? Are you fidgeting in your chair? Is your face flushed and hot? Are you holding your breath? These are just a few examples of the nonverbal signals (body language) you send to yourself and your listener when you are in the grip of a strong emotion.

If you don't feel comfortable saying how you feel in the moment, take a little time to breathe and calm down. See if your feelings subside before you speak. If not, try to let your listener know—in words—that the subject under discussion evokes some strong feelings for you. You don't have to talk about your feelings if you don't want to. But your body language is bound to send a signal that something is going on, so you'll keep the communication clear by making your verbal statement consistent with your nonverbal one. If even this is impossible, take a break before you continue your discussion.

If you find that your emotional reactions consistently interfere with your communications, you'll probably benefit from spending some time working with a professional counselor. (See "Work With Advisers," below.)

When listening to a statement, be attentive to any emotional content. Just as it's important to check your understanding of the informational content of a statement, it's also critical to verify your assessment of the emotions being communicated. Including your understanding of the emotional content of a statement in your feedback is what communication specialists call "reflective listening." Reflective listening has dual benefits: It ensures that there is no misunderstanding in the communication and it promotes respectful and constructive dialogue by demonstrating an understanding of the speaker's feelings.

Reflective listening takes some care and practice. Here are three points to remember:

- **Put your feedback about the emotion in the form of a question.** Putting your feedback in the form of question lets the speaker know what you heard and saw while allowing for the possibility that you got it wrong.

- **Pick a word you think will accurately describe the emotion being expressed without understating or exaggerating it.** Sticking to a word that accurately describes the emotion shows respect for the speaker and allows them the opportunity to clear up any misunderstanding. If you under- or overstate what you perceive, the conversation is likely to turn to your poor perception skills, rather than the speaker's feelings.

- **Accept any correction by the speaker without argument.** The speaker has the final word on how they feel and what they are trying to express. If the speaker corrects your feedback, accept the correction without argument. Otherwise, you'll turn a good communication into an unproductive debate.

Resources for Increasing Your Communication Competence

There is a lot more that can be said about communicating, and fortunately there are plenty of resources available to help you improve your skills. If you want to go further, here are a few suggestions to get you started:

Difficult Conversations: How to Discuss What Matters Most, by Douglas Stone, Bruce Patton, Sheila Heen, and Roger Fisher (Penguin), is a practical approach to communicating about tough subjects based on research from the Harvard Negotiation Project.

Taking the War Out of Our Words, by Sharon Ellison (Voices of Integrity), explains the process of Powerful Non-Defensive Communication (PNDC), an effective tool for improving communication.

Messages: The Communication Skills Book, by Patrick Fanning, Matthew McKay, and Martha Davis (New Harbinger Publications). This book describes in detail the basic skills involved in communicating, including expressing, self-disclosing, and listening.

Nonviolent Communication: A Language of Compassion, by Marshall B. Rosenberg (PuddleDancer Press), describes a system of communication based on empathic listening.

Safe Conversations–Transform Your Relationships offers online workshops for couples wanting to improve their communications; see https://safeconversations.com.

For an interesting take on gender differences in communication, see *You Just Don't Understand: Women and Men in Conversation*, by Deborah Tannen (William Morrow Paperbacks).

Negotiating Lovingly

If at any point in the process of making a premarital agreement you find that the two of you see things differently, you will probably need to negotiate those differences to decide how to address them in your prenup.

Negotiating the terms of a prenup is different from many other kinds of negotiation. For you, the goal of the negotiation is to find a solution that meets the needs of both of you and that provides a solid foundation for your marital partnership. So the two of you will want your negotiations to be caring. In this section, we show you how to use general negotiating techniques in a loving way.

Everyone Negotiates

We all negotiate in our daily lives. Any time we ask someone to cooperate with us in accomplishing something we can't (or don't want to) do on our own, we are negotiating. When we respond to another person's request for our cooperation by stating the conditions under which we will participate, we are also negotiating. Almost all of us have negotiated some major issue in our lives, perhaps buying a house or a car, taking on a new job, or asking for a raise. We also conduct personal negotiations on a regular basis. For example, we might negotiate with friends about what movie to go see Saturday night or where to meet for dinner. For the most part, we conduct these daily negotiations with overall success and without a great deal of thought about how we are negotiating.

When negotiating with each other about your prenup, you will use the same basic techniques you've developed in your daily negotiations, overlaid with your love for one another and your strong motivation to make things work. So negotiating in this context will mostly be a question of staying focused on your ultimate goal: a prenup that represents your common interests and your individual aspirations.

How to Negotiate Successfully

Not only do you want to end up with a premarital agreement that works for you both, you also want the process of making the agreement to be mutually supportive and caring. You have an excellent chance of success if you keep these four basic guidelines in mind:

- Be patient.
- Be clear about your interests.
- Balance assertiveness and attentiveness.
- Seek solutions that meet both persons' interests.

Be patient. One of the best ways to doom a negotiation is to push for a resolution without fully exploring each person's concerns and all of the possible solutions. Conversely, the route to a successful negotiation is to allow enough time to fully understand the dimensions of the problem, how each person views it, and the pros and cons of all potential solutions.

Be sure to allow yourselves enough time to hear each other out, ponder the options, and negotiate an outcome that will be lasting and fair.

Be clear about your interests. An effective negotiation results in an agreement that meets the interests of both people. What is an interest? An interest is someone's need, goal, concern, or aspiration that the agreement must address to be acceptable to that person.

Ted and Grace

Ted's interests include passing a significant portion of his estate, (including family heirlooms) to his children, providing for Grace if he dies before her, and living a lifestyle that includes travel with Grace. Among Grace's interests are leaving her share of a family farm to her sister, traveling with Ted, and financial security (including owning her own home) if she and Ted divorce or if she outlives Ted. They need to address each of these interests in the terms of their prenup.

Typical negotiations begin with each party promoting a position (solution) that meets that person's interests, often at the expense of the other person's interests. If there is never any discussion of each person's interests, the negotiation will—at best—result in a compromise that is not entirely satisfactory to either person. At worst, the negotiators will reach an impasse.

If the focus of the negotiation shifts from your stated positions to your underlying interests, you can try to come up with options that satisfy both of you. This is often referred to as "interest-based negotiation."

In order to focus on your interests, you first need to be very clear about what they are. To do this, try asking yourself the following questions about the issue being negotiated:

- What do I want the prenup to say about this?
- Why do I want the prenup to say this?
- What concerns of mine would be addressed by this solution?
- How will this meet my needs?
- What dreams or aspirations of mine are furthered by the position I am taking?
- How would I be affected if my solution were *not* accepted?

Balance assertiveness and attentiveness. Another essential component of a successful negotiation is maintaining a healthy balance between asserting what's important to you (your interests) and attending to what is important to your fiancé (your fiancé's interests). This requires you to build on the communication skills we discussed earlier in this chapter.

Assertiveness is a two-part process. First, you must get very clear about what is important to you about the issue you are negotiating (see above). Second, you must speak up about your interests during the negotiation. This means specifically and accurately describing your interests, and it might mean being persistent in standing up for them.

Attentiveness is also a two-part process. First, you must listen carefully to what your fiancé says about their interests. Then you must be open to considering options that address your fiancé's interests as well as your own.

Maintaining the proper balance between these two modes—asserting your interests and attending to your fiancé's interests—isn't always easy. At times, it can be very tempting to either give up on your own desires or close your ears to your fiancé's needs. But if you can stay the course, chances are good that the two of you will find some way to accommodate the most important points on both sides.

The best way to make sure you balance these modes as you negotiate is to pay attention. Make a mental inventory from time to time: Am I asserting my important interests? Is something being overlooked? Do I understand what's important to my fiancé? Am I considering my fiancé's interests?

If you pay attention, and if you resist the urge to either abandon your own interests or ignore your fiancé's, you'll find the right balance. The result will be well worth the effort: a premarital agreement that truly addresses each person's needs and concerns.

Seek solutions that meet both persons' interests. Once both of you have identified and clearly expressed your interests, you can shift your attention to exploring options that might address them. Have faith that you will find some way to support each other in what you want. Then commit yourselves to considering all possible options before rejecting any of them. Here is a step-by-step approach to finding the optimum solution:

1. **Gather your ideas.** Together, brainstorm a complete list of all conceivable options. Write down each idea as it comes, without stopping to evaluate it.

2. **Rank your options.** When your list is as complete as you can make it, make a copy of the list for each of you. Then—separately—rank the options, based on their ability to satisfy the most important needs of both of you on a sliding scale of one to five (one being the most desirable and five being the least desirable).

3. **Compare results.** When you are finished ranking each option, compare your results. Look for the options that ranked high for both of you, starting with any that received a combined rank of one/one, then one/two, then two/two, and so forth. This will highlight the most promising options.

4. Choose the best approach. Talk about whether these options seem to work for both of you and why. Which interests do they address? Are any important interests not addressed? Can the options be improved? As you do this, you might find that some compromises are in order. That's okay as long as you're still taking into account the most important concerns you each have. Before you know it, you'll zero in on an agreeable solution to the issue at hand.

What to Do When Problems Arise

What should you do if you hit a snag while putting together your prenup? If the problem is between the two of you, you need to diagnose it and figure out the best way to address it.

Diagnose the Problem

The problem is likely a communication problem or a negotiation problem—or a combination of both. By figuring out which kind of problem you're facing, you can tailor your approach to resolving it.

What Kind of Problem Is It?

How to spot a **communication problem**: One or both of you feel misheard, misunderstood, or confused.

How to spot a **negotiation problem**: You seem to understand each other, but you disagree about what to put in the agreement, and you can't find a solution that works for both of you.

Where Are You Stuck?

Whether the problem derives from a communication failure or a negotiation difficulty will depend in large part on where you are in the process of making your prenup. There are four possible places where you can have trouble:

- **Introducing the idea of a prenup.** The first time you discuss the possibility of having a prenup is one place where you can get off track. If so, your problem primarily concerns communication.

- **Sharing your positions.** Another place you can run into difficulties is when sharing your financial information, goals, and ideas, following the steps outlined in Chapter 3. If you get stuck at this stage, you are likely to have encountered a communication problem.
- **Drafting.** Some couples run into trouble when working through the clauses of the draft agreement. If you have trouble at this point, you probably have a negotiation issue—perhaps compounded by a communication problem.
- **Sealing the deal.** You might have difficulties putting together the final draft. This is likely to involve both communication and negotiation.

Decide on Your Approach

If you're having communication trouble, follow the suggestions for resolving communication problems, just below. If you are hung up at the negotiation stage, see if you can fix the problem using the tips in "Resolve Negotiation Problems," below. If you're not sure what the problem is, or if you know you've got problems with communicating and negotiating (don't worry—you won't be the only ones), cover your bases by reading through the next two sections and implementing all the suggestions that seem to apply.

Resolve Communication Problems

To address a communication problem, you'll want to discuss the issue that caused the disconnect, making sure each of you clearly understands what the other person intends to say.

Agree to take as long as you need for your discussion, and set aside a time when you won't feel pressured to finish quickly. Pick a comfortable place to have the conversation. Make sure you are both rested and refreshed before you begin. Review the guidelines for effective communication above.

Karen and Russ: Breaking an Impasse

Karen and Russ run into a stumbling block when talking about potential community property rights in Karen's veterinary practice and the emergency clinic she's thinking of buying into. They resolve the question of what to do with the practice fairly easily, but the issue of the emergency clinic has them stumped. Here's how it happens.

Karen has been approached by some other veterinarians who are starting a limited liability company to operate an emergency clinic. They plan to have a group practice and have invited Karen to join. Each member will be required to be on call for a certain number of hours per month and to contribute a percentage of the start-up costs. Profits from the company will be shared according to the partners' percentages. Karen is still mulling over whether to get involved, but if she does, she will be putting $15,000 of her own premarital savings into it, and she feels that it should be her separate property. She is unwilling to use the same approach they have come up with for her practice—allocating a share of any increase in value to community property—because she considers the clinic primarily an investment opportunity. She will be paid a salary for her on-call time and Russ will not work in the business (as he will in her regular practice), so it makes no sense to her to consider the return on her investment to be community property.

Russ feels equally strongly that the clinic should be considered at least part community property. If Karen decides to go forward, everything will take place while they are married, and the time she spends on the clinic during their marriage is time she won't spend on other community property endeavors. Russ suggests they agree to give Karen a right of reimbursement for any premarital funds she puts in and call the whole investment community property. This is completely unacceptable to Karen.

After several tense conversations about the clinic, Karen and Russ seem no closer to agreement than before. They realize they are stuck. They decide to try looking again at what each of them has at stake regarding this issue—that is, to examine their interests more closely. They agree that Russ will start by talking about his interests. Karen will listen and then feed back to Russ what she's heard. Then Karen will talk and Russ will listen and give feedback. They agree to keep taking turns like this until both of them feel

Karen and Russ: Breaking an Impasse (continued)

they've said everything that's on their minds. Only then will they try to come up with a solution that works for both of them.

Russ starts by saying that he feels it's important for Karen's investment of time in the marriage to be fully compensated. He's also concerned that if the emergency clinic partners are required to contribute more money, those funds will have to come from community property, which would mean a community property investment in the business. Karen makes sure she's understood these concerns by telling Russ in her own words what she's heard.

Karen then says that in addition to the fact that the investment in this clinic will be funded with her separate property, she's worried about the potential for problems if her partners must cooperate in appraising the practice if she and Russ divorce or if she dies before he does. Russ hears her out, and feeds back what she's said. Then it's Russ's turn to speak again. He tells Karen how important it is to him to feel that they are building something together.

Slowly, it becomes clear that Russ's main concerns are reimbursing any community property funds spent on additional contributions to the emergency clinic and building up a community property investment together. Adequate compensation for Karen's work at the clinic is not such a big deal to Russ, especially once Karen explains she will receive overtime pay for extra hours, in addition to salary.

On Karen's part, she realizes that in addition to her interest in avoiding a valuation hassle, her biggest concern is making sure she can be free to deal with the clinic partners in making business decisions about the clinic without having to consult Russ.

Based on this new understanding of each other's interests, they agree that the clinic (and any other new veterinary business opportunity that comes up) will be Karen's separate property, but that if they divorce or if Karen dies before Russ, he will be entitled to one-half of any community property funds invested in the business, plus an amount equal to 1% of the amount of Karen's original separate property investment in the business multiplied by the number of years of the marriage, up to a maximum of $15,000.

Karen and Russ: Breaking an Impasse (continued)

Clearly identifying the clinic as Karen's separate property will give her the discretion she needs to make business decisions. At the same time, determining (and capping) the amount Karen or her estate would have to pay Russ meets her interest in avoiding valuation hassles and keeping the buyout affordable. Providing for reimbursement of community property funds plus an increasing share of equity addresses Russ's interest in getting back a share of community property funds and building up some equity together.

When you are ready, revisit the conversation in which you had trouble. Don't try to repeat the exact conversation you had before, and don't try to analyze where you went wrong. Just focus on taking turns expressing yourselves and listening attentively. Use feedback (reflective listening) to make sure that you truly understand each other. Go slowly and take breaks. Remember: The goal of communicating is to understand each other, not to determine who's right or wrong.

If you're still having trouble after trying this approach, consider getting some help. (See "Work With Advisers," below.)

Resolve Negotiation Problems

Often, what seems to be a problematic negotiation has its roots in a miscommunication.

If you're satisfied that your communications have been clear and that each of you understands the other person's point of view, then you'll need to take a similar approach to solving the negotiation problem that we described for addressing communication problems, above.

First, set aside a comfortable time and place so that you can take as long as you need to resolve the problem.

Next, review the tips for negotiating discussed in "Negotiating Lovingly," above. The problem might be that one or both of you isn't entirely clear about what's most important to you in the negotiation—in other words, what your interests are. Look carefully at the position each of you is taking. What are your reasons for taking those positions? What are you hoping to accomplish? What concerns do you have that would be addressed by adopting your position? These and similar questions will help you uncover your true interests in the matter.

When you feel sure that you know what your interests are, write them down: List one person's interests on the left-hand side of a piece of paper, and the other person's interests on the right-hand side. Double-check to be sure the list of each person's interests is accurate and that both of you understand each interest. Then take a few moments, silently, to prioritize your own list. On a scale of one to five, which interests are most important to you? Which are less important? Write the number for each interest's priority next to it. This will help you evaluate whether a particular solution is going to meet your most important interests.

Now both of you should try to think of as many different ways as possible to structure your prenup so that it satisfies the interests you've listed. Use the brainstorming and ranking techniques described above, in "Negotiating Lovingly."

If you follow this approach, you'll likely work the kinks out of the negotiation and find some promising alternatives for shaping your prenup. If you try the method described here and find you're still hung up, consider getting some help. (See "Work With Advisers," below.)

Deal With Serious Roadblocks

There are a couple of situations that deserve special attention, beyond simply focusing on your communication and your negotiating skills. If you reach an impasse, there are particular steps you can take to keep things moving forward. Similarly, if you find yourselves in a take-it-or-leave-it situation, there might be a unique way to address the problem.

Breaking an Impasse

What happens if you reach a point where you seem to be stuck? Each of you is clear about what you want, and no compromise seems possible. There are two possibilities here. First, it could be that you've come up against a truly irreconcilable difference. For example, if your discussions have led you to discover that one of you wants to have children and the other doesn't, you might simply need to acknowledge a difference that cannot be reconciled. You'll then have to decide whether the issue is one that you can simply agree to disagree about (at least for now) or whether it is more fundamental. With topics like these, you might wish to consider getting help from a qualified counselor to help you consider and decide on the consequences for your relationship.

The other possibility is that the impasse stems from an incomplete consideration of each person's interests. Even if you think you've identified your interests regarding the issue in question, try looking a little more deeply to see whether that helps you break the logjam.

Avoiding the Take-It-or-Leave-It Syndrome

It's unlikely that you'll encounter this problem if the two of you have worked together to draft your prenup. But if just one of you has prepared the draft, or worse yet, a lawyer representing one of you has prepared a draft without any input from the other party, you might find yourselves in what appears to be a take-it-or-leave-it situation.

You can avoid this problem by working together from the outset. If you don't have that luxury, the next best option is to agree to set aside the proposed draft and go back to the drawing board.

Start by examining your individual situations. Share your information with each other, discuss your goals and concerns, and work together to create the outlines of an agreement that will be acceptable to both of you. Use the clauses offered in Chapters 5 through 9 to put your outline into written form and use the resulting draft as a basis for making revisions to what was presented as a one-sided offering.

Work With Advisers

If you're stuck and need some help, there are a number of options, depending on what you need and who is available. For example, one or both of you could work with a counselor to improve your communication skills. Or, if you want help negotiating a particular issue, you might find it more useful to seek advice from your lawyers or financial advisers. You could also hire a mediator to help you work out the terms of your prenup.

In this section, we review some of the most common options for getting help and suggest ways to make the experience of working with an adviser as productive as possible.

Guidelines for Working With Advisers

Whatever type of adviser you choose, following these general guidelines will help you get the most from your experience.

- **Check qualifications.** Make sure you pick someone who is qualified to help you by asking about the adviser's licenses, credentials, or certifications. Find out if the adviser has any specialties and ask how long the adviser has been in practice. If possible, get personal references from satisfied clients or other professionals.
- **Conduct interviews.** Consider interviewing more than one candidate. If you can afford it—or if free interviews are an option—meet with two or more potential advisers before settling on one. Regardless of a professional's qualifications, style and personality can make a difference. See how comfortable you feel with two or three different candidates. Then pick one who is qualified and who seems easy to work with.
- **Set clear expectations.** Let your adviser know what you want help with. Make sure that this is something your adviser is able and willing to assist with.
- **Agree in advance about fees.** Avoid unpleasant surprises or misunderstandings by finding out about fees at the beginning. Does the adviser charge by the hour? If so, what is the rate? Does the advisor charge for time spent on the phone or consulting other

professionals on your behalf? Will you be expected to pay at the time of each meeting or will you be billed? Is an advance deposit required? Can you pay by credit card? Can you make monthly payments? Ask your adviser to put the fee arrangement in writing, or prepare a memo summarizing your understanding of the arrangement and ask your adviser to look it over and approve it.

- **Be prepared for every meeting.** Prior to each meeting with your adviser, think about what you want to accomplish. Jot down some notes to refer to. If you have questions you want to raise, write them down, too. Take your notes with you to the meeting and check them occasionally to make sure you've covered everything.

- **Follow through.** Working with advisers can involve "homework" on your part. If you agree to assemble information or to practice a skill in between meetings, make a point of following through. You'll get the most out of the advice you're paying for only if you hold up your end.

- **Take seriously the advice you receive.** If your adviser makes a suggestion, consider it carefully. If you don't understand the advice, ask for clarification. If you disagree with the advice, share your reservations with your adviser. Perhaps there is an angle you've overlooked, or maybe there's some piece of information your adviser is unaware of that would make a difference. Get the most out of the time and money you're investing by taking the time to try to fully understand your adviser's opinion rather than rejecting it out of hand.

Licensed Marriage and Family Counselors

One option, especially if you need help with communication, is consulting with a licensed marriage and family counselor. These counselors typically include licensed clinical psychologists, psychiatrists, marriage and family counselors, and licensed social workers. Generally, the fees of a marriage and family counselor or social worker will be lower than those of psychiatrists and clinical psychologists. Some insurance companies will cover part of the expense of counseling; check with your health insurance provider to find out.

The best way to find a counselor is through personal referrals from friends, neighbors, family, and other trusted sources. Follow the guidelines outlined at the beginning of this section to get the most out of using a counselor.

Premarital Counselors

Another choice, especially for help with communication problems, is to work with a premarital counselor. Many churches, temples, and other religious communities offer premarital counseling.

Secular counselors also offer premarital counseling. In at least one state (Minnesota), the fee for a marriage license is reduced if the couple attends premarital counseling with an approved counselor.

If you're already working with a premarital counselor whom you like and trust, that might be the right person to help one or both of you improve your communication skills or even negotiate the terms of your prenup.

If you aren't working with a premarital counselor but are interested in doing so, the best way to find one is through personal referrals from friends, family, business associates, or other people whose opinions you trust. You might also be able to locate a premarital counselor through a church, a synagogue, or another religious community, or even through a search of premarital counseling programs using an Internet search engine.

Whether or not you already have a relationship with a premarital counselor, follow the guidelines outlined above to ensure that you get the most out of the experience.

Attorneys or Financial Advisers

To get help negotiating the terms of your prenup, you might consider consulting a lawyer or a financial adviser. Before you do, be sure to look for someone who is willing to give you nonadversarial advice. Adversarial advice focuses exclusively on what is to your best advantage, regardless of the potential disadvantages to your fiancé and your relationship. Instead, your adviser should be prepared to help you find ways to negotiate a premarital agreement that supports the needs and interests of both of you.

Unless you have already selected a lawyer to work with, refer to Chapter 10 for help finding a good one. If you don't have a financial adviser, use personal referrals to find a qualified person.

Whether you opt for help from a lawyer, a financial adviser, or both, follow the guidelines outlined at the beginning of this section for working with any legal or financial adviser you select.

Mediators

Mediation can be an ideal way to hammer out the details of a prenup. That's because it is nonadversarial—the mediator is neutral and has no power to decide for or against a party.

Historically, mediation has been used to resolve labor disputes and international disagreements. The last 20 years have seen an expansion of the use of mediation to resolve various interpersonal and community disagreements. More and more professionals—in fields ranging from law to psychology to accounting to business—are becoming trained to mediate disputes in their fields. Mediating premarital agreements is a relatively new option for couples, but its use is increasing.

Mediators who are also lawyers or who have other expertise in the legal and financial aspects of preparing premarital agreements are especially helpful. They can draft the final agreement from a neutral point of view so that your advising lawyers will have to review the document only to ensure its clarity and thoroughness. When choosing a mediator, try to find someone who has experience with prenups. Look for referrals from family, friends, colleagues, and other trusted sources. Then follow the approach outlined at the beginning of this section to ensure a successful mediation experience.

After You've Made a Prenup

The process of making a prenup doesn't end when you sign on the dotted line. This chapter discusses steps you can take to ensure the continued effectiveness of the agreement for years to come.

Storing the Original Agreement and Copies

The first thing you should do with your prenup is agree on a safe place to store the original document, in case you ever need to present it to a judge, a county clerk, or another official. Typically, an original prenuptial agreement will be stored with other important family papers, such as real estate deeds, certificates of title for vehicles or other assets, and birth certificates. A good storage place might be a safe deposit box or a filing cabinet in your home. Whatever location you choose, make sure that both of you know where to find the original agreement quickly. It's also a good idea to keep a copy in another location. Even better, you can scan the agreement so you can store a digital copy in the cloud—that way you'll be able to access it from anywhere, in case the original is ever misplaced or destroyed.

Recording an Abstract or Memorandum of the Agreement

Occasionally, a couple signing a prenup also prepares and signs what is known as an "abstract" of the agreement, which they file with the public land records office. (In some states the term "memorandum" is used instead of "abstract." For simplicity, we use "abstract" here.)

The abstract is shorter than the agreement and usually summarizes only the provisions relating to real estate. The purpose of the abstract is to enable one or both spouses to buy and sell separate property real estate without having to obtain the other spouse's signature.

If you prepare an abstract, you will record (file) it in the county where one or both of you owns separate property real estate. The land records office is called the county recorder's office in most places, but in some states it might go by another name, such as the registry of deeds.

Sample Prenup Abstract

RECORDING REQUESTED BY AND
WHEN RECORDED RETURN TO

Barry Agha
123 Main St.
Hayesville, NC 28904

[LEAVE THIS SPACE BLANK
FOR RECORDER'S STAMP]

Abstract of Prenuptial Agreement

We, Barry Agha (Barry) and Chantelle Agha (Chantelle), declare:

1. We were married on December 20, 20xx and are now husband and wife.

2. We entered into a prenuptial agreement on November 12, 20xx.

3. The prenuptial agreement became effective on the date of our marriage and it remains in full force and effect as of the date of execution of this abstract.

4. Among the provisions of the prenuptial agreement are the provisions that follow:

   a. Paragraph 6A provides that the real property described on Exhibit A to this abstract, which is incorporated by reference, is and shall be Barry's separate property, and Barry has the sole right to manage and dispose of the property described on Exhibit A.

   b. Paragraph 7E provides that any real property acquired by Barry in his sole name during our marriage shall be considered Barry's separate property, and Barry has the sole right to manage and dispose of any such property.

   c. Paragraph 2B provides that the prenuptial agreement will remain in full force and effect indefinitely.

We sign this abstract on January 20, 20xx at Hayesville, North Carolina.

Barry Agha
_____
Barry Agha

Chantelle Agha
_____
Chantelle Agha

Certificate of Acknowledgment of Notary Public

_____ COOK _____ County, North Carolina

I certify that the following person(s) personally appeared before me this day, each acknowledging to me that he or she signed the foregoing document.

_____ Barry Agha _____
Name(s) of principal(s)

Date _____ January 20, 20xx _____

[Official Seal]   _____ *Melinda Washington* _____
Official Signature of Notary

_____ melinda washington _____ , Notary Public
Notary's printed or typed name

My commission expires _____ April 6, 20xx _____

Certificate of Acknowledgment of Notary Public

_____ COOK _____ County, North Carolina

I certify that the following person(s) personally appeared before me this day, each acknowledging to me that he or she signed the foregoing document.

_____ Chantelle Agha _____
Name(s) of principal(s)

Date _____ January 20, 20xx _____

[Official Seal]   _____ *Melinda Washington* _____
Official Signature of Notary

_____ melinda washington _____ , Notary Public
Notary's printed or typed name

My commission expires _____ April 6, 20xx _____

Because any document that is recorded in the county's official records is available to the public, using an abstract instead of the entire prenuptial agreement allows you to keep the other details of your prenup private.

> EXAMPLE: Barry is a licensed real estate broker. In the course of his business, he occasionally buys and sells real estate in his own name, and he owns several rental properties. Barry and Chantelle have signed a prenup providing that Barry's rental properties and any new real estate he purchases will be his separate property. To avoid having to obtain Chantelle's signature on the deed every time he sells a property or borrows against it, Barry and Chantelle prepare and sign an abstract of their prenuptial agreement summarizing just the clauses relating to Barry's separate property real estate. They record the abstract in each county where Barry owns real estate so that title companies, lenders, and potential purchasers will know that Barry has the right to sell or borrow against the property without Chantelle's involvement. Because the abstract contains only provisions relating to real estate, the rest of their prenup can be kept private. You can find a sample of their abstract above.

When you prepare your final agreement, you might want to ask your lawyers if preparing and filing an abstract is something you should do in your state or county. If so, your lawyers can help you draw it up at the same time as your prenup, or you can make one later, with help or on your own.

The abstract must be signed and notarized. This is usually done after the wedding, so that the abstract can include a provision stating that the prenup is in effect. If you own real estate in more than one county or expect to in the future, you should sign enough originals of the abstract so that you can record one in each county.

After you record the abstract, the land records office will return the original to you, stamped to show that they've recorded it. You should store the recorded original abstract with your original prenup.

TIP

Check the laws in your location. Laws and procedures dealing with title to real estate vary from state to state and even from county to county within a given state. If you think you need an abstract, it's best to check the legal requirements, including the correct terminology, before preparing the document and taking it to the land records office.

Following Your Own Rules

Once you have made a prenup, it's important to avoid doing anything that is inconsistent with the terms of your agreement. Otherwise, you could find yourselves in a position where your agreement says one thing and your actions indicate another arrangement. At best this creates confusion, and it could even lead to genuine disagreement over the meaning and validity of your prenup.

Even the simplest prenup requires consistent follow-through. For example, the prenup signed by Steven and Freda (see Chapter 9) states that the premarital assets listed on their disclosure schedules will remain their separate property after they marry. Their prenup does not attempt to carve out special rules regarding new property or debts incurred during their marriage. Nevertheless, to ensure that their premarital assets continue to be considered separate property, Steven and Freda need to keep those assets in separate names and not mix them together with marital assets. And if one of them decides to contribute separate property funds to a marital asset, they should consider writing up a separate loan agreement unless the one contributing the funds intends to convert them to marital property.

Be Sure to Complete Any Tasks You Agreed To Do in the Prenup

In addition to acting in a way that is consistent with your prenup, you might need to follow through on specific steps you've agreed to take. If so, it's a good idea to make a list of those steps and a plan for completing them. Again, not doing so could create confusion and could even lead to a result you do not intend.

For example, Ted and Grace agreed to several provisions that require them to take action after they marry, including writing up their estate plans (see below) and signing waivers of surviving spouse rights to each other's retirement benefits. Before putting their prenup away in a safe place, they make a list of all the steps they need to take. When they get back from their honeymoon, they will refer to the list and agree upon a timetable for completing everything.

Similarly, you might have agreed in your prenup that you will do certain things on a regular basis, such as putting money away for your children's college education or paying certain recurring expenses. It's important to continue to follow through with those items. For instance, Ted and Grace's prenup contains two such provisions in Paragraph 8. One clause sets up a process for deciding how to handle their income taxes each year. The agreement also includes a clause stating that Ted will pay the household expenses by contributing the necessary amount each month to a joint bank account. If Ted and Grace decide to deal with the income taxes or household expenses in a manner that differs from the terms of their prenup, they should formalize the decision with a written addendum or modification (see "Changing Your Prenup: Postnuptial Agreements," below).

Completing Your Estate Plan

You might have used your prenup to set out some of the ways you want to leave your property when you die. In addition, you might have waived some or all of the rights you have to receive property from each other's estates. If your prenup touches on estate planning issues such as these, it's critically important that you prepare the necessary documents—wills, trusts, or other paperwork—that will actually transfer your property as you intend. Your prenup doesn't take the place of these important transfer documents, and if you neglect to complete them, it could lead to a lot of confusion and extra work for your inheritors after your death.

For instance, if one or both of you has agreed in the prenup to leave some money or property to the other when you die—perhaps in exchange for giving up some spousal inheritance rights—you'll need to follow up by making wills (and perhaps trusts) soon after you marry. Depending on the complexity of your plan and the size of your estate, you might want to enlist your lawyers to help you choose the best estate planning devices and draw up your papers. If your needs are simple—for example, you don't have significant assets and want to make a moderate gift to your spouse—you can probably prepare your own will or living trust with a good self-help book or software.

Even if you decide to enlist your lawyers for this part of the process, there are many resources available to help you learn more about estate planning and perhaps handle some of the necessary tasks on your own.

RESOURCE

More information about estate planning. Nolo offers many tools designed to help with your estate planning tasks. At Nolo.com, you'll find lots of helpful (and free) information about estate planning. You can also turn to the following products.

Quicken WillMaker & Trust (software for Mac and Windows) allows you to use your computer to prepare a comprehensive will, health care directive, and durable power of attorney for finances. It also enables you to prepare a document setting out your wishes for final arrangements and provides many other useful forms.

Plan Your Estate, by Denis Clifford, offers in-depth coverage of all significant elements of estate planning, from simple wills to probate avoidance and complex tax-saving trusts.

Make Your Own Living Trust, by Denis Clifford, provides a complete explanation of how to prepare a living trust. The book contains forms that allow you to create a probate avoidance living trust.

8 Ways to Avoid Probate, by Mary Randolph, offers a thorough discussion of all the major ways to avoid probate by transferring property at death outside of a will.

Reviewing the Agreement

It's a good idea to take a look at your prenup from time to time to be sure it still works for you. If your prenup includes a clause requiring review at specified intervals, then you already have a plan in place and you just need to remember to do it. If you have a "sunset clause" that automatically terminates your prenup after a specified period of time, you will certainly want to review the prenup prior to the expiration date and decide whether you want to extend your agreement or let it lapse.

Even if you haven't provided for a formal review or termination date, we recommend that you revisit the provisions of your prenup every so often. An ideal time to do this is whenever you update your estate plans—for example, if the two of you have kids together or if there are other major changes in your family or your assets. Often the terms of your estate plans will need to be coordinated with those of your prenup, because a change made in one can affect the other.

Just as you did when you first began to discuss the terms of your prenup, be sure to choose a time and place for your review that will be free of distractions and conducive to a relaxed conversation. Prepare separately for your discussion by reading through the agreement with a fresh attitude and writing down notes of any thoughts or questions that come to mind.

The reviewing process might result in a mutual affirmation of the terms of your prenup. If so, put the agreement away until the next review and just remember to follow its terms.

If the review leads you to conclude that some changes to the agreement are in order, you'll need to make those changes in a written amendment or addendum.

Changing Your Prenup: Postnuptial Agreements

An agreement changing the terms of a prenuptial agreement may be called an amendment or addendum to the agreement. Because it's signed during marriage, it's governed by state laws that apply to postnuptial (sometimes called "postmarital" or even just "marital") agreements, rather than by laws that apply to prenups. After you are married, the laws of your state may hold you to a higher standard in your dealings with each other than you had before you were married. In many states, spouses are considered to have a "confidential" or "fiduciary" relationship to one another. Each spouse is expected to have the other person's interests at heart in dealing with financial matters, and any agreement that appears to be to only one person's advantage can be set aside.

SEE AN EXPERT

Get help with a postnup. An examination of state laws relating to postnuptial agreements (including those modifying prenups) is beyond the scope of this book. Suffice it to say that you should check the legal requirements of your state carefully before attempting to amend your prenup. In all likelihood, you will each need the assistance of a competent lawyer to ensure that the amendment will be binding, just as you did with the prenup itself. In fact, if you were happy with the lawyers who represented you in making your prenup, it might be a very simple matter to go back to them for help with drawing up and signing an amendment.

Closing Thoughts

Making a prenup can be a lot of work. It can be stressful and scary at times. It can also be very satisfying and even exciting to find that you can work together as partners in your financial affairs. Even if your prenup does little more than identify your premarital assets, by dealing directly and respectfully with each other about some tough financial and legal issues, you will have laid a firm foundation for your future relationship as life partners.

We hope that this book plays a part in building that foundation, and that your marriage will be stronger and more secure as a result.

How to Use the Downloadable Forms on the Nolo Website

You can download the Worksheets and sample clauses in Appendixes B and C, along with a PDF of the Summary of State Laws, at:

www.nolo.com/back-of-book/PNUP.html

To use the files, your computer must have specific software programs installed. Here is a list of types of files provided with this book, as well as the software programs you'll need to access them:

- **RTF.** You can open, edit, print, and save these form files with most word processing programs, such as Microsoft *Word*, Windows *WordPad*, and recent versions of *WordPerfect*. On a Mac, you can use Apple *TextEdit* or Apple *Pages*. You can also work with the forms using a cloud-based word processing app such as Google Docs (www.docs.google.com).

- **PDF.** You can view these files with Adobe *Actobat Reader*, free software from Adobe.com. Although you can complete some PDFs on your computer, most PDFs are designed to be printed out and completed by hand.

Editing RTFs

Here are some general instructions about editing RTF forms in your word processing program. Refer to the book's instructions and sample agreements for help about what should go in each blank.

- **Underlines.** Underlines indicate where to enter information. After filling in the needed text, remove the underline. In most word processing programs you can do this by highlighting the underlined portion and typing CTRL-U (Command-U on a Mac).

- **Bracketed and italicized text.** Bracketed and italicized text indicates instructions. Be sure to remove all instructional text before you finalize your document.
- **Optional text.** Optional text gives you the choice to include or exclude text. Delete any optional text you don't want to use. If necessary, renumber numbered items.
- **Alternative text.** Alternative text gives you the choice between two or more text options. Delete those options you don't want to use. If necessary, renumber numbered items.
- **Signature lines.** Signature lines should appear on a page that includes at least some text from the document itself. In other words, try not to have a page that contains only signatures.

Every word processing program uses different commands to open, format, save, and print documents, so refer to your software's help documents for more information. Nolo cannot provide technical support for questions about how to use your computer or your software.

CAUTION

In accordance with U.S. copyright laws, the forms provided by this book are for your personal use only.

Accessing the Summary of State Prenuptial Laws

A file containing summaries of each state's prenuptial laws is included with the downloadable files in Adobe *Acrobat Reader* PDF format.

List of Forms Available on the Nolo Website

Go to: **www.nolo.com/back-of-book/PNUP.html**

Files on the Book's Companion Page	
The following files are included in rich text format (RTF) on the book's companion page (and are in Appendixes B and C):	
Form Title	**File Name**
Worksheet 1: Financial Inventory	Worksheet1.rtf
Worksheet 2: Credit History and Spending Habits	Worksheet2.rtf
Worksheet 3: Financial Outlook	Worksheet3.rtf
Worksheet 4: Prenup Goals	Worksheet4.rtf
Worksheet 5: The Basics of Our Prenup	Worksheet5.rtf
Worksheet 6: Comparison of Prenup to Law	Worksheet6.rtf
Simple Prenuptial Agreement	SimplePrenup.rtf
Custom Prenuptial Outline	Outline.rtf
1. Introductory Facts	Introductory.rtf
2. Effective Date and Term	Term.rtf
3. Legal Representation	Representation.rtf
4. Disclosures	Disclosures.rtf
5. Definitions	Definitions.rtf
6. Ownership of Premarital Assets	Ownership.rtf
7. Rights in Assets Acquired During Marriage	MarriageAssets.rtf
8. Responsibility for Debts and Expenses	Expenses.rtf
9. Estate Planning Matters—Optional	Estate.rtf
10. Property Transfers or Purchases Upon Marriage—Optional	Transfers.rtf

Files on the Book's Companion Page (continued)	
Form Title	**File Name**
11. Provisions Applicable to Divorce—Optional	Divorce.rtf
12. Other Matters—Optional	Other.rtf
13. Interpretation, Modification, Review, and Enforcement of This Agreement	Interpretation.rtf
14. Signatures, Attorneys' Certifications, and Acknowledgments	Signatures.rtf
Abstract of Prenup	Abstract.rtf
Schedule 1—Financial Disclosures	Schedule1.rtf
Schedule 2—Financial Disclosures	Schedule2.rtf
Schedule 3—Jointly Owned Premarital Assets	Schedule3.rtf
The following files are included in portable document format (PDF):	
Form Title	**File Name**
Summary of State Prenup Laws	StateLaw.pdf

Worksheets

Y ou can copy these worksheets and use them as described in the chapters above. You can also download the worksheets at:

www.nolo.com/back-of-book/PNUP.html

When there are important changes to the information in this book, we'll post updates on the same dedicated page.

Date Prepared _____   Your Name _____

Worksheet 1: Financial Inventory

1. **Assets**

   ### Real Estate

Address or Description	Percentage Owned	Current Market Value
_____	_____%	$_____
_____	_____%	$_____
_____	_____%	$_____

   ### Cash and Bank Accounts (Checking, Savings, or Money Market Accounts, CDs)

Type of Account	Current Balance
_____	$_____
_____	$_____
_____	$_____

   ### Other Investment Assets (Stocks and Stock Options, Bonds, Mutual Funds, Annuities, Life Insurance)

Description	Current Market Value
_____	$_____
_____	$_____
_____	$_____
_____	$_____

   ### Retirement Assets (Pension, IRA, 401(k), Deferred Compensation Plans)

Description	Current Market Value
_____	$_____
_____	$_____

   ### Personal Property (Vehicles, Household Goods, Art, Antiques, Jewelry, Tools, Equipment, Animals, Other Items)

Description	Current Market Value
_____	$_____
_____	$_____
_____	$_____
_____	$_____
_____	$_____
_____	$_____

Business Ownership

Business Name	Form (Corporation, LLC, Partnership, Sole Proprietorship)	Percentage Owned	Current Market Value
_____	_____	_____%	$_____
_____	_____	_____%	$_____
_____	_____	_____%	$_____

Other Assets (Including Money Owed to You)

Description	Current Market Value
_____	$_____
_____	$_____
_____	$_____

Total Assets $_____

2. Debts

Secured Loans (Mortgages, Auto Loans, Other Loans Secured by Assets)

Owed To	Secured by (Asset Description)	Current Balance	Date Due
_____	_____	$_____	_____
_____	_____	$_____	_____
_____	_____	$_____	_____
_____	_____	$_____	_____

Credit Card Debts

Owed To	Current Balance	Date Due
_____	$_____	_____
_____	$_____	_____
_____	$_____	_____
_____	$_____	_____
_____	$_____	_____

Bank Loan/Lines of Credit

Owed To	Current Balance	Date Due
_____	$_____	_____
_____	$_____	_____
_____	$_____	_____
_____	$_____	_____

Private Loans

Owed To	Current Balance	Date Due
_____	$_____	_____
_____	$_____	_____
_____	$_____	_____
_____	$_____	_____

Student Loans

Owed To	Current Balance	Date Due
_____	$_____	_____
_____	$_____	_____
_____	$_____	_____
_____	$_____	_____

Child Support/Alimony

Owed To	For	Monthly Amount	Date Ends
_____	_____	$_____	_____
_____	_____	$_____	_____
_____	_____	$_____	_____

Divorce Settlement or Other Judgment Debt

Owed To	For	Current Balance	Date Due
_____	_____	$_____	_____
_____	_____	$_____	_____

Other Debts

Owed To	For	Current Balance	Date Due
_____	_____	$_____	_____
_____	_____	$_____	_____
_____	_____	$_____	_____
_____	_____	$_____	_____
_____	_____	$_____	_____
_____	_____	$_____	_____

Total Debts $_____

3. Income

Type of Income	Annual Amount (Before Tax)
Salary/Wages	$
Business Income (Sole Proprietorship)	$
Dividends, Interest	$
Capital Gain (or Loss) Income	$
Pension or Annuity Income	$
Rental or Partnership, S Corporation Income	$
Social Security Benefits	$
Tax-free Income	$
Other (specify):	$
	$
	$
	$
Total Income	$

4. Personal Expenses (indicate monthly or annual)

	Annual Expense	Monthly Expense
Housing Expenses		
Rent or Mortgage	$	$
Property Tax	$	$
Insurance	$	$
Utilities and Maintenance	$	$
Other Housing Expenses (specify):		
	$	$
	$	$
Transportation and Auto		
Auto Payment	$	$
Registration and Insurance	$	$
Repairs and Maintenance	$	$
Gas, Parking	$	$
Other Transportation Expenses (specify):		
	$	$
	$	$

Necessities

	Annual Expense	Monthly Expense
Food and Supplies	$_____	$_____
Clothing	$_____	$_____
Medical/Dental	$_____	$_____
Personal Hygiene	$_____	$_____

Other Necessities (specify):

_____	$_____	$_____
_____	$_____	$_____
_____	$_____	$_____
_____	$_____	$_____
_____	$_____	$_____
_____	$_____	$_____
_____	$_____	$_____
_____	$_____	$_____
_____	$_____	$_____

5. Other

	Annual Expense	Monthly Expense
Entertainment and Travel	$_____	$_____
Dues, Subscriptions, and Hobbies	$_____	$_____
Gifts and Donations	$_____	$_____
Insurance	$_____	$_____

Other (specify):

_____	$_____	$_____
_____	$_____	$_____
_____	$_____	$_____
_____	$_____	$_____
_____	$_____	$_____
_____	$_____	$_____
_____	$_____	$_____
_____	$_____	$_____
_____	$_____	$_____
_____	$_____	$_____
_____	$_____	$_____
_____	$_____	$_____
Total Expenses	$_____	$_____

_____   _____
Date Prepared   Your Name

Worksheet 2: Credit History and Spending Habits

A. Credit History

    1. a. Do you currently owe any debt that is more than 60 days overdue? ☐ yes ☐ no

        b. If so, specify the debt and the amount you owe.

        _____

        _____

        _____

        _____

    2. a. Have you been turned down for a loan or credit card in the last two years? ☐ yes ☐ no

        b. If so, give details (when, by whom, and the reason given for the denial of credit).

        _____

        _____

        _____

        _____

    3. a. Have you ever been sued for failing to pay a debt? ☐ yes ☐ no

        b. If so, give details (when, by whom, what court, amount of the claim, and the outcome).

        _____

        _____

        _____

B. Spending and Saving Habits

    1. How important is it to you to set aside savings on a regular basis? (circle one)

        Not important   1   2   3   4   5   Very important

    2. How comfortable are you with going into debt in order to take advantage of an investment opportunity? (circle one)

        Not comfortable   1   2   3   4   5   Very comfortable

    3. How do you usually pay bills? ☐ Early ☐ On time ☐ A little late ☐ Very late

4. Of the following methods, which ones do you use to pay bills and everyday expenses? (check all that apply):

☐ Cash ☐ Check ☐ Automatic Transfer ☐ Online Bill Pay ☐ Credit Card

☐ Other (specify): _____

5. How many credit cards do you currently have? _____

6. Do you pay credit card bills in full each month?

☐ Always ☐ Frequently ☐ Occasionally ☐ Never

7. How often do you balance your checkbook?

☐ Always ☐ Frequently ☐ Occasionally ☐ Never

8. Do you participate in a voluntary savings program? ☐ yes ☐ no

9. Have you set aside money in a savings account or another investment in the past 12 months?

☐ yes ☐ no

10. How many secured loans have you obtained in the past 12 months? (include details)

_____

_____

11. How many unsecured loans have you obtained in the past 12 months? (include details)

_____

_____

12. Other information you consider significant:

_____

_____

_____

_____

_____

_____

_____

_____

_____   _____
Date Prepared   Your Name

Worksheet 3: Financial Outlook

	Yes	No

1. a. Do you plan to make a major purchase or an investment of more than $10,000 in the next two years? ☐ ☐

   b. If so, give details.

   _____

   _____

   _____

   _____

2. a. Are you planning a career change in the next two years? ☐ ☐

   b. If so, give details.

   _____

   _____

   _____

   _____

3. a. Are you planning to retire from your current occupation in the next five years? ☐ ☐

   b. If so, give details.

   _____

   _____

   _____

   _____

4. a. Are you planning to enter a college, vocational, or professional school in the next few years? ☐ ☐

   b. If so, give details.

   _____

   _____

   _____

   _____

	Yes	No

5. a. Do you expect to receive a significant inheritance or gift in the next few years? ☐ ☐

b. If so, give details.

_____

_____

6. a. Do you know of any other approaching events that are likely to affect your financial status? ☐ ☐

b. If so, give details.

_____

_____

_____

_____

_____

_____

_____

_____

_____

_____

_____

_____

_____

_____

_____

_____

_____

Date Prepared   Your Name

Worksheet 4: Prenup Goals

[Check all that apply; highlight or mark those that are most important to you]

Property Ownership

☐ 1. Keep my premarital assets separate

Exceptions: _____

☐ 2. Have the following assets acquired during marriage considered separate property, marital property, or community property:

		Separate	Marital Property	Community Property
☐	a. Real estate purchased	☐	☐	☐
☐	b. Each person's salary earned during marriage	☐	☐	☐
☐	c. My retirement benefits earned during our marriage	☐	☐	☐
☐	d. Stock options and other employment benefits	☐	☐	☐
☐	e. Any increase in the value of a premarital business	☐	☐	☐
☐	f. Other investments	☐	☐	☐
☐	g. Joint bank accounts	☐	☐	☐
☐	h. Other:_____	☐	☐	☐

Comments: _____

_____

_____

☐ 3. Include the following special provisions regarding assets acquired during marriage:

_____

_____

_____

Debts

☐ 4. Protect one or both of us from the other person's premarital debts

☐ 5. Protect one or both of us from the other person's business debts or other debts incurred during marriage

Financial Responsibilities During Marriage

☐   6. Specify a process for filing income tax returns each year

☐   7. Specify each person's responsibility for household expenses

☐   8. Other: _____

        _____

        _____

Estate Planning

☐   9. Provide for my children

☐ 10. Pass on family property

☐ 11. Avoid disagreements between my spouse and my other heirs after my death by including certain terms in my estate plan

☐ 12. Provide for my support if my spouse dies

☐ 13. Provide for my spouse when I die

Divorce

☐ 14. Avoid an expensive and complicated divorce by deciding property issues in advance

☐ 15. Specify that I will/will not [*circle one*] receive alimony if we get divorced

Other Goals

☐ 16. _____

        _____

        _____

        _____

        _____

        _____

        _____

        _____

        _____

        _____

_____   _____
Date Prepared   Your Names

Worksheet 5: The Basics of Our Prenup

1. Premarital assets will be:

   ☐ Separate property

   ☐ Marital property

   ☐ Community property

   ☐ Exceptions or special provisions (specify): _____

2. Any of the following assets we acquire during our marriage will be:	Separate	Marital Property	Community Property
a. Real estate purchased	☐	☐	☐
b. Each person's salary earned during marriage	☐	☐	☐
c. Retirement benefits earned during our marriage	☐	☐	☐
d. Stock options and other employment benefits earned during our marriage	☐	☐	☐
e. Any increase in the value of a premarital business	☐	☐	☐
f. Other investments	☐	☐	☐
g. Joint bank accounts	☐	☐	☐
h. Other: _____	☐	☐	☐

3. Special provisions concerning assets acquired during marriage. Details:

   _____

   _____

   _____

   _____

4. Our prenup will provide the following regarding each person's premarital debts. Details:

   _____

   _____

   _____

   _____

5. Our prenup will provide the following regarding business debts or other debts incurred during marriage. Details:

_____

_____

_____

_____

_____

6. Our prenup will spell out a process for deciding whether to file joint tax returns and how to allocate income, deductions, taxes, and refunds. Details:

_____

_____

_____

_____

7. Our prenup will define each person's responsibility for household expenses. Details:

_____

_____

_____

_____

_____

8. This is how our prenup will support our intended estate plans (this might require waivers of surviving spouse rights). Details:

_____

_____

_____

_____

_____

_____

_____

_____

9. Our prenup will provide for our estate plans to include the following terms. Details:

_____

_____

_____

_____

10. Our prenup will provide for support of the surviving spouse. Details:

_____

_____

_____

_____

11. Our prenup will specify what should happen to our property if we separate and divorce. Details:

_____

_____

_____

_____

_____

12. Our prenup will limit, avoid, or provide for alimony if we separate and divorce. Details:

_____

_____

_____

13. Our prenup will include other agreements that apply if we divorce. Details:

_____

_____

_____

_____

_____

14. Other provisions of our prenup. Details:

_____

_____

_____

_____

_____

_____

_____

_____

_____

_____

_____

_____

_____

_____

_____

_____

_____

_____

_____

_____

_____

_____

_____

_____

_____

_____

_____

_____

_____

_____

Date Prepared   Your Name

Worksheet 6: Comparison of Prenup to Law

[Use a separate sheet for each item identified on Worksheet 5]

Prenup Item Number and Description:

_____

_____

_____

_____

1. What does the law say about this item?

_____

_____

_____

_____

_____

_____

2. Will the law allow us to create a different result in our premarital agreement?

_____

_____

_____

_____

_____

3. Is there any special legal restriction, procedure, or consideration that applies to this item?

_____

_____

_____

_____

_____

_____

Clauses for Building Your Prenup

This appendix contains all of the clauses you'll need to assemble your prenup. The clauses are organized into ten basic paragraphs that should be included in every prenuptial agreement, followed by a series of optional paragraphs and clauses. After the clauses, you'll find suggested formats for the financial disclosures you will attach to the agreement. And at the end of the appendix, there is a template you can use to create an abstract of your prenup, as explained in Chapter 9.

CAUTION

Use this appendix with Chapters 5 and 6. Refer to the detailed instructions and examples found in those chapters before attempting to create your prenup with the clauses in this appendix.

TIP

Completing your agreement: names and pronouns. To avoid confusion, we suggest you decide whose name will come first throughout the agreement. When you complete the clauses this appendix, put that person's name in all the blanks labeled "Spouse 1." The other spouse's name goes in the blanks for "Spouse 2." As you put together your document, you must also choose the appropriate pronouns—for example, "she," "he," and "they" or "her," "his," and "their"—as you go along. We've indicated each spot where you must make a choice.

SKIP AHEAD

Creating a simple prenup. To create a very simple prenup that identifies your premarital Separate Property assets and debts and leaves everything else to state law, use the clauses that have already been checked ☑ and those marked with a ✳. (If a group of alternative clauses is marked with a ✳, choose the clause that is most appropriate for your agreement.) Making a simple prenup is discussed in Chapter 5. You can also download and use a file containing a simple prenup template on the book's companion page (see Appendix A for details). Look for the simple prenuptial agreement file (SimplePrenup.rtf).

Your Prenup's Title (Mandatory for All Agreements)

Choose one:

☐   **Premarital Agreement**

☐   **Prenuptial Agreement**

☐   **Antenuptial Agreement**

☐   *[Other]*

The Ten Basic Paragraphs (Mandatory for All Agreements)

* ☑   **Paragraph 1:**   **Introductory Facts**

* ☑   **A. Parties**

This Agreement is between [*Spouse 1 first and last name*] and [*Spouse 2 first and last name*]. We refer to ourselves by our first names in This Agreement.

* ☑   **B. Purpose of Agreement**

We plan to marry on [*date*]. The purpose of This Agreement is: [*choose all that apply, or insert your own provisions*]

* ☑   to identify our premarital assets and debts,

* ☑   to define our mutual rights and obligations regarding property and finances after we marry,

☐   to support our estate plans through waiver of certain spousal rights,

☐   to set forth our rights and obligations if we separate or divorce.

☐   This Agreement also covers [*specify*].

* ☑   **C. Current Circumstances**

[*Spouse 1*] currently resides at [*address*]. [*Choose a possessive pronoun*] occupation is [*occupation*]. [*Choose a possessive pronoun*] has [*number*] children: [*names and ages*]. [*Insert optional additional information*].

[*Spouse 2*] currently resides at [*address*]. [*Choose a possessive pronoun*] occupation is [*occupation*]. [*Choose a pronoun*] has [*number*] children: [*names and ages*]. [*Insert optional additional information*].

☐   **D. Future Plans**

[*Insert any specific plans to relocate, change jobs, attend college, or similar matters*].

* ☑ **Paragraph 2: Effective Date and Term**

* ☑ **A. Effective Date of Agreement**

This Agreement will be effective on the day we marry. If we do not marry, This Agreement will be null and void.

* *Choose one:*

Alternative 1: Prenup Continues Indefinitely

☐ **B. Term of Agreement**

After we marry, This Agreement will remain in full force and effect indefinitely, unless and until we sign a new written agreement revoking or modifying This Agreement.

Alternative 2: Prenup Ends on a Specified Date (Retroactive)

☐ **B. Term of Agreement**

After we marry, This Agreement will remain in full force and effect until [*date when agreement will no longer apply*], unless prior to that date we sign a new written agreement revoking or modifying This Agreement. On [*date when agreement will no longer apply*], This Agreement will be automatically terminated and it will no longer have any force and effect, unless we sign a new written agreement extending This Agreement. After the automatic termination of This Agreement, our rights and obligations will be governed by applicable laws as if we had never signed This Agreement.

Alternative 3: Prenup Ends on a Specified Date (Not Retroactive)

☐ **B. Term of Agreement**

After we marry, This Agreement will remain in full force and effect until [*date when agreement will no longer apply*], unless prior to that date we sign a new written agreement revoking or modifying This Agreement. On [*date when agreement will no longer apply*] This Agreement will be automatically terminated and it will no longer have any force and effect, unless we sign a new written agreement extending This Agreement. After the automatic termination of This Agreement, our rights and obligations will be governed by applicable laws without regard to the terms of This Agreement, except that whatever property rights and obligations we have accrued by that date will not be retroactively affected. That is, any property defined by This Agreement as Separate Property and any debt defined by This Agreement as a separate debt shall remain separate, and any property or debts defined by This Agreement as [*choose one:* Marital/Community] Property and debts shall remain so.

* ☑ Paragraph 3:   Legal Representation

Choose one:

Alternative 1: Representative for Spouse 1

* ☐   A. Representation of [*Spouse 1*]

[*Spouse 1*] has been represented by [*name of attorney for Spouse 1*] in the negotiation and drafting of This Agreement. [*Spouse 1*] has fully discussed the terms of This Agreement with [*choose a possessive pronoun*] attorney and is voluntarily choosing to sign This Agreement.

Alternative 2: Waiver of Independent Advice for Spouse 1

☐   A. Representation of [*Spouse 1*]

[*Spouse 1*] understands that [*choose a pronoun*] has a right to be represented by an independent attorney in the negotiation and drafting of This Agreement. [*Spouse 1*] does not want to be represented by an independent attorney, even though [*choose a pronoun*] has had ample time and has sufficient funds to hire an attorney. [*Spouse 1*] understands the terms of This Agreement and [*choose a pronoun*] is voluntarily choosing to sign This Agreement without obtaining independent legal representation.

Choose one:

Alternative 1: Representative for Spouse 2

* ☐   B. Representation of [*Spouse 2*]

[*Spouse 2*] has been represented by [*name of attorney for Spouse 2*] in the negotiation and drafting of This Agreement. [*Spouse 2*] has fully discussed the terms of This Agreement with [*choose a possessive pronoun*] attorney and is voluntarily choosing to sign This Agreement.

Alternative 2: Waiver of Independent Advice for Spouse 2

☐   B. Representation of [*Spouse 2*]

[*Spouse 2*] understands that [*choose a pronoun*] has a right to be represented by an independent attorney in the negotiation and drafting of This Agreement. [*Spouse 2*] does not want to be represented by an independent attorney, even though [*choose a pronoun*] has had ample time and has sufficient funds to hire an attorney. [*Spouse 2*] understands the terms of This Agreement and [*choose a pronoun*] is voluntarily choosing to sign This Agreement without obtaining independent legal representation.

Choose one:

Alternative 1: Prenup Drafted Together

* ☐   C. Drafting of Agreement

This Agreement was drafted through the joint efforts of [*first names of spouses*].

Alternative 2: Prenup Not Drafted Together

☐ C. **Drafting of Agreement**

This Agreement was drafted by [*name*].

* ☑ **Paragraph 4:   Disclosures**

Choose one:

Alternative 1: Formal Written Disclosure

* ☐ A. **[*Spouse 1*]'s Disclosures**

All of [*Spouse 1*]'s assets [*optional:* having a value greater than $_____] and all of [*choose a possessive pronoun*] debts [*optional:* exceeding $_____] are listed on Schedule 1, attached to This Agreement. [*Spouse 1*]'s income for the calendar year [*insert year*] [*optional:* and the approximate amount of [*choose a possessive pronoun*] personal expenses for that year] [*choose one:* is/are] also listed on Schedule 1. [*Spouse 1*] has provided the information on Schedule 1 in good faith. The values and other financial information on Schedule 1 are approximations and might not be exact, but they are intended to present a full, fair, and reasonable disclosure of [*Spouse 1*]'s assets, debts, income, and personal expenses as of the time they were presented to [*Spouse 2*].

* ☐ B. **[*Spouse 2*]'s Disclosures**

All of [*Spouse 2*]'s assets [*optional:* having a value greater than $_____] and all of [*choose a possessive pronoun*] debts [*optional:* exceeding $_____] are listed on Schedule 2, attached to This Agreement. [*Spouse 2*]'s income for the calendar year [*insert year*] [*optional:* and the approximate amount of [*choose a possessive pronoun*] personal expenses for that year] [*choose one:* is/are] also listed on Schedule 2. [*Spouse 2*] has provided the information on Schedule 2 in good faith. The values and other financial information on Schedule 2 are approximations and might not be exact, but they are intended to present a full, fair, and reasonable disclosure of [*Spouse 2*]'s assets, debts, income, and personal expenses as of the time they were presented to [*Spouse 1*].

☐ C. **Jointly Owned Premarital Assets** [*optional:* and Jointly Owed Premarital Debts]

All of our jointly owned premarital assets [*optional:* having a value greater than $_____] [*optional:* and all jointly owed premarital debts] are listed on Schedule 3, attached to This Agreement. The values stated on Schedule 3 are reasonably accurate as of [*date you prepared Schedule 3*].

☐ __. **Documents Provided by [*Spouse 1*]**

In addition to the information listed on Schedule 1, [*Spouse 1*] has given [*Spouse 2*] copies of the following documents [*list all documents that apply*]:

☐ 1. Federal and state individual income tax returns filed by [*Spouse 1*] for the year(s) [*insert year(s)*].

☐ 2. The following appraisals: [*for each appraisal, specify property appraised, date, and appraiser*].

☐ 3. [*List any additional documents provided*].

☐ __. **Documents Provided by [*Spouse 2*]**

In addition to the information listed on Schedule 2, [*Spouse 2*] has given [*Spouse 1*] copies of the following documents [*list all documents that apply*]:

☐ 1. Federal and state individual income tax returns filed by [*Spouse 2*] for the year(s) [*insert year(s)*].

☐ 2. The following appraisals: [*for each appraisal, specify property appraised, date, and appraiser*].

☐ 3. [*List any additional documents provided*].

* ☐ __. **Acknowledgment of Receipt of Disclosures**

[*Spouse 1*] received a copy of Schedule 2 [*insert if applicable:* and the documents described in Paragraph __] on [*date*]. [*Spouse 1*] reviewed this information before signing This Agreement.

[*Spouse 2*] received a copy of Schedule 1 [*insert if applicable:* and the documents described in Paragraph __] on [*date*]. [*Spouse 2*] reviewed this information before signing This Agreement.

☐ __. **Mutual Waiver of Further Disclosure**

Each of us understands that the values and other information on Schedules 1 and 2 are approximate. We consider this information [*insert if applicable:* and the documents described in Paragraphs __ and __] sufficient and each of us voluntarily waives the right to be given any additional information.

Alternative 2: Waiver of Formal Written Disclosure

☐ **A.** **[_Spouse 1_]'s Waiver of Formal Written Disclosure**

[_Spouse 1_] is aware of [_Spouse 2_]'s financial circumstances. [_Choose a pronoun_] voluntarily waives the right to be given a formal written disclosure or any other information about [_Spouse 2_]'s finances.

☐ **B.** **[_Spouse 2_]'s Waiver of Formal Written Disclosure**

[_Spouse 2_] is aware of [_Spouse 1_]'s financial circumstances. [_Choose a pronoun_] voluntarily waives the right to be given a formal written disclosure or any other information about [_Spouse 1_]'s finances.

Optional: Acknowledgment of Receipt of Agreement

☐ **__. Acknowledgment of Receipt of Agreement**

[_Spouse 1_] first received a draft of This Agreement on [_date_]. This Agreement [_choose one_: has/ has not] been revised since that date [_optional_: and [_Spouse 1_] received the final draft of This Agreement on [_date_].] [_If no revisions, choose "has not" and add a period after "since that date."_]

[_Spouse 2_] first received a draft of This Agreement on [_date_]. This Agreement [_choose one_: has/ has not] been revised since that date [_optional_: and [_Spouse 2_] received the final draft of This Agreement on [_date_].] [_If no revisions, choose "has not" and add a period after "since that date."_]

* ☑ **Paragraph 5:   Definitions**

* ☑ **A. This Agreement**

The term "This Agreement" refers to the provisions of this document, once signed by us, as modified by any subsequent amendments in writing signed by us.

* ☑ **B. Separate Property**

Any asset designated as one person's "Separate Property" in This Agreement belongs exclusively to that person. A spouse has the sole right to manage and dispose of their Separate Property assets. Separate Property is not subject to division between us if we divorce. However, if the owner of Separate Property dies, the surviving spouse may have a legal claim to it, unless they have signed a valid written waiver in This Agreement or in another document.

* *Choose one:*

Alternative 1

☐ **C. Marital Property**

An asset designated as "Marital Property" in This Agreement might be subject to division between us by a court if we divorce, unless we provide otherwise in This Agreement or in another document. Any asset designated as Marital Property might be subject to a claim by a surviving spouse, unless the surviving spouse has signed a valid written waiver of such claims in This Agreement or in another document. [*Optional:* We will both have equal rights to manage and control any Marital Property held in our joint names. If an asset designated as Marital Property is held in only one of our names, the sole title holder will have the exclusive right to manage, control, transfer, or sell that property, to the extent allowed by state law.]

Alternative 2

☐ **C. Community Property**

Any asset designated as "Community Property" in This Agreement belongs to both of us equally. Our Community Property will be subject to division between us by a court if we divorce, taking into account any requirements for division spelled out in This Agreement.

We will both have equal rights to manage and control any Community Property, subject to any exceptions provided by state law. [*Optional*: If an asset designated as Community Property is held in only one of our names, the sole title holder will have the exclusive right to manage, control, transfer, or sell that property, to the extent allowed by state law.]

* ☐ **D. Divorce**

The term "Divorce" in This Agreement refers to any legal proceeding to end or alter our marital relationship, including a proceeding for divorce, dissolution of marriage, total or absolute divorce, legal separation, or separate maintenance [*Optional:* , or annulment].

* ☑ **Paragraph 6:   Ownership of Premarital Assets**

Choose one:

Alternative 1

* ☐ **A. All Premarital Assets and Property Traceable to Them Remain Separate Property**

Except as specified elsewhere in This Agreement, [*Spouse 1*]'s premarital assets (which are listed on Schedule 1), and all property traceable to those assets, shall continue to be [*choose a possessive pronoun*] Separate Property after we marry. "All property traceable to those assets" means any growth in value of those assets [*choose one:* including/not including] growth in value arising as a direct or indirect result of the efforts of one or both of us during our marriage. It also means any sales proceeds of those assets, any asset purchased with the sales proceeds, or any asset(s) acquired in exchange for those assets, as long as the sales proceeds or any such new asset is held in the sole name of [*Spouse 1*] [*add if applicable:* or if held in joint names, as long as it is traceable to the premarital asset].

Except as specified elsewhere in This Agreement, [*Spouse 2*]'s premarital assets (which are listed on Schedule 2), and all property traceable to those assets, shall continue to be [*choose a possessive pronoun*] Separate Property after we marry. "All property traceable to those assets" means any growth in value of those assets [*choose one:* including/not including] growth in value arising as a direct or indirect result of the efforts of one or both of us during our marriage. It also means any sales proceeds of those assets, any asset purchased with the sales proceeds, or any asset(s) acquired in exchange for those assets, as long as the sales proceeds or any such new asset is held in the sole name of [*Spouse 2*] [*add if applicable:* or if held in joint names, as long as it is traceable to the premarital asset].

Alternative 2

☐ **A. All Premarital Assets Remain Separate Property but Not Property Traceable to Them**

Except as specified elsewhere in This Agreement, [*Spouse 1*]'s premarital assets, which are listed on Schedule 1, shall continue to be [*choose a possessive pronoun*] Separate Property after we marry. However, all property traceable to those assets shall be considered [*choose one:* Marital/ Community] Property. "All property traceable to those assets" means any growth in value of those assets, including growth in value arising as a direct or indirect result of the efforts of one or both of us during our marriage. It also means any sales proceeds of those assets, any asset purchased with the sales proceeds, or any asset(s) acquired in exchange for those assets, even if the sales proceeds or any such new asset is held in the sole name of [*Spouse 1*].

Except as specified elsewhere in This Agreement, [*Spouse 2*]'s premarital assets, which are listed on Schedule 2, shall continue to be [*choose a possessive pronoun*] Separate Property after we marry. However, all property traceable to those assets shall be considered [*choose one:* Marital/ Community] Property. "All property traceable to those assets" means any growth in value of those assets, including growth in value arising as a direct or indirect result of the efforts of one or both of us during our marriage. It also means any sales proceeds of those assets, any asset purchased with the sales proceeds, or any asset(s) acquired in exchange for those assets, even if the sales proceeds or any such new asset is held in the sole name of [*Spouse 2*].

Alternative 3

☐ **A. All Premarital Assets Will Be Considered [_choose one_: Marital/Community] Property**

Except as specified elsewhere in This Agreement, all of our premarital assets, which are listed on Schedules 1 and 2, and all property traceable to those assets, will be considered [_choose one:_ Marital/Community] Property as soon as we marry. "All property traceable to those assets" means any growth in value of those assets, including growth in value arising as a direct or indirect result of the efforts of one or both of us during our marriage. It also means any sales proceeds of those assets, any asset purchased with the sales proceeds, or any asset(s) acquired in exchange for those assets, even if the sales proceeds or any such new asset is held in the sole name of one of us.

Optional Clause for Jointly Owned Premarital Assets

☐ **__. Jointly Owned Premarital Assets Will Be Considered [_choose one:_ Equally Owned Separate/ Marital/Community] Property**

Except as specified elsewhere in This Agreement, all of our jointly owned premarital assets, which are listed on Schedule 3, and all property traceable to those assets, will be considered [_choose one:_ equally owned Separate/Marital/Community] Property as soon as we marry. "All property traceable to those assets" means any growth in value of those assets, including growth in value arising as a direct or indirect result of the efforts of one or both of us during our marriage. It also means any sales proceeds of those assets, any asset purchased with the sales proceeds, or any asset(s) acquired in exchange for those assets, even if the sales proceeds or any such new asset is held in the sole name of one of us.

Optional Clause for Premarital Real Estate

Choose one:

Alternative 1

☐ **__. [_Choose one:_ Real Estate/_Specify Certain Real Estate_] Will Remain Separate Property**

During our marriage, [_name_]'s real estate located at [_address_] shall continue to be [name]'s Separate Property after we marry [_if it is a home you will live in together, add_: regardless of whether we refer to it as "our" home and no matter how long we live there]. Use of [_choose one:_ Marital/Community] Property funds to pay any mortgage payments, property taxes, insurance, improvements, repairs, or other expenses for the property [_optional:_ or time spent by one or both of us fixing it up] will not alter the Separate Property nature of the home. Such payments will not be reimbursable to the [_choose one:_ Marital/Community] Property estate unless we sign a written agreement expressly providing otherwise. [_Optional:_ Any increase in the property's value shall also be [_name_]'s Separate Property. If [_name_] sells the property or exchanges it for another asset, any sales proceeds or asset acquired in exchange will be [_choose a possessive pronoun_] Separate Property.]

Alternative 2

☐ __. Equity in [*choose one:* Real Estate/*Specify Certain Real Estate*] Will Be Apportioned Between Separate Property and [*choose one:* Marital/Community] Property

The equity in [*name*]'s real estate located at [*address*] will be apportioned between [*name*]'s Separate Property and [*choose one:* Marital/Community] Property as follows: [*specify the percentage that will be Separate Property and the percentage that will be Marital or Community Property, or the method to be used to apportion the asset*]. [*Add if applicable:* The above provisions will apply to any sales proceeds or assets acquired in exchange for the property during our marriage.]

Alternative 3

☐ __. [*Choose one:* Marital/Community] Property Contributions to [*choose one:* Real Estate/ *Specify Certain Real Estate*] Will Be Reimbursed

If [*choose one:* Marital/Community] Property funds are used to pay for certain expenses related to [*name*]'s real estate located at [*address*], the property will remain [*name*]'s Separate Property, but the [*choose one:* Marital/Community] Property payments will be reimbursed as follows: [*specify how and when the reimbursement would be payable, such as all or one-half of what was paid, with or without interest, to the estate or to the nonowner, upon death and/or upon divorce. If applicable, cross-refer to any paragraphs relating to estate planning or divorce*]. The reimbursable expenses referred to in this clause shall include only payments for [*specify types of payments that qualify, such as payments reducing the principal balance owed on a mortgage, mortgage interest, property taxes, repairs, or capital improvements*].

Alternative 4

☐ __. [*Choose one:* Real Estate/*Specify Certain Real Estate*] Will Become [*choose one:* Marital/ Community] Property

[*Name*]'s real estate located at [*address*] will become [*choose one:* Marital/Community] Property [*specify when this will happen, such as on a certain date or "as soon as we marry"*].

Optional Clause for a Premarital Business

Choose one:

Alternative 1

☐ __. Premarital [*choose one:* Business/Professional Practice] Will Remain Separate Property

During our marriage, [*name*] plans to continue to operate the [*choose one:* business/ professional practice] known as [*name of business/professional practice*]. The [*choose one:* business/professional practice] shall continue to be [*name*]'s Separate Property after we marry. Any increase in its value shall also be [*name*]'s Separate Property, regardless of how we refer to it or how much time either or both of us devotes to it. If [*name*] sells the [*choose one:* business/practice] or exchanges it for another asset, any sales proceeds or asset acquired in exchange will be [*choose a possessive pronoun*] Separate Property.

Alternative 2

☐ __. Premarital [*choose one:* Business/Professional Practice] Will Be Subject to Apportionment Between Separate and [*choose one:* Marital/Community] Property

During our marriage, [*name*] plans to continue to operate the [*choose one:* business/professional practice] known as [*name of business/professional practice*]. After we marry, the [*choose one:* business/professional practice] will be subject to apportionment between [*name*]'s Separate Property and [*choose one:* Marital/Community] Property as follows: [*specify the method to be used to apportion the asset*]. [*Add if applicable:* If the [*choose one:* business/practice] is sold during our marriage, the above provisions will apply to apportionment of any sales proceeds.]

Optional Clause for Premarital Retirement Benefits

Choose one:

Alternative 1

☐ __. Premarital Retirement or Employee Benefits Will Be Separate Property

All retirement or employee benefits earned by (or in the name of) one of us before we marry, as listed on Schedules 1 and 2, will be the Separate Property of the person who earned them or in whose name those benefits are vested. This applies to all benefits in all retirement, pension, deferred compensation, stock options, and other employee benefit or tax deferred plans, whether qualified according to IRS regulations or nonqualified.

Each of us hereby waives all present and future legal claims regarding the other person's premarital retirement or employee benefits referred to above. Each of us understands that this waiver might not be effective under applicable laws unless reaffirmed after we marry in a written waiver in a form approved by the retirement or employee benefit plan. Therefore, we agree that after we marry, upon request by the other party, each of us will sign any document necessary to carry out the intent of this clause, including a written waiver in a form approved by the plan.

Alternative 2

__. Premarital Retirement or Employee Benefits Will Be [*choose one:* Marital/Community] Property

All retirement or employee benefits earned by (or in the name of) one of us before we marry, as listed on Schedules 1 and 2, will be considered [*choose one:* Marital/Community] Property. This applies to all benefits in all retirement, pension, deferred compensation, stock options, and other employee benefit or tax deferred plans, whether qualified according to IRS regulations or nonqualified.

Each of us understands that under applicable laws title to any retirement or employee benefit account can be held in the name of only one person, and that the written consent of both spouses might be required prior to making any election of benefits under a retirement or employee benefit plan. We agree that after we marry, upon request by the other party, each of us will sign any document necessary to carry out the intent of this clause.

Optional Clauses for Other Premarital Assets

Choose all that apply:

Alternative 1

☐ ___. **Certain Premarital Assets Will Remain Separate Property**

The following premarital asset(s) will remain the Separate Property of the spouse who owns the asset(s) prior to marriage and will not be converted to [*choose one:* Marital/Community] Property when we marry: [*for each person, list each asset from Schedule 1 or 2 to which this applies*].

Alternative 2

☐ ___. **Certain Premarital Assets Will Be Apportioned Between Separate and [*choose one:* Marital/Community] Property**

The following premarital asset(s) will be apportioned between [*name*]'s Separate Property and [*choose one:* Marital/Community] Property [*choose one:* as soon as we marry/*specify when this will take effect*] as follows: [*for each person, list each asset from Schedule 1 or 2 to which this applies, and specify the method to be used to apportion the asset(s)*]. [*Add if applicable:* If any asset listed in this clause is sold during our marriage, the above provisions will apply to apportionment of any sales proceeds.]

Alternative 3

☐ ___. **Certain Premarital Assets Will Become [*choose one:* Marital/Community] Property**

The following premarital assets will become [*choose one:* Marital/Community] Property [*choose one:* as soon as we marry/*specify when this will take effect*]: [*list the assets from Schedule 1 or 2 to which this applies*].

* ☑ **Paragraph 7:   Ownership of Assets Acquired During Marriage**

Choose one:

Alternative 1

* ☐ **A. Our Rights in Assets Acquired During Marriage Will Be Determined According to State Law**

Except as specified elsewhere in This Agreement, our rights in every asset acquired after we marry, and in any profits or growth in value or any sales proceeds or asset acquired in exchange for those assets, will be determined in accordance with the laws of [*name of state*].

Alternative 2

☐ **A. Our Rights in Assets Acquired During Marriage Will Be Determined According to How Title Is Held**

Except as specified elsewhere in This Agreement, every asset acquired after we marry, and any profits or growth in value or any sales proceeds or asset acquired in exchange for those assets, will be owned as specified in the document of title. If an asset is tangible personal property that does not have a document of title, the person who paid for the asset will be the owner.

Each of us understands that if it were not for This Agreement, certain assets acquired during our marriage may be considered [*choose one:* Marital/Community] Property despite the name in which title is held, and we knowingly agree to waive our [*choose one:* Marital/Community] Property rights in such assets and be bound by This Agreement instead, unless a [*choose one:* Marital/Community] Property form of ownership is specified in the title.

Alternative 3

☐ **A. All Property to Be Separate—No [*choose one:* Marital/Community] Property Rights Accrue**

We intend to own every asset acquired during our marriage, including property acquired in joint names and any profits or growth in value, or any sales proceeds or asset acquired in exchange for those assets, as Separate Property and not as [*choose one:* Marital/Community] Property, as if we were unmarried. Each of us understands that if it were not for This Agreement, certain assets acquired during our marriage may be considered [*choose one:* Marital/Community] Property despite the name in which title is held, and we knowingly agree to be bound by This Agreement instead.

Alternative 4

☐ **A. Assets Acquired During Marriage Will Be [*choose one:* Marital/Community] Property**

Except as specified elsewhere in This Agreement, every asset acquired by one or both of us after we marry, and any profits or growth in value, or any sales proceeds or asset acquired in exchange for these assets, will be considered [*choose one:* Marital/Community] Property, regardless of how title is held. Each of us understands that if it were not for This Agreement, certain assets acquired in the name of only one person during our marriage may be considered Separate Property of the person in whose name it is held, and we knowingly agree to be bound by This Agreement instead.

Alternative 5

☐ **A. Our Rights in Assets Acquired During Marriage Will Be Apportioned**

Except as specified elsewhere in This Agreement, our rights in every asset acquired during our marriage in the name of one or both of us, and any profits or growth in value or any sales proceeds or asset acquired in exchange for that asset, will be apportioned between us, according to the following formula: [*insert formula*].

Optional Clause for Income

Choose one:

Alternative 1

☐ __. **All Income Will Be [*choose one:* Marital/Community] Property**

Except as specified elsewhere in This Agreement, our wages and other earned or unearned income will be considered [*choose one:* Marital/Community] Property. This clause applies to wages or income earned during our marriage even if received at a later time. It also applies to all unearned income such as dividends, interest, rents, and partnership distributions received during our marriage, regardless of whether it is derived from Separate Property or [*choose one:* Marital/Community] Property.

Alternative 2

☐ __. **All Income Will Be Separate Property**

Except as specified elsewhere in This Agreement, our wages and other earned or unearned income will be considered the Separate Property of the person who earned or received the income. This clause applies to wages or income earned during our marriage even if received at a later time. It also applies to all unearned income such as dividends, interest, rents, and partnership distributions received during our marriage.

Alternative 3

☐ __. **Earned Income Will Be [*choose one:* Marital/Community] Property; Unearned Income Will Be Separate Property**

Except as specified elsewhere in This Agreement, our wages and other income earned during our marriage, even if received at a later time, will be considered [*choose one:* Marital/Community] Property. Except as specified elsewhere in This Agreement, all unearned income such as dividends, interest, rents, and partnership distributions received during our marriage will be considered the Separate Property of the person who received the income,

Choose one:

☐ provided that any unearned income derived from an asset held in our joint names shall be owned by us in the same manner and proportions as the asset from which it is derived is owned.

OR ☐ provided that any unearned income derived from [*choose one:* Marital/Community] Property or an asset held in our joint names shall be considered [*choose one:* Marital/Community] Property.

Alternative 4

☐ __. **Earned Income Will Be Separate Property; Unearned Income Will Be [*choose one:* Marital/Community] Property**

Except as specified elsewhere in This Agreement, our wages or other income earned during our marriage, even if received at a later time, will be considered the Separate Property of the person who earned or received the income. Except as specified elsewhere in This Agreement, all unearned income such as dividends, interest, rents, and partnership distributions received during our marriage will be considered [*choose one:* Marital/Community] Property, including income derived from Separate Property.

Optional Clause for Inheritances

Choose one:

Alternative 1

☐ __. **Inheritances Received by One Party During Marriage Will Be Separate Property**

If one of us receives an asset as an inheritance, bequest, trust distribution, or other death benefit during our marriage, that asset will be that individual's Separate Property.

Choose one:

☐ Any profits or growth in value or any sales proceeds or assets acquired in exchange for a Separate Property inheritance described above will also be Separate Property.

OR ☐ However, any profits or growth in value or any sales proceeds or assets acquired in exchange for a Separate Property inheritance described above will be considered [*choose one:* Marital/Community] Property.

Alternative 2

☐ __. **Inheritances Received by One Party During Marriage Will Be [*choose one:* Marital/Community] Property**

If one of us receives an asset as an inheritance, bequest, trust distribution, or other death benefit during our marriage, that asset will be [*choose one:* Marital/Community] Property. Any profits or growth in value, and any sales proceeds or assets acquired in exchange for that asset will also be [*choose one:* Marital/Community] Property.

Optional Clause for Gifts

Choose one:

Alternative 1

☐ __. **Gifts Received During Marriage Will Be Separate Property**

Except as specified elsewhere in This Agreement, any asset received by one us during our marriage as a gift from a third party or from the other spouse will be the Separate Property of the spouse who receives the gift.

Any gift given to both of us jointly will be owned by us jointly in equal Separate Property shares unless at the time of making the gift the person making the gift specifies in writing a different percentage of ownership.

Choose one:

☐ Any profits or growth in value or any sales proceeds or assets acquired in exchange for a Separate Property gift described above will also be Separate Property.

OR ☐ However, any profits or growth in value or any sales proceeds or asset acquired in exchange for a Separate Property gift described above will be considered [*choose one:* Marital/Community] Property.

Alternative 2

☐ __. **Gifts Received During Marriage Will Be [*choose one:* Marital/Community] Property**

Except as specified elsewhere in This Agreement, any asset received by one of us during our marriage as a gift from a third party or from the other spouse, and any gift given to both of us jointly, will be [*choose one:* Marital/Community] Property. Any profits or growth in value or any sales proceeds or assets acquired in exchange for that asset will also be [*choose one:* Marital/Community] Property.

Alternative 3

☐ __. **Third-Party Gifts Will Be Separate Property; Interspousal Gifts Will Be [*choose one:* Marital/Community] Property**

Except as specified elsewhere in This Agreement, any asset received by one of us during our marriage as a gift from a third party will be the Separate Property of the spouse who receives the gift. Any gift given to both of us jointly will be owned by us jointly in equal Separate Property shares unless at the time of the gift the person making the gift specifies in writing a different percentage of ownership.

Except as specified elsewhere in This Agreement, any asset received by one of us during our marriage as a gift from the other spouse will be [*choose one:* Marital/Community] Property, unless at the time of the gift the spouse making the gift specifies in writing that the gift is intended to be the Separate Property of the receiving spouse.

Choose one:

☐ Any profits or growth in value or any sales proceeds or assets acquired in exchange for a Separate Property gift described above will also be Separate Property [*if applicable, add:* if it has a value of greater than $_____ at the time of the gift].

OR ☐ However, any profits or growth in value or any sales proceeds or asset acquired in exchange for a Separate Property gift described above will be considered [*choose one:* Marital/Community] Property.

Alternative 4

☐ __. Third-Party Gifts Will Be [*choose one:* Marital/Community] Property; Interspousal Gifts Will Be Separate Property

Except as specified elsewhere in This Agreement, any asset received by one of us during our marriage as a gift from a third party, and any gift given to both of us jointly, will be [*choose one:* Marital/Community] Property. Any profits or growth in value or any sales proceeds or assets acquired in exchange for that asset will also be [*choose one:* Marital/Community] Property.

Except as specified elsewhere in This Agreement, any asset received by one of us during our marriage as a gift from the other spouse will be the Separate Property of the spouse who receives the gift.

Choose one:

☐ Any profits or growth in value or any sales proceeds or assets acquired in exchange for a Separate Property gift described above will also be Separate Property.

OR ☐ However, any profits or growth in value or any sales proceeds or asset acquired in exchange for a Separate Property gift described above will be considered [*choose one:* Marital/Community] Property.

Optional Clause for Joint Accounts

Choose one:

Alternative 1

☐ __. Joint Accounts Will Be [*choose one:* Marital/Community] Property

Any funds deposited into a joint bank or other deposit account established by and between us will be considered [*choose one:* Marital/Community] Property, even if one or both of us deposits Separate Property funds into the account.

Choose one:

☐ There will be no right of reimbursement for any Separate Property funds deposited into a joint account unless we expressly agree in writing to a right of reimbursement regarding a particular account or specific deposit.

OR ☐ Whoever deposits Separate Property funds into a joint account will have a right of reimbursement for the amount of the funds contributed unless that person signs a written waiver of the right to be reimbursed. Any reimbursement owed shall be payable as follows: [*specify how and when the reimbursement is payable—for example, at certain times of year, upon death or divorce, with or without interest; if applicable, cross-refer to paragraphs relating to estate planning or divorce*].

Alternative 2

☐ ___. **Joint Accounts Will Consist of Shares of Separate Property**

If a bank or other deposit account is acquired by us jointly (in both of our names), each of us will own an undivided share of the funds in the account as Separate Property and not as [*choose one:* Marital/Community] Property, as follows: [*specify each person's percentage or the method to be used to determine percentages, such as equal shares or in proportion to the total amount contributed by each spouse to the account*].

This clause shall apply to any joint account, even if we deposit [*choose one:* Marital/Community] Property funds into the account, unless we sign a separate written agreement expressly specifying a different form or percentage of ownership regarding a particular account.

Choose one:

☐ There will be no right of reimbursement for deposits of any [*choose one:* Marital/Community] Property funds unless we expressly agree in writing to a right of reimbursement regarding a particular account or a specific deposit.

OR ☐ There will be a right of reimbursement for any deposit of [*choose one:* Marital/Community] Property funds unless the spouse who did not make the deposit of [*choose one:* Marital/Community] Property funds signs a written waiver of the right to be reimbursed. Any reimbursement owed shall be payable as follows: [*specify how and when the reimbursement is payable—for example, at certain times of year, upon death or upon divorce, with or without interest; if applicable, cross-refer to paragraphs relating to estate planning or divorce*].

Optional Clause for Retirement and Employee Benefits

Choose one:

Alternative 1

☐ ___. **Retirement or Employee Benefits Earned During Marriage Will Be Separate Property**

All retirement or employee benefits earned by (or in the name of) one of us during our marriage will be the Separate Property of the person in whose name those benefits are vested. This applies to all benefits in all retirement, pension, deferred compensation, stock options, and other employee benefit or tax deferred plans, whether qualified according to IRS regulations or nonqualified.

Each of us hereby waives all legal claims to the other person's retirement or employee benefits referred to above. Each of us understands that this waiver might not be effective under applicable laws unless reaffirmed after we marry in a written waiver in a form approved by the retirement or employee benefit plan. We agree that after we marry, upon request by the other party, each of us will sign any document necessary to carry out the intent of this clause, including a written waiver in a form approved by the plan.

Alternative 2

☐ __. Retirement or Employee Benefits Earned During Marriage Will Be [*choose one:* Marital/ Community] Property

All retirement or employee benefits earned by (or in the name of) one of us during our marriage will be considered [*choose one:* Marital/Community] Property. This applies to all benefits in all retirement, pension, deferred compensation, stock options, and other employee benefit or tax deferred plans, whether qualified according to IRS regulations or nonqualified.

Each of us understands that under applicable laws, title to any retirement or employee benefit account can be held in the name of only one person, and that the written consent of both spouses might be required prior to making any election of benefits under a retirement or employee benefit plan. We agree that after we marry, upon request by the other party, each of us will sign any document necessary to carry out the intent of this clause.

Optional Clause for Other Assets Acquired During Marriage

Choose one:

Alternative 1

☐ __. [*Choose one:* Certain Assets/*Insert Name of Asset(s)*] Will Be Separate Property

After we marry, [*name*] [*choose one:* plans to/might] acquire [*choose one:* certain assets or types of assets/*insert the name of the asset, such as "a home"*]. [*Choose one:* Any such asset/*asset name*] may otherwise be [*choose one:* Marital/Community] Property, but instead will be [*name*]'s Separate Property. [*Add if applicable:* This also applies to any profits or increase in value or any sales proceeds or assets acquired in exchange for [*choose one:* any such asset/*asset name*].] [*If specific asset covered is not inserted above, add:* The assets or types of assets to which this applies are listed below:

Insert list of assets or types of assets that will be separate property and insert any additional conditions that apply.]

Alternative 2

☐ __. [*Choose one:* Certain Assets/*Insert Name of Asset(s)*] Will Be [*choose one:* Marital/ Community] Property

After we marry, we [*choose one:* plan to/might] acquire [*choose one:* certain assets or types of assets/*insert the name of the asset, such as "a home"*]. [*Choose one:* Any such asset/*asset name*] may otherwise be Separate Property but instead will be considered [*choose one:* Marital/ Community] Property. [*Add if applicable:* This also applies to any profits or increase in value or any sales proceeds or assets acquired in exchange for [*choose one:* any such asset/*asset name*].] [*If specific asset covered is not inserted above, add:* The assets or types of asset to which this applies are listed below:

Insert list of assets or types of assets that will be considered marital or community property and insert any additional conditions that apply].

Optional Clauses for Contributions of Separate Property to Marital or Community Assets

Alternative 1

☐ __. Contributions of Separate Property to [*choose one:* Marital/Community] Property: Ownership Will Be Apportioned

During our marriage, one or both of us may contribute Separate Property funds to the acquisition or improvement of [*optional:* or payment of other expenses related to] [*choose one:* Marital/Community] Property. If so, ownership of any such property will be apportioned between Separate Property and [*choose one:* Marital/Community] Property as follows: [*specify the percentages that will be separate property and marital or community property, or the method to be used to apportion the asset*]. [*Add if applicable:* There will be no apportionment for Separate Property funds paid for expenses related to Community Property other than for acquisition or improvement of the property.]

Alternative 2

☐ __. Separate Property Contributions to [*choose one:* Marital/Community] Property Will Be Reimbursed

During our marriage, one or both of us may contribute Separate Property funds to acquire or improve [*optional:* or to pay other expenses related to] [*choose one:* Marital/Community] Property. In the absence of a contrary written agreement, we will consider any such contribution to be subject to a right of reimbursement payable [*specify how and when the reimbursement would be payable—for example, at certain times of year, upon death or divorce, with or without interest; if applicable, cross-refer to paragraphs relating to estate planning or divorce*]. The reimbursable contributions referred to in this clause shall include only payments for [*specify types of payments that qualify, such as down payments, payments reducing the principal balance owed on a mortgage or other financing, interest and finance charges, property taxes, repairs, or capital improvements*].

Alternative 3

☐ __. Waiver of Reimbursement for Separate Property Contributions

During our marriage, one or both of us may contribute Separate Property funds to acquire or improve [*optional:* or to pay other expenses related to] [*choose one:* Marital/Community] Property. In the absence of a contrary written agreement, we will consider any such contribution to be a gift of Separate Property. Neither of us shall be entitled to reimbursement for any such contribution, and each of us hereby waives any right to reimbursement otherwise granted by law.

* ☑ **Paragraph 8: Responsibility for Debts and Expenses**

Choose all that apply:

* ☐ __. Each Person Solely Responsible for Own Premarital Debts

[*Spouse 1*]'s debts listed on Schedule 1 are [*choose a possessive pronoun*] sole and separate debts. [*Spouse 2*] will not be responsible for them, nor may [*choose a possessive pronoun*] Separate Property [*add if applicable:* or [*choose one:* his/her] share of any [*choose one:* Marital/Community] Property be used to pay them without [*choose a possessive pronoun*] written consent. [*Spouse 1*] will indemnify and hold [*Spouse 2*] harmless from any proceeding to collect on [*Spouse 1*]'s debts from [*Spouse 2*]'s property, and [*choose a pronoun*] will be solely responsible for any expenses, including attorneys' fees, incurred by [*Spouse 2*] in connection with such a proceeding.

[*Spouse 2*]'s debts listed on Schedule 2 are [*choose a possessive pronoun*] sole and separate debts. [*Spouse 1*] will not be responsible for them, nor may [*choose a possessive pronoun*] Separate Property [*add if applicable:* or [*choose one:* his/her] share of any [*choose one:* Marital/Community] Property be used to pay them without [*choose a possessive pronoun*] written consent. [*Spouse 2*] will indemnify and hold [*Spouse 1*] harmless from any proceeding to collect on [*Spouse 2*]'s debts from [*Spouse 1*]'s property, and [*choose a pronoun*] will be solely responsible for any expenses, including attorneys' fees, incurred by [*Spouse 1*] in connection with such a proceeding.

☐ __. Each Spouse Solely Responsible for Debts Incurred by That Spouse During Marriage

Except as specified elsewhere in This Agreement, all debts incurred by [*Spouse 1*] in [*choose a possessive pronoun*] sole name during our marriage will be [*choose a possessive pronoun*] sole and separate debts. [*Spouse 2*] will not be responsible for them, nor may [*choose a possessive pronoun*] Separate Property [*add if applicable:* or [*choose a possessive pronoun*] share of any [*choose one:* Marital/Community] Property] be used to pay them without [*choose one:* his/her] written consent. [*Spouse 1*] will indemnify and hold [*Spouse 2*] harmless from any proceeding to collect on [*Spouse 1*]'s debts from [*Spouse 2*]'s property, and [*choose a pronoun*] will be solely responsible for any expenses, including attorneys' fees, incurred by [*Spouse 2*] in connection with such a proceeding.

Except as specified elsewhere in This Agreement, all debts incurred by [*Spouse 2*] in [*choose a possessive pronoun*] sole name during our marriage will be [*choose a possessive pronoun*] sole and separate debts. [*Spouse 1*] will not be responsible for them, nor may [*choose a possessive pronoun*] Separate Property [*add if applicable:* or [*choose a possessive pronoun*] share of any [*choose one:* Marital/Community] Property] be used to pay them without [*choose a possessive pronoun*] written consent. [*Spouse 2*] will indemnify and hold [*Spouse 1*] harmless from any proceeding to collect on [*Spouse 2*]'s debts from [*Spouse 1*]'s property, and [*choose a pronoun*] will be solely responsible for any expenses, including attorneys' fees, incurred by [*Spouse 1*] in connection with such a proceeding.

☐ __. Debts Incurred During Marriage for Mutual Benefit Will Be [*choose one:* Marital/Community] Debts

Any debt incurred by either or both of us for our mutual benefit during our marriage will be considered a [*choose one:* Marital/Community] debt and will be paid from [*choose one:* Marital/Community] Property funds. A debt will be considered incurred for our mutual benefit if it covers any of the following expenses: [*insert the types of expenses included*]; but not the following expenses: [*insert expenses not included*]. If one of us uses [*choose one:* his/her] Separate Property funds to pay all or part of the debt, they [*choose one:* will/will not] be entitled to be reimbursed from [*choose one:* Marital/Community] Property funds. [*If separate property funds are to be reimbursed, specify how and when the reimbursement is to be made.*]

☐ __. Taxes

We agree to confer each year prior to the deadline for filing federal [*add if applicable:* and state] income tax returns for the preceding year in order to determine whether it is to our mutual advantage to file joint or separate returns. We will determine this by preparing draft joint and separate returns and then comparing the overall taxes that would be due on the joint and separate draft returns. Each of us will provide all information necessary to prepare the draft returns.

If we agree that it is to our mutual benefit to file joint returns, we will do so. Any taxes owed on joint returns, and any accountants' fees or other expenses incurred in preparing the draft and final returns, will be [*choose one:* paid from an account held in both our names/paid by [*name*]/ [*specify some other method for allocation*]]. Any refund received shall be [*choose one:* shared equally/paid to [*name*]/[*specify some other method for allocation*]].

If we file separately:

1. Our income and deductions will be allocated as follows [*include all that apply; letter sequentially*]:

☐   a. Any earned income will be allocated between us according to applicable tax laws;

☐   b. Any unearned income, gain, loss, or credit from any investment held in both our names will be allocated between us according to our percentage of ownership;

☐   c. Any unearned income, gain, loss, or credit from any investment that is [*choose one:* Marital/Community] Property will be allocated equally;

☐   d. Any unearned income from Separate Property investments will be allocated to the person whose Separate Property investment produced the unearned income;

☐   e. Any deductible expense paid from [*choose one:* Marital/Community] Property funds will be allocated between us [*choose one:* equally/[*specify allocation*]];

☐   f. Any deductible expense paid from Separate Property funds will be allocated to the person from whose funds they were paid.

☐   2. Any taxes owed on any separate return will be paid by the person filing the separate return. Any refund on any separate return will be paid to the person filing the separate return. Any accountants' fees or other expenses incurred in preparing the draft and final returns will be [*choose one:* paid by [*name*]/shared equally/[*specify how the expenses will be paid or allocated*]].

Add if applicable:

☐   3. If one of us elects to file separate returns and the other does not, and if this results in greater taxes for the other person than that person would have owed on a joint return for the same year, [*choose one:* the person who elected to file separately will pay the additional amount owed by the other party/the additional amount owed will be paid from an account held in both our names].

☐   __. [***Choose one:*** **Name**/**Each Spouse**] **Solely Responsible for Own Business Debts**

Choose one or both:

☐   All debts incurred by [*Spouse 1*] in connection with [*name of business belonging to Spouse 1*] before or during our marriage will be [*choose a possessive pronoun*] sole and separate debts. [*Spouse 2*] will not be responsible for them, nor may [*choose a possessive pronoun*] Separate Property [*add if applicable:* or [*choose a possessive pronoun*] share of any [*choose one:* Marital/Community] Property] be used to pay them without [*choose a possessive pronoun*] written consent. [*Spouse 1*] will indemnify and hold [*Spouse 2*] harmless from any proceeding to collect on [*Spouse 1*]'s debts from [*Spouse 2*]'s property, and [*choose a pronoun*] will be solely responsible for any expenses, including attorneys' fees, incurred by [*Spouse 2*] in connection with such a proceeding.

☐ All debts incurred by [*Spouse 2*] in connection with [*name of business belonging to Spouse 2*] before or during our marriage will be [*choose a possessive pronoun*] sole and separate debts. [*Spouse 1*] will not be responsible for them, nor may [*choose a possessive pronoun*] Separate Property [*add if applicable:* or [*choose a possessive pronoun*] share of any [*choose one:* Marital/Community] Property] be used to pay them without [*choose a possessive pronoun*] written consent. [*Spouse 2*] will indemnify and hold [*Spouse 1*] harmless from any proceeding to collect on [*Spouse 1*]'s debts from [*Spouse 2*]'s property, and [*choose a possessive pronoun*] will be solely responsible for any expenses, including attorneys' fees, incurred by [*Spouse 1*] in connection with such a proceeding.

Optional Clause for Payment of Household Expenses

Choose one:

Alternative 1

☐ __. Household Expenses Will Be Paid by [*Name*]

[*Name*] will be responsible for paying all reasonable household expenses from [*choose a possessive pronoun*] [*choose one:* earnings/Separate Property funds]. Household expenses will include [*specify included expenses*], but will not include [*specify any excluded expenses*]. [*Add if applicable:* For convenience, we will establish a joint checking account into which [*name*] will deposit [*choose one:* sufficient funds/[*specify amount*]] per month to cover the regular household expenses, plus additional amounts as necessary to cover extraordinary household expenses. Either one of us may write checks on the joint account to pay for household expenses. [*Name*] will be responsible for balancing and reconciling the joint account on a regular basis.] [*Add if applicable:* The household expenses listed above include reasonable living expenses for [*name*]'s children, [*names of children*], while they are living with us. [*Name*] will deposit [*choose one:* all/[*specify amount/percentage*]] of any child support payments received into the account established for payment of household expenses.]

Alternative 2

☐ __. Household Expenses Will Be Shared

We will be responsible for paying all reasonable household expenses on [*choose one:* an equal/a pro rata] basis. [*Add if pro rata:* [*Name*]'s share will be [*specify percentage*] and [*name*]'s share will be [*specify percentage*]. Household expenses will include [*specify included expenses*], but will not include [*specify excluded expenses*].

Add if applicable:

☐ For convenience, we will establish a joint checking account into which we will each deposit every month our share of [*choose one:* an amount we will agree upon from time to time/[*specify amount*]] to cover the regular household expenses, plus additional amounts as necessary to cover extraordinary household expenses. Either one of us may write checks on the joint account to pay for household expenses. [*Name*] will be responsible for balancing the joint account on a regular basis.

Add if applicable:

☐ The household expenses listed above include reasonable living expenses for [*name*]'s children, [*names of children*], while they are living with us. [*Name*] will deposit [*choose one:* all/[*specify an amount or percentage*]] of any child support payments received into the account established for payment of household expenses.

* ☑ Paragraph __: Interpretation, Modification, Review, and Enforcement of This Agreement

* ☑ A. Entire Agreement

This Agreement contains our entire agreement on the matters covered. Any oral representations made concerning This Agreement shall be of no force or effect. [*Optional:* This Agreement supersedes any written or oral agreements or understandings between us prior to the date of This Agreement. Each of us hereby waives any and all claims we might have against the other arising out of our cohabitation prior to the date of our marriage.]

* ☑ B. Binding Effect of Agreement

Once we sign This Agreement, it shall be binding on us and our respective inheritors and estate representatives.

* ☑ C. Commitment to Carry Out This Agreement

Each of us shall take any steps that are reasonably necessary to carry out the terms and intent of This Agreement, including signing, notarizing, and delivering any necessary documents, upon request by the other party.

* ☑ D. Modification of This Agreement

This Agreement may be modified only by a subsequent written agreement signed by both of us. Any oral or written statements made by us (other than express representations in a subsequent written agreement), including but not limited to statements referring to Separate Property as "ours" or to [*choose one:* Marital/Community] Property as "mine," "yours," "his," or "hers" (or another possessive) will be only for convenience and will not be deemed to modify This Agreement in any way. The filing of joint or separate tax returns during our marriage will not be deemed to modify This Agreement in any way.

* ☑ **E. Voluntary Transfers and Restoration of Rights**

Nothing in This Agreement prevents either of us from making a voluntary transfer of an interest in property to the other party, and any such transfer, once completed, shall be deemed a gift, unless This Agreement or a subsequent written agreement provides otherwise.

During our marriage, or upon death, either of us is free to restore to the other party any legal right waived in This Agreement.

Absent an express written agreement modifying This Agreement, any voluntary transfer or restoration of a right will not be deemed an amendment of This Agreement nor a waiver of the terms of This Agreement.

* ☑ **F. Interpretation and Choice of Law**

This Agreement has been drafted and entered into in the State of [*state name*]. It shall be interpreted fairly and simply, and enforced according to the laws of [*state name*]. A copy of the signed agreement may be submitted to the court and admitted into evidence in place of the original in any proceeding to enforce or interpret This Agreement.

* ☑ **G. Severability**

If any part of This Agreement is determined by a court to be invalid, illegal, or unenforceable, the validity and enforceability of the remaining parts of This Agreement shall not be affected.

* ☑ **H. Attorneys' Fees**

In any proceeding to enforce or interpret the terms of This Agreement, the prevailing party shall be entitled to recover their reasonable expenses incurred in connection with the proceeding, including reasonable attorneys' fees.

Optional Clauses for Periodic Reviews and Dispute Resolution

Choose all that apply:

☐ __. **Periodic Reviews**

We agree to review the terms of This Agreement [*specify frequency*].

☐ __. **Mediation of Disputes**

If any dispute arises between us concerning terms of This Agreement, we will first try to resolve the dispute in mediation with a qualified mediator acceptable to both of us. We will share the expenses of mediation equally. The mediation sessions shall be confidential, and neither of us may subpoena the records of the mediator or call the mediator as a witness in any arbitration or other legal proceeding between us.

☐ __. **Arbitration of Disputes**

[*Choose one:* If any dispute arises between us concerning This Agreement/If a dispute between us concerning This Agreement cannot be resolved in mediation], we agree to submit the dispute to [*choose one:* advisory/binding] arbitration within [*number*] days after either of us makes a written demand. If we cannot agree upon an arbitrator, each of us shall appoint one person and the persons so appointed shall select the arbitrator. Participation in arbitration or a waiver of arbitration by both of us shall be a prerequisite to any legal action brought by either of us concerning the matters covered by This Agreement, unless applicable law prohibits arbitration of the disputed issue(s).

* ☑ **Paragraph __: Signatures, Attorneys' Certifications, and Acknowledgments**

Each of us has read This Agreement carefully and is signing it freely after obtaining all advice we each consider appropriate.

Dated: _____   _____
                                                    [*Name*]

Dated: _____   _____
                                                    [*Name*]

Alternative 1

* ☐

Certificate of Attorney for [*Spouse 1*]

I certify, as attorney for [*Spouse 1*] only, that [*choose a pronoun*] has freely and voluntarily signed the attached premarital agreement. I have advised [*Spouse 1*] about the legal effects of the terms of This Agreement, and [*choose a pronoun*] has had a full opportunity to discuss it with me and with any other advisers of [*choose a possessive pronoun*] own choosing. I believe that [*choose a pronoun*] has been fully advised and that [*choose a pronoun*] is aware of all the legal effects of This Agreement.

Dated: _____   _____
                                                [*Attorney's Name*]

Alternative 2

☐

Certificate of Attorney for [*Spouse 1*]

I certify, as attorney for [*Spouse 1*] only, that I have advised [*Spouse 1*] about the legal effects of the terms of the Agreement, and that [*choose a pronoun*] has had a full opportunity to discuss it with me.

Dated: _____   _____
                                              [*Attorney's Name*]

Alternative 1

* ☐

Certificate of Attorney for [*Spouse 2*]

I certify, as attorney for [*Spouse 2*] only, that [*choose a pronoun*] has freely and voluntarily signed the attached premarital agreement. I have advised [*Spouse 2*] about the legal effects of the terms of This Agreement, and [*choose a pronoun*] has had a full opportunity to discuss it with me and with any other advisors of [*choose a possessive pronoun*] own choosing. I believe that [*choose a pronoun*] has been fully advised and that [*choose a pronoun*] is aware of all the legal effects of This Agreement.

Dated: _____   _____
                                              [*Attorney's Name*]

Alternative 2

☐

Certificate of Attorney for [*Spouse 2*]

I certify, as attorney for [*Spouse 2*] only, that I have advised [*Spouse 2*] about the legal effects of the terms of This Agreement, and that [*choose a pronoun*] has had a full opportunity to discuss it with me.

Dated: _____   _____
                                              [*Attorney's Name*]

[We provide the following notary certificates as examples only. Your state might use a different certificate. If your state requires you to have the signatures on your prenup notarized, the notary public will provide and attach a certificate of acknowledgment here. Please delete these sample certificates from your agreement before finalizing your document.]

* ☑

Certificate of Acknowledgment of Notary Public

State of _____ ⎫
County of _____ ⎬ ss
　　　　　　　　　　　　　　　　　⎭

On _____, before me, _____ ,
personally appeared _____ ,
who proved to me on the basis of satisfactory evidence to be the person(s) whose name(s) is/
are subscribed to the within instrument and acknowledged to me that he/she/they executed the
same in his/her/their authorized capacity and that by his/her/their signature on the instrument
the person, or the entity on behalf of which the person(s) acted, executed the instrument.

I certify under PENALTY OF PERJURY under the laws of the state of _____
that the foregoing paragraph is true and correct.

WITNESS my hand and official seal.

_____

[NOTARIAL SEAL]　　　　　　　Notary Public for the state of _____
　　　　　　　　　　　　　　　My commission expires _____

* ☑

Certificate of Acknowledgment of Notary Public

State of _____

}ss

County of _____

On _____, before me, _____,
personally appeared _____,
who proved to me on the basis of satisfactory evidence to be the person(s) whose name(s) is/
are subscribed to the within instrument and acknowledged to me that he/she/they executed the
same in his/her/their authorized capacity and that by his/her/their signature on the instrument
the person, or the entity on behalf of which the person(s) acted, executed the instrument.

I certify under PENALTY OF PERJURY under the laws of the state of _____
that the foregoing paragraph is true and correct.

WITNESS my hand and official seal.

_____

[NOTARIAL SEAL]

Notary Public for the state of _____
My commission expires _____

Optional Paragraphs (Insert After Paragraph 8, Above)

☐ **Paragraph __: Estate Planning Matters**

Optional Clause for Waiver of Surviving Spouse Rights

Choose one:

Alternative 1

☐ __. **Mutual Waiver of Rights in Each Other's Estate—Complete Waiver**

Each of us waives and forever gives up any and all rights and claims to the Separate Property of the other person due to our marriage, including but not limited to:

1. Rights or claims of dower, curtesy, or any substitute for those rights or claims provided by any applicable state statute at the time of the other person's death;

2. The right of election to take against the will of the other;

3. The right to a share in the Separate Property estate of the other person if the other person dies without a will;

4. The right to act as administrator of the estate of the other;

5. The right to a probate homestead or homestead allowance;

6. The right to a family allowance and to a personal property allowance.

Nothing in This Agreement shall be deemed to constitute a waiver by either of us of any gift one of us might choose to make to the other by will or other estate planning document, or to act as executor designated in the will of the other. However, we acknowledge that no promises of any kind have been made by either of us to the other person regarding any such gift or designation, except for any specific provisions included in This Agreement.

Alternative 2

☐ __. **Mutual Waiver of Rights in Each Other's Estate—Partial Waiver**

Each of us waives and forever gives up the following rights or claims that we might acquire in the Separate Property of the other person due to our marriage [*choose all that apply*]:

☐ 1. Rights or claims of dower, curtesy, or any substitute for those rights or claims provided by any applicable state statute at the time of the other person's death;

☐ 2. The right of election to take against the will of the other;

☐ 3. The right to a share in the Separate Property estate of the other person if the other person dies without a will;

☐ 4. The right to act as administrator of the estate of the other;

☐ 5. The right to a probate homestead or homestead allowance;

☐ 6. The right to a family allowance and to a personal property allowance.

☐ Nothing in This Agreement shall be deemed to constitute a waiver by either of us of any gift that one of us might choose to make to the other by will or other estate planning document, or to act as executor designated in the will of the other. However, we acknowledge that no promises of any kind have been made by either of us to the other person regarding any such gift or designation, except for any specific provisions included in This Agreement.

Additional Estate Planning Clauses

Choose all that apply:

☐ __. **Provision for [*Name*] Upon [*Name*]'s Death**

Upon [*name*]'s death, if no proceeding for Divorce, dissolution, legal separation, or annulment is pending at the date of death, [*name*] shall be entitled to receive the following distribution(s) from [*name*]'s estate [*choose all that apply*]:

☐ A lump sum payment of $ [*insert amount*].

☐ An amount equal to [*percentage*]% of [*name*]'s gross estate. The term "gross estate" as used here does not include life insurance proceeds, retirement benefits, or other death benefits payable on the death of [*name*].

☐ An amount based on the following formula: [*insert formula*].

☐ The following described property: [*insert property description*].

☐ In addition, [*name*] shall be entitled to [*insert any other agreed provision, such as a life estate, payments for a certain period of time, or a right to use or occupy certain property*].

☐ At all times during our marriage, [*name of person whose estate is responsible*] shall maintain in effect a valid will, trust, or other estate planning document that includes the foregoing provisions.

☐ __. **Estate Plans to Be Consistent With This Agreement**

We acknowledge the importance of making valid estate plans that are consistent with This Agreement. Therefore, as soon as possible after our marriage, each of us will establish and maintain in effect a valid will, trust, or other estate planning document or combination of documents that will be consistent with, and will carry out the terms of, This Agreement. We further agree to review our estate plans periodically to ensure that our estate planning documents remain consistent with This Agreement and to modify our estate planning documents if necessary to keep them consistent with This Agreement.

☐ **Paragraph __: Property Transfers or Purchases of Insurance Upon Marriage**

Choose all that apply:

☐ **__.Transfer of Real Estate**

Within [*number*] days after our marriage, [*name*] will sign, deliver, and record a deed granting to [*name*] a [*percentage*]% interest, as [*specify how title will be held, for example, tenants in common, joint tenants, or his or her sole and separate property*] in the following real estate: [*address and legal description of the property*]. [*Name(s)*] will pay [*specify share, such as all, half, or some other proportion*] of any expenses related to the transfer, including the cost of obtaining title insurance on the property.

☐ **__.Transfer of Cash, Securities, or Other Personal Property**

Within [*number*] days after our marriage, [*name*] will deliver and assign to [*name*] ownership of the following property: [*describe property or cash to be transferred*]. [*Name(s)*] will pay [*specify share, such as all, half, or some other proportion*] of any expenses related to the transfer.

☐ **__.Assignment of Life Insurance**

Within [*number*] days after our marriage, [*name*] will deliver and assign to [*name*] ownership of the following [*optional: fully paid*] life insurance [*choose one: policy/policies*] on [*name*]'s life: [*insert insurance company name, policy number, and face amount*]. [*Name(s)*] will pay [*specify share, such as all, half, or some other proportion*] of any expenses related to the assignment. [*Optional: [*Name(s)*] will pay [*specify share, such as all, half, or some other proportion of*] of any premiums due on the policy after the assignment.*]

☐ **__.Purchase of Annuity**

Within [*number*] days after our marriage, [*name*] will purchase and maintain in effect for [*specify time period*] an annuity contract that will pay at least $[*annual amount*] per year beginning [*specify the event or date that will trigger payments to begin, such as a certain number of years following the purchase, or when the beneficiary reaches a certain age*], and continuing until the death of [*name*], who shall be designated as sole primary beneficiary of the annuity. [*Name(s)*] will pay [*specify share, such as all, half, or some other proportion*] of the costs of purchasing and maintaining the annuity.

☐ **__.Purchase of Life Insurance Policy**

Within [*number*] days after our marriage, [*name*] will purchase and maintain in effect for [*specify time period*] a life insurance policy that will pay at least $[*insert amount*] on [*choose a possessive pronoun*] death. [*Name*] shall be designated as sole primary beneficiary of the policy. [*Name(s)*] will pay [*specify share, such as all, half, or some other proportion*] of the costs of purchasing and maintaining the policy.

☐ **Paragraph __: Provisions Applicable to Divorce**

A. Terms of This Agreement to Control

In the unhappy event that our marriage ends in Divorce, as that term is defined in Paragraph 5 of This Agreement, we want to resolve all issues as amicably and efficiently as possible.

Therefore, if we divorce, we agree to the following:

1. This Agreement will control all issues addressed by This Agreement.

2. As soon as possible after the case is filed, we will file This Agreement (or a true copy of it) in court and we will sign and file a stipulation acknowledging the validity of This Agreement.

3. Any dispute about the validity or interpretation of This Agreement will be separated from all other issues in the case and submitted to the court for determination before any issues addressed in This Agreement are decided.

Optional Clause for Distribution of Marital or Community Property Assets

☐ **__.Distribution of Separate Property Assets**

In any Divorce proceeding, our Separate Property assets will be distributed as follows:

1. Each party's Separate Property assets, as defined in This Agreement, shall be confirmed to that party absolutely, without being included in any division of [*choose one:* Marital/Community] Property.

Add if applicable:

☐ 2. Each jointly owned Separate Property asset shall be divided between us in proportion to our respective ownership interests in the asset ("in kind"), if that is possible without making us co-owners of the same asset after the asset is divided. If an in-kind division of any asset is not possible, the asset shall be sold and the net proceeds divided in proportion to our respective ownership interests in the asset.

Optional Clause for Distribution of Marital or Community Property Assets

Choose one:

Alternative 1

☐ **__. Equal Distribution of [*choose one:* Marital/Community] Property Assets**

In any Divorce proceeding, except as provided elsewhere in This Agreement or in a written agreement signed by both of us at the time of the divorce, any [*choose one:* Marital/Community] Property assets shall be distributed between us in such a way as to achieve a monetarily equal division of the aggregate net value of the [*choose one:* Marital/Community] Property assets. If we so agree, certain assets may be distributed to one of us in exchange for a distribution of offsetting assets to the other party. Otherwise, each asset will be divided between us equally ("in kind"), if that is possible without making us co-owners of the same asset after the asset is divided. If an asset cannot be divided in kind and there is no agreement to assign the asset to one party, it shall be sold and the net proceeds divided so as to accomplish an equal division of all the assets. In determining whether the assets have been equally divided, any asset not sold will be valued at its fair market value as of the date the assets are divided.

Alternative 2

☐ __. **Equitable Distribution of [*choose one:* Marital/Community] Property Assets**

In any Divorce proceeding, except as provided elsewhere in This Agreement or in a written agreement signed by both of us at the time of the Divorce, any [*choose one:* Marital/Community] Property assets shall be distributed between us in such a way as to achieve an equitable division of the aggregate net value of the [*choose one:* Marital/Community] Property assets, as determined by written agreement signed by both of us or by the court in the Divorce case. If we so agree, certain assets may be distributed to one of us in exchange for a distribution of offsetting assets to the other. Otherwise, each asset will be divided between us ("in kind"), if that is possible without our ending up as co-owners of the same asset after the asset is divided. If an asset cannot be divided in kind and there is no agreement to assign the asset to one party, it shall be sold and the net proceeds divided so as to accomplish an equitable division of all the assets. In determining whether the assets have been equitably divided, any asset not sold will be valued at its fair market value as of the date the assets are divided.

Optional Clause for Division of Retirement Benefits

Choose one:

Alternative 1

☐ __. **Retirement or Employee Benefits to Be Divided—Offset Method**

If we divorce, the terms of the Divorce decree or judgment shall provide that any [*choose one:* Marital/Community] Property interest in retirement, pension, deferred compensation, stock options, and other employee benefit or tax deferred plans, whether qualified according to IRS regulations or nonqualified, shall be divided so that the person who earned the benefits or in whose name those benefits are held receives all of the benefits and the other person receives other property or funds as an offset in the [*choose one:* equal/equitable] division of the [*choose one:* Marital/Community] Property.

Alternative 2

☐ __. **Retirement or Employee Benefits to Be Divided—In-Kind Method**

If we divorce, the terms of the Divorce decree or judgment shall provide that any [*choose one:* Marital/Community] Property interest in retirement, pension, deferred compensation, stock options, and other employee benefit or tax deferred plans, whether qualified according to IRS regulations or nonqualified, shall be divided so that each of us receives a share of the benefits payable, with each person's share calculated in a manner consistent with the [*choose one:* equal/equitable] division of the [*choose one:* Marital/Community] Property. Each of us will cooperate in preparing any court order for division of the benefits required by the plan or as provided by applicable law.

Alternative 3

☐ ___. **No Division of Retirement or Employee Benefits**

If we divorce, the terms of the Divorce decree or judgment shall provide that any [*choose one:* Marital/Community] Property interest in retirement, pension, deferred compensation, stock options, and other employee benefit or tax deferred plans, whether qualified according to IRS regulations or nonqualified, shall be confirmed to the person who earned the benefits or in whose name those benefits are vested and shall not be included in the [*choose one:* equal/equitable] division of the [*choose one:* Marital/Community] Property.

Alternative 4

☐ ___. **Retirement or Employee Benefits to Be Divided—Method to Be Determined**

If we divorce, the terms of the Divorce decree or judgment shall provide that any [*choose one:* Marital/Community] Property interest in retirement, pension, deferred compensation, stock options, and other employee benefit or tax deferred plans, whether qualified according to IRS regulations or nonqualified, shall be divided in a manner consistent with the [*choose one:* equal/equitable] division of the [*choose one:* Marital/Community] Property, as determined by a written agreement signed by both of us or by the court in the Divorce case.

Optional Clause for Division of Specific Assets

☐ ___. [*Insert Title of Clause, such as Family Residence, Business, or Joint Securities*]

[*Insert applicable terms of clause*].

Optional Clause for Division of Premarital Debts

☐ ___. **Responsibility for Premarital Debts**

If we divorce, the terms of the Divorce decree or judgment shall provide that any outstanding premarital debt will be allocated to the person who incurred the debt, and the person who incurred the debt shall be required to pay the debt and to indemnify and hold the other person harmless from the debt and all costs related to it.

Optional Clause for Responsibility for Debts Incurred During Marriage

Choose one:

Alternative 1

☐ ___. **Equal Responsibility for Debts Incurred During Marriage—General Rule**

Except as provided elsewhere in This Agreement, if we divorce, the terms of the divorce decree or judgment shall provide that any outstanding debts incurred by one or both of us during our marriage will be paid and allocated between us equally, to the extent an equal allocation is practical, as specifically determined by written agreement signed by both of us, or by the court in the Divorce case. If the allocation is unequal, there shall be a corresponding offset in the division of our [*choose one:* Marital/Community] Property assets, in order to equalize the overall division of assets and debts.

If a debt is allocated to one of us in accordance with this clause, the person to whom it is allocated shall be required to indemnify and hold the other person harmless from the debt and all costs related to it.

Alternative 2

☐ __. Equitable Allocation of Responsibility for Debts Incurred During Marriage—General Rule

Except as provided elsewhere in This Agreement, if we divorce, the terms of the Divorce decree or judgment shall provide that any outstanding debt incurred by one or both of us during our marriage will be paid and allocated between us equitably, as determined by written agreement signed by both of us or by the court in the divorce case.

If a debt is allocated to one of us in accordance with this clause, the person to whom it is allocated shall be required to indemnify and hold the other person harmless from the debt and all costs related to it.

Optional Clause for Student Loans

Choose one:

Alternative 1

☐ __. Sole Responsibility for Student Loans

If we divorce, the terms of the Divorce decree or judgment shall provide that any outstanding student loan debt will be allocated to the person whose education was financed by the loan, who shall be required to pay the debt and to indemnify and hold the other person harmless from the debt and all costs related to it.

Alternative 2

☐ __. Shared Responsibility for Student Loans

If we divorce, the terms of the Divorce decree or judgment shall provide that any outstanding student loan debt will be allocated between us in the same manner as any other debts incurred during our marriage for which we are mutually responsible, and not solely to the person whose education was financed by the loan.

Optional Clause for Certain Debts Incurred During Marriage

☐ __. Sole Responsibility for Certain Debts Incurred by One Party During Marriage

If we divorce, the terms of the Divorce decree or judgment shall provide that any of the following outstanding debts incurred by one of us during our marriage will be allocated solely to the person who incurred the debt: [*specify debt or type of debt to be allocated to one spouse, such as one spouse's business debts, any debt incurred without the knowledge and consent of the other party, or debts related to certain activities*].

If a debt is allocated to one of us in accordance with this clause, the person to whom it is allocated shall be required to indemnify and hold the other person harmless from the debt and all costs related to it.

Optional Clause for Reimbursement for Debts or Expenses Paid

Choose one:

Alternative 1

☐ __. **Reimbursement for Debts or Expenses Paid**

In any Divorce proceeding, each of us will be entitled to reimbursement from the other for [*choose all that apply*]:

☐ 1. Payments made during our marriage from Separate Property funds of one of us for for premarital debts [*optional:* including child support or alimony] owed by the other;

☐ 2. One-half of payments made during our marriage from [*choose one:* Marital/Community] Property funds for premarital debts [*optional:* or child support or alimony] owed by the other;

☐ 3. Payments made from Separate Property funds of one of us for necessary expenses incurred by the other in connection with attendance at an accredited educational institution (including tuition, fees, books, and supplies [*choose one:* but not including/and] living expenses), whether paid directly or by payments on student loans incurred for those expenses;

☐ 4. One-half of payments made during our marriage from [*choose one:* Marital/Community] Property funds for necessary expenses incurred by the other in connection with attendance at an accredited educational institution (including tuition, fees, books, and supplies [*choose one:* but not including/and] living expenses), whether paid directly or by payments on student loans incurred for those expenses;

☐ 5. [*Insert any additional reimbursements*];

☐ 6. Any other amounts expressly agreed to be reimbursable as provided elsewhere in This Agreement.

Neither of us will be entitled to any reimbursement from the other for paying any debts or expenses except those listed above, whether paid from Separate Property funds or [*choose one:* Marital/Community] Property funds or both.

Alternative 2

☐ __. **No Reimbursement for Debts or Expenses Paid**

In any Divorce proceeding, neither of us will be entitled to any reimbursement from the other for paying debts or expenses of the other during our marriage except as may be provided elsewhere in This Agreement, whether paid from Separate Property funds or [*choose one:* Marital/Community] Property funds or both.

Optional Clauses for Alimony (Check State Law for Specific Requirements or Limitations)

Choose all that apply:

Alternative 1 (If Both Spouses Are Waiving Alimony, Include a Separate Clause for Each)

☐ ___. Waiver of [<u>choose one</u>: Alimony/*Other Term*] by [*Name*]

[*Name*] expects to have sufficient earning capacity, income, and assets to provide for [*choose a possessive pronoun*] reasonable needs if we divorce. Therefore, [*name*] hereby waives absolutely any and all rights to request [*optional:* temporary and] permanent [*choose one:* alimony/*other term*] from [*name*] [*insert if applicable:* , except in the following limited circumstances only: [*specify circumstances—for example, if waiving spouse would be eligible for welfare without alimony*]. [*Name*] understands that this waiver could later result in a hardship, and has taken that risk into account in making this waiver.

Alternative 2 (Include a Separate Clause for Each Spouse to Whom This Applies)

☐ ___. Specified [<u>choose one</u>: Alimony/*Other Term*] to [*Name*]

If we divorce, [*name*] shall be entitled to [*optional:* temporary or] permanent [*choose one:* alimony/*other term*] payments of [*optional:* no more than] $[*amount*] per month from [*name*] [*optional:* for a period of [*number of years or months*], beginning [*specify starting point, such as the date when we stop living together or the date the case is filed*] and ending absolutely on [*specify ending point, such as remarriage, death, or a certain date or number of months or years; if more than one event or date could end alimony payments, add "whichever occurs first" after listing the possible ending dates or events*]. This clause may not be modified except by a written agreement signed by both of us. [*Name*] hereby waives absolutely any and all rights to request [*optional:* temporary and] permanent [*choose one:* alimony/*other term*] from [*name*] except as provided in this clause. [*Name*] understands that this waiver could later result in a hardship and has taken that risk into account in making this waiver.

Other Clauses for Divorce

☐ ___. [*Insert Title of Clause*]

[*Insert applicable terms of clause*].

☐ **Paragraph ___: Other Matters**

[*Insert any clauses for matters not covered in other paragraphs; insert sequential letters if you use more than one, starting with letter A*].

☐ ___. [*Insert Title of Clause*]

[*Insert applicable terms of clause*].

Financial Disclosures

* ☑   **Schedule 1—[_Spouse 1_]'s Disclosures**

ASSETS

Description _____

Approximate
Value _____

[_Optional Section_]

DEBTS

To Whom Owed _____

Approximate
Balance _____

[_Spouse 1_]'s annual income (calendar year [_insert year_]): $ _____

[_Optional_] [_Spouse 1_]'s annual personal expenses: $ _____

_____   _____

Date Prepared   _Initials_

_____   _____

Date Received   _Initials_

* ☑

Schedule 2—[*Spouse 2*]'s Disclosures

ASSETS

Description _____ Approximate Value _____

DEBTS

To Whom Owed _____ Approximate Balance _____

[*Spouse 2*]'s annual income (calendar year [*insert year*]): $ _____

[*Optional*] [*Spouse 2*]'s annual personal expenses: $ _____

_____   _____
Date Prepared   *Initials*

_____   _____
Date Received   *Initials*

* ☑

Schedule 3—Jointly Owned Premarital Assets
[*Optional:* and Jointly Owed Premarital Debts]

ASSETS

Description   Approximate Value

[*Optional Section*]

DEBTS

To Whom Owed   Approximate Balance

_____   _____

Date Prepared   *Initials*

_____   _____

Date Received   *Initials*

☐ Abstract of Prenup

RECORDING REQUESTED BY
AND WHEN RECORDED RETURN TO

[LEAVE THIS SPACE BLANK FOR
RECORDER'S STAMP]

[*Insert name and address of spouse whose
property is referred to*]

[**Choose one:** Abstract/Memorandum] of [*Title of Prenup*] Agreement

We, [*full name of Spouse 1, followed by first name of Spouse 1 in parentheses*] and [*full name of
Spouse 2, followed by first name of Spouse 2 in parentheses*], declare:

1. We were married on [*date*] and are now [*choose one:* husband and wife/legal spouses].

2. We entered into a [*title of prenup*] on [*date*].

3. The [*title of prenup*] became effective on the date of our marriage and it remains in full
   force and effect as of the date of execution of this abstract.

4. Among the provisions of the [*title of prenup*] are the provisions that follow:

   a. [*Insert paragraph number and letter of clause*] provides that the real property described
      on Exhibit A to this abstract, which is incorporated by reference, is and shall be [*insert
      owner's first name*]'s Separate Property, and [*owner's first name*] has the sole right to
      manage and dispose of the property described on Exhibit A.

   b. [*Insert a summary of any additional clauses you want to include in the abstract, such as
      a clause providing for real estate acquired during marriage to be considered the separate
      property of a spouse*].

   c. Paragraph [*number and letter of clause*] provides that the [*title of prenup*] will remain in
      full force and effect [*choose one:* indefinitely/until *specify date*].

We sign this abstract on _____[Date]_____ at _____[Place]_____

_____   _____
[*Name*]   [*Name*]

[We provide the following notary certificates as examples only. Your state might use a different certificate. If your state requires you to have the signatures on your prenup notarized, the notary public will provide and attach a certificate of acknowledgment here. Please delete these sample certificates from your agreement before finalizing your document.]

* ☑

Certificate of Acknowledgment of Notary Public

State of _____ ⎫

County of _____ ⎬ ss

On _____, before me, _____,

personally appeared _____,

who proved to me on the basis of satisfactory evidence to be the person(s) whose name(s) is/are subscribed to the within instrument and acknowledged to me that he/she/they executed the same in his/her/their authorized capacity and that by his/her/their signature(s) on the instrument the person, or the entity on behalf of which the person(s) acted, executed the instrument.

I certify under PENALTY OF PERJURY that the foregoing paragraph is true and correct.

WITNESS my hand and official seal.

_____

[NOTARIAL SEAL]   Notary Public for the state of _____

My commission expires _____

* ☑

Certificate of Acknowledgment of Notary Public

State of _____

County of _____ } ss

On _____, before me, _____,

personally appeared _____,

who proved to me on the basis of satisfactory evidence to be the person(s) whose name(s) is/are subscribed to the within instrument and acknowledged to me that he/she/they executed the same in his/her/their authorized capacity and that by his/her/their signature(s) on the instrument the person, or the entity on behalf of which the person(s) acted, executed the instrument.

I certify under PENALTY OF PERJURY that the foregoing paragraph is true and correct.

WITNESS my hand and official seal.

_____

[NOTARIAL SEAL]

Notary Public for the state of _____

My commission expires _____

Exhibit A

[*Attach the legal description (from the deed) of any property you refer to in Paragraph 4a*].

Index

D

N

O

On Nolo.com you'll also find:

Books & Software

Nolo publishes hundreds of great books and software programs for consumers and
business owners. Order a copy, or download an ebook version instantly, at Nolo.com.

Online Forms

You can quickly and easily make a will or living trust, form an LLC or corporation,
apply for a provisional patent, or make hundreds of other forms—online.

Free Legal Information

Thousands of articles answer common questions about everyday legal issues,
including wills, bankruptcy, small business formation, divorce, patents,
employment, and much more.

Plain-English Legal Dictionary

Stumped by jargon? Look it up in America's most up-to-date source for
definitions of legal terms, free at Nolo.com.

Lawyer Directory

Nolo's consumer-friendly lawyer directory provides in-depth profiles of lawyers all
over America. You'll find information you need to choose the right lawyer.

PNUP7